STORIES TO LIGHT THE NIGHT

A GRIEF AND LOSS COLLECTION FOR CHILDREN, FAMILIES AND COMMUNITIES

SUSAN PERROW

Hawthorn Press

Stories to Light the Night: A Grief and Loss Collection for Children, Families and Communities
© 2021 Susan Perrow.

Susan Perrow is hereby identified as the author of this work in accordance with section 77 of the Copyright, Designs and Patent Act, 1988. She asserts and gives notice of her moral right under this Act.

Hawthorn Press
Published by Hawthorn Press, Hawthorn House,
1 Lansdown Lane, Stroud, Gloucestershire, GL5 1BJ, UK
Email: info@hawthornpress.com
www.hawthornpress.com

Stories to Light the Night © Hawthorn Press 2021
Cover illustration and design by Lucy Guenot
Typesetting by Lucy Guenot
Printed by Short Run Press Ltd, Exeter

Every effort has been made to trace the ownership of all copyrighted material. If any omission has been made, please bring this to the publisher's attention so that proper acknowledgement may be given in future editions.

The views expressed in this book are not necessarily those of the publisher.

The stories are reproduced with kind permission from the 34 authors listed on pages 6–7. These and Susan Perrow's own stories cannot be reproduced in any form without the written permission of the publisher.

British Library Cataloguing in Publication Data applied for

ISBN 978-1-912480-27-2

Dedication

To Nancye

My Mother, My Rose

Acknowledgements

This book has been many years in the making. I have struggled with the responsibility of such an important collection but have been urged forward by the contributions from others, the positive responses to my own stories, and personal experiences at my therapeutic story seminars.

Thank you to the 34 teachers, psychologists, social workers, storytellers, parents and grandparents from across the globe who took the time to share their stories and story outcomes with me, then generously agreed to contribute them to this book. And much gratitude to Benjamin Aukram, Austin Clark-Smith and Katie Hepton for allowing their healing words from the 'Our Kids Project' (Lismore Base Hospital) to be shared in this collection.

A heartfelt 'thank you' to my loving husband John Adam for his patience and support, including many shoulder massages, through the long journey of crafting this book. And to my children and grandchildren for their enduring love and encouragement of my story passion, and especially to my youngest son Jamie Perrow for his help shaping the cover with his designer 'eye'.

To my publisher Martin Large for his trust in me and my work, to Claire Percival for her prompt replies to my many emails, to Katie Bevan for her artistic formatting, to Lucy Guenot for her talent with the beautiful cover image, and to Alida Gersie for her helpful suggestions on the introduction. Especial thanks to Richard House for his generosity and insight during his thorough and encouraging copy-edit process, helping to polish this book in readiness to shine out to the world.

A collection like this has required dedicated mentoring and guidance from several colleagues and friends. I am especially indebted to Paula Bowles (Member of the Australian Psychology Society) for our discussions on the sensitive challenges of compiling this collection. And to Julie McVeigh, Di Kelly and Margaret King for their feedback and reflections.

Last, but definitely not least, a mighty 'thank you' to my special Byron Writers Group – the Zinklings – Lynton Burger, Jenni Cargill-Strong, Vicky King, Mitchell Kelly, Jay McKenzie and Ana Davis. You cared for me like family, nursing my stories through the ups and downs of writing's many challenges.

CONTENTS

List of Contributors

Name, story title(s) and biographical details (listed by first name).

Dr Aimee Chua – 'The Bamboo Family'; child and adolescent psychiatrist, Iloilo City, The Philippines

Dr Alys Mendus – 'The Migratory Bird'; independent scholar and Casual Academic at the University of Melbourne. Originally from the UK, now living in Moreton Bay, QLD, Australia

Ana Barišić, M.Sc. – 'Miss Burble'; writer and educator, Rijeka, Croatia

Andreja Krenek – co-author of 'The Black Stone'; office manager and storyteller, Zagreb, Croatia

Anja Jarh – 'The Lavender Nest'; educator, Ljubljana, Slovenia

Annie Bryant – 'The Tale of Little Fawn and Dear Friend'; professional storyteller and musician, Quaama, NSW, Australia

Bandana Basu – 'And Thus Came the Restful Night' and 'A New Dawn'; author, poet, blogger, teacher mentor and school advisor, Mumbai, India

Beate Steller M.A.Ed., B.S.W. (Hon), R.N. – 'The Space between the Moon and the Stars'; social worker, counsellor, adult educator, spiritual carer and registered nurse, Grays Point, NSW, Australia

Becky Whitcombe – 'The Rainbow Stone' and 'Little Singing Bunny'; postnatal consultant and playgroup leader, Sydney, Australia

Diana Petrova – 'When Grandma Passed Away'; contemporary children's author and editor, Sofia, Bulgaria

Didi A. Devapriya – 'Uprooted', 'The Nest Builders' and 'Healing Bones'; neo-humanist educator, AMURTEL Romania, Bucharest

Elodie Guidou – 'The Rainbow Gnomes' and 'The Cave of Secrets'; early childhood teacher, Bowral, NSW, Australia

Erika Katačić Kožić – co-author of 'The Black Stone'; pharmaceutical scientist and storyteller, Zagreb, Croatia

Esther Moreno – 'A Nest in the Stars'; early childhood teacher, Malla, Spain

Jenni Cargill-Strong – 'The Mulberry Tree'; professional storyteller, teacher and coach, with a special interest in teaching 'Storytelling for Changemakers', Northern NSW, Australia

Jill Tina Taplin – 'The Little Fish'; author and teacher trainer (UK and internationally), Staffordshire, UK

Kaitlyn Tighe – 'The Whale and the Pearl'; social worker / child safety officer, Central Queensland, Australia

Lyn McCormick – 'Whisper Sweet Dreams'; educator and grandmother, Ocean Shores, NSW, Australia

Mayumi Murphy – 'The Lake and the Sky'; Japanese language teacher, South Coast, NSW, Australia

Mohini Frankel-Hutton – co-author of 'The Beavers and the Oak Tree'; spiritual response therapist, Findhorn, Scotland

Ninna Nygaard – 'The Crack'; architect and storyteller, Præstø, Denmark

Pamela Celestine Perkins, M.Ed. – 'The Little Star Who Could Not Stay'; educator, writer, puppeteer and grandmother, Vermont, USA

Paula Bowles – 'The Garden'; psychologist and Fellow of the APS College of Counselling Psychologists, Byron Shire, NSW, Australia

Petra Kapović Vidmar – 'The Cup Tower'; educator and author, Rijeka, Croatia

Saška Klemenčič, M.Sc., NLP – 'Little Shell and the Dancing Pearls'; Master Praktik and NLP coach, trainer for self-management, Ljubljana, Slovenia

Scarlet Cheng – translator of 'The Gannan Orange' (by Bai Chun Yan); English language translator and special needs teacher, Beijing, China

Silke Rose West – 'Wolf Boy's Journey Home'; author, kindergarten teacher and supporter of the Golden Willow Grief Group, Taos, New Mexico, USA

Stephen Sharpe – co-author of 'The Beavers and the Oak Tree'; musician and drumming teacher, Forres, Scotland

Suzette Ellison – 'The Little Candle'; early childhood teacher, Australia

Tabitha Wangeci-Gikingo – 'Taji La Lipendo – The Crown of Love'; early childhood teacher and mentor, Nairobi, Kenya

Tjenka Murray – 'The Memory Blanket'; primary school teacher, Bega, NSW, Australia

Toni Wright-Turner – 'Apple Leaf'; educator and Greens councillor, Bellingen, NSW, Australia

Yvonne Donohoe – 'Goodbye Shelly' and 'Sylvie and the Stars'; retired school principal, life and business coach, author and grandmother, North Coast, NSW, Australia

Zavet Monroy Little – 'Little Star's Journey' (co-written with the author) and 'Mexican Cultural Thoughts on "Cycles of Life"'; illustrator, puppeteer, oneiromancer, Mexico City, Mexico

Stories created by Susan Perrow

Stories re-written or transcribed by Susan Perrow

FOREWORD

Every year in the UK around 40,000 children are sadly told about the death of their mum or dad. Many more children will hear that their brother or sister, grandparent, teacher, friend or much-loved pet has died. All these children are bereaved. They will have to come to grips with the lasting absence of somebody who was important to them. Even though so many children experience bereavement, general recognition of this fact is very limited indeed. Many voluntary organisations are trying to change this through initiatives such as the annual *National Grief Awareness Week*, driven by the *Good Grief Trust*. There are also excellent specialized support and training organizations such as *Grief Encounter* and *Winston's Wish*. But in the public domain progress is slow. At present fewer than 10 percent of British teachers receive any training about the specific needs of bereaved children, and just one in five teachers says that there is specialist support in their school.

Internationally the situation is the same or worse. This, despite the fact that in every class in every school worldwide there is at least one child whose parent(s) or sibling has recently died. Even more children in that same class will be actively mourning the death of another person close to them, or another grievous loss or agonizing separation of some kind.

Loss, death, mourning and grief are as much part of childhood as birth, learning, routines, new arrivals, boredom and excitement. However, in the industrialized world many adults feel intense cultural pressure to treat childhood as a flawless time of carefree innocence. Here children generally don't participate in family-talk about people who died. They may also be kept away from funerals or cemeteries. Such well-intentioned shielding of children against the realities of death, loss and grief can make their bereavement more difficult than it otherwise might be.

The social silence also prevents grieving children from finding answers to their often urgent questions about death and other significant losses. They want to know what happened, what is now going to happen, who knew what, why they weren't told earlier, will they too get sick and die, will someone else leave, and above all who is going to take care of them now. Honest answers to these questions by a trusted adult can greatly ease their anxiety. But many of children's questions like these are left hanging in the saddened air. Other cultures or families may as a matter of practice tell children about such things, include them in a mourning ritual or involve them in talk about grief. That helps.

The death of a person who matters to us, or other serious loss experiences, have in their wake numerous, often painful, ripple-effects. These cause us significant inner and interpersonal pain. It hurts even more when the person who died is young, or if a death is untimely, violent, sudden and unexpected, or when several people die at once. If coping with mourning and grief is really tough for adults, it is truly hard for children. The more so if they already face other daunting challenges, such as physical and/or learning difficulties, poverty, or a precarious family home. The greater the number of adverse life-events that a child has experienced, the harder it will be for them to cope with the numerous complexities following the death of someone who is important to them. Moreover, life continues and promises to present new adversities and new blessings.

The stories in this book can help adults to open up conversations about loss, death, dying and bereavement; conversations that so many can find extremely difficult to initiate, let alone conduct.

Death, Loss and Bereavement Always Have Ripple-effects

The raw impact of such ripples is of course greater when there are also serious financial problems. The desire to give the dead person a great send-off causes many bereaved people to get into debt that they later find hard, if not impossible, to repay. To make matters worse – when a parent dies, the spouse/partner/carer often faces a significant drop in income. Children quickly notice that there are money worries. This tends to frighten an already-unsettled child even more. Most surviving parents find it initially very hard to cope with their children's intense needs. Some sink into deep depression. Others rely on drugs or alcohol to get through the day. Yet others desperately want a new beginning. They decide to move house, find another job or a new partner. Some of this happened to Emily (8), an only child whose mother died in a traffic accident.

Within a year of her mother's sudden death Emily's father met someone through an online dating-service. They grew to love each other. One day her dad told Emily that his new partner was a man. Emily had not known that prior to marrying her mother, her father had also lived with men. The new partner lived in a town 100 miles away and could for various reasons not move. Emily's dad decided to apply for a new job in his partner's town. When he got it they told Emily that they wanted to create a joint family-home. Every care was taken to involve Emily in the house-hunting, which she gamely did. However, shortly after the move, Emily began to feel very lost, saying that she was very confused about her father's loving relationship with a man. Due to the move she had also lost contact with her previous childhood friends, her school and gym-club, her familiar neighbourhood, as well as the more or less daily contact with her much-loved grandparents on her mother's side who had lived just around the corner from her former home. All in all, she had a lot to deal with.

The school was able to put her in touch with one of their specialist support-staff. Together they made up stories, did crafts activities and talked. After some months Emily found a new balance. She was relatively lucky. She had not grown up in poverty. Nor had she suffered the effects of health inequalities. Moreover, she got on well with her dad's new partner. She liked her new school, and before long she made new friends. Over time she also found new ways of staying in regular touch with her former friends and grandmother. Of course she continued to miss her mother, sometimes sorely, and the move to the new town was without a doubt very tough for

   STORIES TO LIGHT THE NIGHT

her. But like the majority of bereaved children she was gradually able to create links, emotionally and cognitively, between her former and her current experiential worlds. There were many bumps along her road towards emotional well-being. But that was to be expected. Her ability to deal with these bumps depended in large part on her school's and her new parents' joint willingness to address the complexity of her grief.

A Lesson from Hare

If we live long enough and love well enough, we will, at some point, have to come to grips with the death of people or animals we care for. By honestly facing the universal presence of death, birth and renewal we are likely to experience a greater resilience and joy in living, than if we were to persist in trying to pretend that death does not happen, or at least not to anyone we love. When we know about death, we will no longer be like Hare, the great culture-hero in the Winnebago Trickster-Cycle.

> When Hare discovered Death he ran back to the place where he lived. He shouted and cried: 'My people must not die!' And then he suddenly thought: 'All things will one day die!' He imagined cliffs and crags. They fell away. He imagined big mountains. They fell apart. He imagined the place below the earth. All that lived in the soil stopped scurrying about and died. He imagined the skies high above and the birds that flew stopped flying and fell to earth, dead. He entered the place where he lived. He reached for his blanket, and rolled himself into it. He lay there and wept. There will not be enough earth for all that dies, he thought. There is not enough earth for all that dies. He buried himself in his blanket. He made no sound.

Hare's overwhelmed response to his realization that death was inevitable and ubiquitous raises several important issues for the practice of storytelling with bereaved children. The first concerns a query about what the adults must do to comfort their own inner 'Hare'. This is necessary so that they can be with a child's grief in a centred, caring way. The second is that such adults need to be able to convey to the child that they truly want to be there for them and want to hear the stories that the child would like to share (Gersie, 1992, 1997).

Fundamental to possible answers to these issues are matters of psychological and social resilience. There are shared elements in different definitions of resilience. Generally speaking, resilient children and adults are able:

- to absorb and recover from shock;
- to face threats and events that are abnormal in terms of scale, form and timing;
- to adapt to changing and often threatening occurrences;
- to marshal their will to survive;
- to rally round a shared set of values.

But something else is needed besides the habits of resilient response, the preparedness to actively listen, and a kind intention, so that the Hare in all of us can move from frightened overwhelm to deep engagement with a grieving child. That something else is the true willingness to understand what bereaved children deserve in addition to having their physical needs met, and being in a safe environment with adults who will take care of them and protect them against misuse or exploitation.

What Grieving Children Most Need

Once their core needs are secure, most children have a profound need for re-connection, social support and involvement in important decisions. They also need to re-learn how to calm themselves when they get hyper-agitated. This is irrespective of their cultural background, the family's financial or social position, or their religious orientation. Below I lift some of their 'key' needs to the fore.

- They need the regular presence of some familiar older children or adults who are reliable, able to listen and chat, play games, make things with them, read stories, explore mementoes, are supportive and kind and maintain routines.
- The children also need to have their grief reactions normalized. They need to feel that it is okay and normal to have intense, and often quickly fluctuating, feelings, such as being sad, angry or feeling guilty; that they can expect to be a bit confused or forgetful, or find it hard to concentrate. Most children also like to know that unhappy dreams and trouble sleeping are part of the grieving process. While they might want adults to take their new aches and pains very seriously, they also seek reassurance that these pains, or a lack of appetite, may well happen to other grieving children too. Above all they need to hear that it is okay for them to carry on playing, to laugh as well as cry, and to do something distracting that helps them to forget what happened for a while.
- In addition, most bereaved children like to be reminded that they cannot control events that are in essence uncontrollable but that they will be asked, wherever practicable, to do things that they can do, such as setting a table, helping with the shopping or meal-preparation, or making a drawing for someone's birthday. Such doing will also help the child to differentiate between things that nobody can fix, that adults can fix, and things that they are expected to sort.
- Finally, every bereaved child needs to see and hear that the adults around them will take care of them and also of themselves. It matters to bereaved children that their caring adults remain well. This can be a difficult task. Bereaved families deserve a lot of support from their relatives, neighbours, colleagues and friends. But such help may not be forthcoming or available. When this is the case I urge you to seek support from the children's school, at work, from a support group, your faith-group or a dedicated organization. Grief is a lonely enough experience as it is, but we do not have to live through it alone. Help is available wherever we live.

How This Books' Stories and Storytelling Can Help

The stories and activities in this book encourage ordinary adults to try and alleviate the most common difficulties that young children and teenagers can have when they experience a serious loss or bereavement. The stories are a simple gift. Nothing more, but also nothing less. Taken together the stories and activities serve at least three functions:

First, if the child likes the story that it is told (and that's an important 'if'), the storytelling itself becomes an intimate interpersonal experience. That matters when someone important has died or you are shaken by an unwanted life-transition that involves major loss.

Secondly, the tales try to normalize a wide range of experiences of grievous loss that may bewilder the child. This too eases their burden of grief.

Thirdly, the stories attempt to offer children as well as their family and community a glimpse of how they might, in due course, be able to live well with their big loss. Many stories try to show them how their loss could become a lighter part of them and make them stronger. The telling of the stories to the children frequently also helps the adults to start to feel less helpless and tongue-tied when talking with the child about their grief. This often increases their own, initially fragile belief that they can support their grieving child despite their own sorrow.

These stories, like all other tales, have a beginning, a middle and an end. So do the lives of people, creatures and plants. And although every story ends, the child and the adult know that it will live on in their respective inner worlds, just like the memory of the person who died. This 'survival in memory' is reassuring. Taken together, the story, its telling and its remembrance help the child and the teller-of-stories to find a new togetherness and solidity in their shaken-up life. And that matters. A lot.

Enfield, December 2020
Alida Gersie Ph.D.
Author and co-editor, *Storytelling for a Greener World : Environment, Community and Story-based Learning*, Hawthorn Press, Stroud, UK, 2014 .

Further Reading
Anthony, S. (1940). *The Child's Discovery of Death. A Study in Child Psychology.*
    London: Routledge and Kegan Paul.
Bowlby, J. (1960). Grief and mourning in infancy and early childhood.
    Psychoanalytic Study of the Child, No. 15, pp. 9–52.
Dyregrov, A. (2008). *Grief in Children: A Handbook for Adults.* London: Jessica
    Kingsley Publishers.
Gersie, A. (1992). *Storymaking in Bereavement. Dragons Fight in the Meadow.*
    London: Jessica Kingsley Publishers.
Gersie, A. (1997). *Reflections on Therapeutic Storymaking. The Use of Stories in Groups.*
London: Jessica Kingsley Publishers.

1 INTRODUCTION

The Healing Power of Words and Stories

In the weeks before my mother died, I captured images of my love and appreciation for her in a poem entitled 'My Mother, My Rose'. While sitting by her hospital bed, while she was still conscious, and even when she was unconscious, I was able to read it to her – over and over... 'My Mother is the rose in the garden of my life....'

Little did I know just how important these images would be for me after she passed, when I was struggling to come to terms with the reality of 'My Mother was the rose in the garden of my life'. One verse especially shone a flicker of a light in the dark night of my grief. This tiny light helped me slowly find my way forward and gave me strength to carry on my responsibilities as a mother and a director of a school.

> *And when comes the time*
> *For the rose in my garden to die –*
> *Not brown and withered will I let it be,*
> *But the sweet petal memories*
> *Will be wrapped in silken haze*
> *To carry close to my heart*
> *For the rest of my days*

Even now, 30 years later, the image of 'sweet petal memories wrapped in silken haze' still lifts me out of my sadness at such a loss. And still, 30 years later, if I am given a bunch of cut roses, once they have lived out their life in a vase in my house I gather their petals into a bowl and then symbolically spread them in my garden.

Many years before experiencing the loss of my mother, a different kind of personal loss was greatly helped by the power of words. I was at an important crossroads in my life and was battling significant anxiety and loss of confidence in my decision-making. To follow my heart or to follow the expectations of others... this was my dilemma at the age of 19 years.

Then a gift came my way – a little book called *Jonathan Livingston Seagull*. The story of a seagull soaring high in the sky gave me strength and confidence to follow my heart direction. I am ever grateful for this modern classic about seeking a higher purpose in life, even if your flock, tribe or neighbourhood finds your ambition threatening. For most gulls, it is not flying that matters, but eating. For Jonathan, it was not eating that mattered, but flight.[1]

In 1671, John Milton wrote:

...apt words have power to swage
The tumours of a troubled mind.
And are as balm to festered wounds[2]

Almost two thousand years before Milton penned this wisdom on the healing power of words, a marble engraving was commissioned by King Ramses ll above the entrance to the royal chamber of an Egyptian palace where books were stored. Considered to be the oldest known library maxim in the world, the translated meaning is 'The house of healing for the soul'.

Bibliotherapists enthusiastically share this as the first recorded evidence of the existence of 'bibliotherapy',[3] a creative arts process that involves the reading of specific texts with the purpose of healing.

However, healing through words and stories dates back a long time before poetry, ballads and stories were ever written down, and an even longer time before the emergence of the term 'bibliotherapy'. Out of deep respect for indigenous cultures worldwide, it is important in this introduction to honour the magnificence of their oral history.

Before books... before writing... for thousands of years, many thousands of years, oral storytelling was integral to our humanity. Ben Okri, a Nigerian poet and novelist, eloquently states that 'The universe began as a story... we are part human, part stories'.[4]

The storyteller was the carrier of folklore and morals, the teacher, and the healer. His or her words were a soothing and strengthening and motivating balm for children and adults alike.

In many indigenous cultures, 'story' embraced, and still embraces, everything – all life, connectedness, nature and community. The stories and the storyteller stitched life and purpose and earth and sky together, mostly using images and motifs from the natural world: animals, birds, trees, mountains, clouds, stars, moon and sun.

In times of grief and loss, strength would be drawn from the stars, solace gained from sitting by a river, pain eased by walking through a forest. Stories were created that wove nature threads into healing journeys, and to this day continue to weave their healing work.

The world has so much to learn from this wisdom.

Intentions

The healing power of words and stories is the underlying premise for this collection of therapeutic stories on grief and loss. However, it is important that the word 'healing' is understood as an intention only... a humble intention to help. One needs to approach this work with humility.

The most effective support for grief offers a range of options, none of which can claim to be 'healing'. Most kinds of grief cannot be healed – but they can be supported, nursed, helped.

Grief is a highly individualized experience. Different ages, different people and different cultures grieve in diverse ways and respond to supportive modalities in individual and different ways. Recent decades have seen a broadening of attention to consider cognitive, social, cultural and spiritual dimensions to the study of grief, as well as the traditional focus on emotional consequences.[5]

A central process in grieving is the attempt to reaffirm or reconstruct a world of meaning that has been challenged by loss.[6] Story therapy can help this process. It can be used together with individual counselling, group support, community support, rituals, psycho-educational programmes and online support.

Story therapy can help navigate the emotions that come with profound loss. By allowing rather than resisting the truth, and by dressing it with the fabric of the imagination (see 'The Story of Truth', p. 41), stories can help the journey of weaving the truth into the wholeness of everyday life. Stories for grief and loss are emphatically not intended to distract from the experience of loss, but can enable a working-through of the experience.

The shortest distance between truth and a human being is a story
Anthony de Mello[7]

Overview

The stories in this collection have been enriched by the wellspring of oral and written story history. Of the 94 stories in the book, as well as many written by me, there are contributions by writers from most continents and cultures. The web of creativity spans from Australia to India, Denmark to Bulgaria, Scotland to Kenya, Slovenia to the UK, Spain to China, the USA to Croatia, Romania to the Philippines, Japan to Mexico and back to Australia.

The stories from the 34 contributors connect strongly to personal situations. They include descriptions of whom the story was written for, the age group and the situation. The writers are psychologists, social workers, nurses, teachers, parents and grandparents, plus three children from the 'Our Kids – Healing with Words' Hospital Project (a creative writing project for children living with chronic and serious illness).

Some have written other therapeutic stories before, but for others their contribution is their first attempt at story therapy, and they have shared it together with the documented help that it provided.

Some of the stories include an activity as an extension to the therapeutic process – making a memory treasure box, a mobile, a felt star, a knitted blanket, a scrapbook, a collage, some painted stones, a photo album, a weaving, planting a tree. Other stories are simply shared – for the reader or listener to digest and work with – in their own way and in their own time.

The comprehensive collection gives the opportunity for the reader to choose a story, or stories, that may resonate with their own personal situation of loss, or the personal situation of their client or family or school or community.

My Journey in Compiling this Collection

For many years I have been running therapeutic story-writing seminars – both nationally and internationally. At almost every seminar, whether the participant number was as low as six or as high as a hundred, the theme of grief and loss has been present. Either there has been a need to write a story for someone else – a child, teenager or adult – or for a group who has suffered trauma or loss, or sometimes grieving participants have been writing stories for themselves.

Often the question has been asked – when will you publish a book to address this theme? I have struggled with the responsibility of this, however the many heartfelt contributions from others and the positive responses to my own stories have encouraged its birth.

My confidence grew when it was pointed out to me, several times by different health professionals, that it is possible to offer a book with the theme of grief and loss that isn't 'clinical'. I am not a psychologist, but I have a talent for writing stories, and to the best of my ability, I am thorough with my documentation of 'when, where, for whom, what for and what happened next'. Such documentation is an integral part of therapeutic story-writing.

Hence I make no apology that this collection and its commentaries are not written from a clinical, explicitly psychotherapeutic and theoretical perspective, but rather from documented lived experiences. Readers seeking more explicitly *clinical-therapeutic* and *theoretical* approaches to 'story' are recommended to consult, respectively, Denborough (2014), Gersie (1997), Golding (2014), Jones & Pimenta (2020), Marr (2019) and Mellon (2019); and Bassil-Morozow (2020), Boyd (2010), Bruner (2002), Kearney (2001) and Rose & Philpot (2004).

I can also share that this collection, unlike my previous ones, is not just for children. From the moment I pondered the writing of this book, it seemed important that the collection would include stories for all ages. The experience of grief and loss has no boundaries: when someone dies, no matter at what age, the close family and the extended family and the friends and the community are often all involved.

Sometimes, for example, with the loss of a loved one there may be a need for a story for the little ones in the family, a different kind of story for the older children, and another kind for the teens and adults. In this collection some stories for use with younger children include 'The Little Candle'; 'Mama Roo and Little Roo'; and 'Little

Singing Bunny'. Others, with more complex story lines intended for older children, include 'When Grandma Passed Away'; 'The Fantastic Flying Machine'; and 'Goodbye Shelly'. Some have been written specifically for teens and adults, e.g. 'The Whale and the Pearl'; 'The Black Stone'; 'Little Shell and the Dancing Pearls'; 'The Garden'; 'The Lavender Nest'. Some have been written to share with all ages in the family, e.g. 'The Memory Treasure Box'; 'The Memory Blanket'; 'The Family Ship'.

The stories on the theme of 'cycles of life and change' and the stories for environmental grief and loss can be used as a springboard for discussion for families, schools and community groups. These could be used with all ages of children, except our very little ones who need as much as possible to stay protected by Mother Tree, as in 'The Little Gnome Who Had to Stay Home' (p. 145), a story written for the Covid-19 pandemic.

How to Use This Book

My advice to readers is to begin at the beginning and read through the pages of the introduction. For those who are interested in creating stories, I have included a theory section to follow this introduction. Here you will find notes on different kinds of therapeutic stories and therapeutic writing processes, and thoughts on metaphor and imagination. Many insights and examples have been included here to introduce you to this genre.

This is not a book intended to be read from cover to cover in one sitting. It is a resource collection with different sections for you to refer to if required. You may only want to look up and read one story, then come back to the book much later when and if you are interested, or have a need to do so. Also, please understand that this collection of 94 stories is not, by any means, a complete offering – there could be thousands of different kinds of therapeutic stories for grief and loss. The ones included here are a small sample of possibilities.*

For practical reasons, the stories in each section appear, in loose progression, as suitable for younger to older, and a suggested age group is identified in the introduction to the story. It did not feel appropriate to categorize them in any other way.

To help you find your way, each section begins with a list of the stories, including a brief description of the background circumstances.

Introducing the Different Story Sections

Loss of a loved one: in this section you will find stories written for children who have lost a sibling or a twin or a parent or a grandparent; stories for families who have

---

*If you have a story you have written on this theme, together with documentation of how the story helped a grief / loss situation, feel welcome to send it to be reviewed for possible inclusion in the second edition of this book.

lost a new baby; stories for parents who have lost children; and stories for a school and/or community where a friend has died from an illness or an accident.

Loss of family connection: this section includes stories for children whose parents have separated, stories for adopted and foster children, and stories for family members who for various reasons can only have limited time with other members of their family.

Loss of a pet: there are only three stories in this section but each of these, and the suggestions in them, can be adjusted to use for a variety of situations concerning the death of a beloved pet, or situations of having to say goodbye to a bird or animal that has been nursed back to health.

Loss of health and well-being: this includes stories for extended illness, anxiety about getting ill, the loss of mobility, the loss of voice (including selective mutism) and the loss of sight.

Loss of place: here you will find stories for children, families and communities who have lost their homes in bushfires, floods and other environmental disasters; stories for those who have had to move out of their home for various reasons; and stories for those who have had to leave their home country and settle elsewhere.

Environmental grief and loss: there are eight stories in this section covering different environmental themes. Some of them have story journeys that begin with greed and lack of caring and end on hopeful tones of sharing and caring. Others plunge deeply into the terrible situations of ocean pollution and loss of species, and end with just a hint of a possibility, in the hope that the message will be heard and acted upon. Eco-grief and eco-loss are a sad reality of our modern time. A collection on grief and loss calls for stories for these new challenges. They provide a contribution to a positive way forward, what Johnston and Macy term, 'active hope'.[8] In the words of Dr Jane Goodall, when asked how to speak effectively on the subject of climate change: 'Use the power of storytelling.... What you have to do is to get into the heart. And how do you get into the heart? With stories.'[9]

Other kinds of loss: there are many other kinds of loss that don't fall into the previous categories, yet it felt important to include stories for the loss of trust, the loss of co-operation, the loss of control, the loss of balance and the loss of respect.

Cycles of life and change: this section includes stories that share the 'bigger picture' of the cycles of life – the metamorphosis of a caterpillar to a butterfly; the cycle of the seasons; the cycle of water and the journey of a snowflake. Some traditional stories from different parts of the world bring their wisdom to this selection.

Patterns and templates: some of the stories are followed by an activity box that may have craft activities with patterns – you will find them in this section.

References and resources: here you will find a list of websites and resource books, and information on Bereavement Clinics and Services for Children and their Families in different countries around the world.

Notes and References

1. Richard Bach, *Jonathan Livingston Seagull*, Macmillan, New York, 1970.

2. *The Poetical Works of John Milton: Paradise Regained. Samson Agonistes. Minor Poems*, Nabu Press, 2012.

3. Originating from the Greek words for a book 'biblion' and healing 'therapeia', Bibliotherapy uses an individual's relationship to the content of books, poetry and other written words as therapy. After the term 'bibliotherapy' was coined by Samuel McChord Crothers in an August 1916 *Atlantic Monthly* article, it eventually found its way into the medical lexicon. Sometimes referred to as book therapy, poetry therapy or story therapy, today bibliotherapy is utilized in many helping professions worldwide, and there is a growing number of trainings incorporated into counselling, teaching and healthcare courses. Some of the trainings specialize in poetry therapy; others in book therapy; others, including my own trainings, specialize in story therapy, with the focus on crafting short stories for specific challenging behaviours and challenging situations.

4. Ben Okri, *Birds of Heaven*, Weidenfeld & Nicolson, London, 1996, p. 22.

5. Christopher Hall, 'Beyond Kübler-Ross: Recent developments in our understanding of grief and bereavement', MAPS, Director, Australian Centre for Grief and Bereavement, extracted from an article in *InPsych*, Vol. 33, Issue 6.

6. R. A. Neimeyer (ed.), *Techniques of Grief Therapy: Assessment and Intervention*, Routledge, New York, 2016.

7. Anthony de Mello (1931–1987) was an Indian Jesuit priest, psychotherapist, writer and public speaker.

8. Joanna Macy and Chris Johnstone, *Active Hope: How to Face the Mess We're in without Going Crazy*, New World Library, Novato, Calif., 2012.

9. Dr Jane Goodall, World Economic Forum, Davos, Switzerland, 2019.

2 THERAPEUTIC STORIES: PROCESS AND EXPERIENCE

Therapeutic stories are a healing medium that allows children, teenagers and adults to embark on an imaginative journey, rather than being lectured or directly addressed about the issue. By identifying with the main character or characters, the listener is empowered as obstacles are overcome and a resolution achieved. This is a gentle, easy, yet often effective means of addressing challenging behaviours and difficult situations.

Working with a creative journey and a specific selection of metaphors, a therapeutic story approach has the potential to shift an out-of-balance behaviour or situation back towards wholeness or balance. The story may help considerably, help a little, soothe, motivate, strengthen resolve and/or sow invaluable seeds for future change.

In my first two print books, *Healing Stories for Challenging Behaviour* and *Therapeutic Storytelling: 101 Healing Stories for Children*, a story-making model is shared in detail – a three-fold framework of 'Metaphor', 'Journey' and 'Resolution' – to guide the writing of therapeutic stories.

In this model, the journey is the formative part of the therapeutic story construction. An eventful journey is a way to build the tension as the story evolves, and can lead the plot into and through the behaviour 'imbalance' and out again to a wholesome, proactive resolution (that is not guilt-inducing).

However, I wish to emphasize the following. **In situations of grief and loss, to offer a specific framework or method for writing therapeutic stories does not seem possible or appropriate. It would be insensitive to suggest that a story journey could lead to a 'wholesome proactive resolution'. It would be inappropriate to claim that a story could be 'healing'.**

A more subtle, reflective, intuitive approach is required in these difficult times.

Story therapy may only give a whisper of comfort, a whisper of support, but is well worth the creative effort if it can offer such whisperings.

A Quality of 'Being Present'

Every story in this collection has a different pathway, a different journey, a different style... but they all share one common quality. Each story has been written out of observation and listening. Each story has been created out of total dedication to being 'present' – both with the individual(s) involved and the situation of grief and loss. Insight into the importance of such 'presence' can be gained from the following definition: 'The word "therapy" comes from both Greek and Latin origins (Modern Latin – therapia; Greek – therapeia), and has the following range of meanings: curing, healing, waiting on, attending, taking care of, doing service.'[1] This gives us an important clue for writing therapeutic stories for grief and loss. We need to take time 'to attend' the situation; and to do this we need a quality of 'being present', a quality of 'listening':[2]

- We need to quietly listen to and observe the situation of the grief and loss.
- We need to 'be present with' and take time to observe the child, adult, family or community involved.
- We need to listen to and respect the religious and or philosophical beliefs of the child, adult, family or community involved (and create our stories with this in mind).
- We need to listen to our intuition.
- We need to listen to our common sense.

We also need the patience and perseverance to be able to play with ideas and have the courage to 'give it a go' – to write down our stories and, when and if appropriate, to share them with others.

Sensing the Right Time and Place to Share a Therapeutic Story

A sensitivity is required in finding the right time and place for sharing a therapeutic story. There can be no exact guidelines. As mentioned above, you need to listen to the situation. I once wrote a story for a friend who had lost her child in an accident. I thought on my first visit to her home that I would share it with her, but it did not feel appropriate. Almost a year passed before the 'right' moment came for its sharing.

The story you write may never be seen or heard by anyone. You certainly need to be careful not to push your stories on the grieving individual or family or community. However, the story may be helpful to you, may support you.

Sometimes your story idea may be a seed for a future story.

Sometimes your story, or a story from this collection, may be shared with a child or family while out walking in the forest, or sitting in a park, or playing in a sandpit, or at a table while drawing together, or by soft candlelight before bedtime.

Sometimes a story may be read out or told at a memorial service or community gathering. Or you may wrap it up in a box, or roll it as a scroll, and give it as a gift to a close friend or family member.

Sometimes a story may be so ready to be heard that it will fly up and out and find a way to reach many readers and listeners, in print and/or oral form – in the home, the classroom, the therapist's clinic, or at a community gathering.

Cautionary notes

- When sharing stories with children, often they will guide you – if the story is not interesting to them, or leaves them feeling uncomfortable, they will usually communicate this. However, with very little ones, you as the adult have to be careful to make age-appropriate choices.[3] In summary, the milder the theme or journey, the more appropriate the tale for younger children (if obstacles are encountered they should not weigh too heavily on the soul of the listener); the greater or more complex the difficulties or journey, the more appropriate the tale is for older children. (The confrontation with negative characters and obstacles may be stronger and more challenging, and there may be more twists and turns along the journey.)
- Be careful about the names you choose for your story characters. I usually avoid 'human' names as much as possible, and use, for example, 'Little Roo' for a baby kangaroo, and not, for example, Rosie Roo: this way prevents the listener making connections between the metaphors and real life, real people. Many years ago when I was finding my way into this story work, I shared a therapeutic story with a child, and without thinking about it I began using the child's real name as the character's name. This altered his listening experience from one of indirect expression (a sharing of someone else's difficulties through a metaphorical story journey) to one of direct expression. It exposed him as the centre of the story, he did not want to hear the full tale, and any therapeutic value was lost.
- Be wary of following a therapeutic story with any kind of interpretation or closed meaning: *leave the story to do its work.* Your comments could interfere with or, worse still, destroy any therapeutic value. However, if the listener or reader (child or adult) is eager to talk about the story, I suggest you let them lead the discussion.
- Even if a therapeutic story is specifically written for a certain age, it will sometimes speak to other age groups – stay open to this possibility. The very nature of a 'story' rebels against being fixed into an age-appropriate box. The metaphors in therapeutic stories have a fluid quality that can often speak to different ages in different ways.

Different Types of Stories

There are no recipes or formulae for writing therapeutic stories for grief and loss. However, several types of stories have emerged in the preparation of this collection. The following are identified and explored – they are a sample of therapeutic stories that could be used in situations of grief and loss:

- Mirroring stories
- Open-ended stories
- Stories that offer 'love in another form'
- Stories addressing challenges as a consequence of grief and loss
- Talismans in stories and stories with practical extensions

Mirroring stories

Sometimes simply acknowledging or mirroring the situation with the use of imagery can be of help. 'Mirroring' is a literary device or technique that can bring depth and meaning to a situation in a safe and subtle way, enabling the story to address otherwise difficult or sensitive topics without lecturing or preaching. The story journey and story metaphors present the truth not in naked form, but clothed in the fabric of the imagination.

A teacher in Spain wrote a story after the death of her nephew Tomás, one of twin boys who sadly lived for only a few days. The story ('A Nest in the Stars' – p. 46) is about two birds, Pio Pio and Cu Cut, who choose to come down from their high nest in the stars to live in the world. Pio Pio is enjoying all his new adventures in the world, but Cu Cut is cautious and uncomfortable and missing the warmth of his star nest, and he wants to return.

> Cu Cut took to the air and soared up, up, up.... all the way to the sky... When night fell, Pio Pio looked up at the stars from the meadow, and Cu Cut gazed at the same stars from his nest.

The teacher illustrated the story as a picture book to give as a supportive gift for the whole family. She also shared it with her five-year old son, after telling him the news of the loss of his little cousin. The images in this 'mirroring' story helped her son make some sense of the situation. His response was immediate: 'Now Tomás will be able to see the stars from above, and Pablo from below'.

A different kind of story journey, but one that used similar imagery of a bird in a high nest, was written for a father of a little girl. It mirrored the situation of regular but very difficult separation times – the father's work in forestry required him to live quite a distance from his daughter ('The Forester and the Bird' – p. 129).

There are so many possibilities for choosing imagery for mirroring stories; in these following examples the writers have used:

- a candle ('The Little Candle' – p. 52)
- a bubbly spring ('Miss Burble' – p. 71)
- a clump of bamboo ('The Bamboo Family' – p. 178)
- a tomato plant ('Uprooted' – p. 198)
- a little fish in a rock pool ('Two Homes for Sparkle' – p. 103)
- a mother and baby kangaroo ('Mama Roo and Baby Roo' – p. 105)

- a yellow train and a blue engine ('The Little Yellow Train' – p. 111)
- a collection of cups in a kitchen cupboard ('The Cup Tower' – p. 122)
- three circle friends in the land of shapes ('The Circle Friends' – p. 252)
- a tailor and an embroidered kimono ('The Flowered Kimono' – p. 192)
- a sweet and juicy orange ('The Gannan Orange' – p. 125)

A mirroring approach can sometimes provide answers to difficult questions that present to the family in times of grief. In the story 'Wolf Boy's Journey Home' (p. 48), written for a young boy dying of an incurable illness, the boy's 'need to know' answers ('where will I be buried?') were woven into the story journey.

> ...The next day Papa Wolf awoke to a hard question from Wolf Boy. 'Papa, where will you bury my bones and my body?' Mama Wolf nodded towards Papa Wolf and spoke, 'What do you think about the old cedar tree, the place where you can look at the beautiful mountain?'.
>
> 'Yes', said Wolf Boy. 'Can we go there today so you can show me the place?' Papa Wolf remembered that the owl had said that Wolf Boy would ask the right questions to get them ready.

A mirroring approach sometimes needs to reflect the dark places and dark experiences as much as including the positive light-filled times. A Danish mother, Ninna, who had adopted twins from China, wrote a story ('The Crack' – p. 118) about the journey of two mouse babies that fell out of their mouse carriage:

> The two little mouse babies fell into a crack in the ground, and suddenly everything was very dark, and all they could feel was cold dirt. Fortunately for the two babies, they both held on to each other's tails. And in the darkness, they rolled up against each other, shaking with fear.

Ninna explains how cathartic it was for both boys to repeatedly hear about the terrible times. In her words, 'it felt like they again and again had to go back to the feeling they had when they were left alone in the foster home, or in some dark and hopeless place'.

Open-ended stories

Sometimes a story requires an open ending, or it may just leave a hint of a suggestion at the end. To offer anything resolved or final in the story journey may not be necessary, possible or appropriate.

In Zagreb a mother attended a seminar on story therapy. Together with a friend she crafted a story for her 17-year old daughter who was suffering from full loss of mobility. The teenager could no longer walk by herself but was refusing the use of a wheelchair. The story, entitled 'The Black Stone' (p. 170), had a remarkable effect on the girl, who is now, many years later, an advocate for disability services in Croatia.

Here are the final few sentences – they help to shine a light on a possible way forward:

> ...as she fell, the stone slipped from her hold and cracked open as it landed on the ground, revealing its brilliant purple from within, its inner colour and shine. Illuminated by the light of her stone, the girl continued her journey through life.

You will notice that the above story doesn't end with a lecture or any kind of message to suggest that the wheelchair should be used. There is no mention of a wheelchair in the whole story. In fact, it is worth noting that this kind of 'lecturing' or 'teacher talk' does not belong in story therapy. The 'Black Stone' story was constructed in a way that left the teenager free to come to her own conclusion.

Another example of an open-ended story is one I wrote for environmental grief and loss. 'Messages in the Sand' (p. 214) uses a multi-armed, multi-mouthed monster to represent the state of pollution in the ocean, a monster that is growing exponentially. There doesn't seem to be a solution. Then great-grandmother turtle has an inspiration. She suggests a way for all the turtles to deliver an important message to the humans, in the hope that the message will be heard and acted upon. The story ends with just a hint of a possibility: six words are left in the sand for the humans to find the next morning. They are only there for a short time, then the tide washes them away.

Stories that offer 'love in another form'

The novelist Franz Kafka[4] one day encountered a young child in the park where he went walking. The girl was crying because she had lost her doll and seemed inconsolable. Kafka immediately began to explain to her what had happened. 'Your doll has gone off on a journey', he said. The surprised girl asked him how he knew that, to which he replied, 'Because she's written me a letter – I'll bring it with me tomorrow'.

When he returned home, Kafka wrote the letter, then met the girl in the park the next day and read it to her. 'Please do not mourn me, I have gone on a trip to see the world. I will write you of my adventures.' This was the beginning of many letters. When he and the little girl met each day, he read to her the imagined adventures of the beloved doll. The little girl was comforted – her loss had been supplanted with a different reality.

This poses the question: 'Did Kafka offer the girl a false reality?' According to the laws of fiction, one could argue his approach was true – the doll had indeed gone on an adventure, even though the descriptions in the letters were different to its real adventure (that no one had any information about).

After some time, Kafka presented the child with another doll that obviously looked different from the original doll. An attached letter explained: 'my travels have changed me...'

The real-life story gets a bit blurry here, but one version says that many years later, the now-grown girl found a letter stuffed inside the much-loved replacement doll. In summary it said: 'Everything that you love, you will eventually lose, but in the end, love will return in a different form.'

Even if the story didn't happen quite this way, the wisdom in Kafka's actions is of interest to those of us writing therapeutic stories. He was trying to help the little girl with her loss, by finding a way to bring back 'love in another form'.

In relation to the loss of material things, we can learn something important from this. Too often if we focus so intently on such a loss, we can miss out on wonderful aspects of life that are right in front of us, within arm's reach. Great sensitivity was demonstrated by Kafka. He had the wisdom to *not* say to the little girl, 'You can always find another doll'.

In the story 'Goodbye Shelly' (p. 85), when Jenny loses her precious shell to a fast-moving incoming tide, grandma comforts her but is careful how she does this:

> The one thing Grandma didn't say was, 'you can always find another shell'. Jenny was so glad that her Grandma was wise and knew that saying that would not have helped.

Some examples of stories in this collection that offer 'love in another form' include:

'A New Dawn' (p. 134) This story was written for a boy in Mumbai who had become attached to a stray dog; then his family moved to another part of the city. Through the journey of the story, his love and attachment are shifted to 'birds' – this was much more feasible as he now lived in a high-rise apartment, with only one balcony as a connection to the outside world. He began to leave seeds on the balcony, and the seeds attracted parrots residing on neighbouring trees. Bird watching continues to be his hobby even today.

'Heavenly Magic' (p. 56) This story was written for a boy in China called Tao Tao who had lost his father in a drowning incident one year earlier. Tao Tao was about to start school and his mother was concerned that he couldn't let go of his special blanket (he was already being teased about this). In the story journey some heavenly magic turned the blanket into a blanket bag, a bag that could easily travel with Tao Tao wherever he went.

'The Beavers and the Oak Tree' (p. 67) This story was written for two boys whose grandfather and cousin were killed in a car accident. It begins with a magnificent tree in the forest that is cracked in half by lightning. It had been a home to many forest creatures – birds, animals and insects – and now they have nowhere to live. Then the Beavers come along. Chanting their song, they busily set to work, gnawing and carving the fallen wood, shaping new homes for the forest creatures. The magnificent tree and all it represented is now in another form.

Stories addressing challenge as a consequence of grief and loss

Some of the stories in this collection have been written to address various behaviour challenges as a consequence of a grief-and-loss situation. For these situations my therapeutic story-writing model[5] has been used, and the relevant stories have helped to shift an out-of- balance behaviour or situation back towards some kind of balance.

This construction model for writing a therapeutic (healing) story works with a framework of 'Metaphor', 'Journey' and 'Resolution'. It is helpful to identify and discuss these separately, even though they intricately weave together to create the finished story.

The framework put forward here is only one suggested approach. Many of the stories included in this book have not been written based on this (or any other) foundation but have followed their own intuitive path. First, you need to be clear what you are trying to achieve when writing a therapeutic story. A story devised to help or heal a behaviour challenge is about trying to re-create wholeness or balance in the child's or teen/adult's own experience. It is also important to understand that behaviour is contextual and relational. Any imbalanced behaviour can rarely be effectively addressed in isolation. When working with challenging behaviour, storytelling is just one of many possible approaches and strategies – one thread in the whole fabric.

Positive resolutions

The resolution in a therapeutic story is the restoration of harmony or balance in a situation or behaviour that has been disruptive or out of balance. It is important for a resolution to offer affirmation rather than inducing guilt. Even though the resolution comes at the end of the story, when planning it is usually helpful to think about this before anything else. If the resolution is not clear, then it is difficult to know what to work towards with your journey and metaphors.

Building tension – the journey and the metaphors

The journey is the formative part of the construction model. As the story evolves an eventful journey helps to build the 'tension'. Stories for young children[6] usually only require simple events and small amounts of tension in the journey, whereas for older children events can be more detailed or complex, and supply greater tension as the journey unfolds.

The use of obstacle and helping metaphors is intricately connected with the journey. The tension or conflict (like pulling back the string on a bow) is usually built up through the involvement of the obstacle metaphors, and the resolution is achieved through the helping metaphors.

Some examples of stories written with this three-part framework are summarized here.

'**The Ballerina and the Music Box**' (p. 54) – this is a story that helped a five-year old girl overcome her fear of going to sleep. One month beforehand she had lost her father to a sudden illness. Because he had died at home in his sleep, the girl was extremely fearful of going to sleep, and very fearful of her mother going to sleep.

Out of balance situation: lack of sleep, fear of sleep
More balanced situation: healthy sleep patterns, confident to sleep[7]

'The Fantastic Flying Machine' (p. 82) – this story was written for a ten-year old boy in Holland whose father was tragically killed in a car accident. The story helped re-channel the boy's anger for what had happened (anger that he was directing at his mother) into something productive for his future.

Out of balance situation: anger, lack of motivation
More balanced situation: reduced anger, motivation to take on new projects

'Little Shell and the Dancing Pearls' (p. 172) – this story was written as self-therapy by a woman in Slovenia. She had suffered extreme difficulties through life, including losing an eye at the age of three.

Out of balance situation: feelings of guilt, anger, shame and pain
More balanced situation: increased confidence, reduced anger

Talismans in stories and stories with practical extensions

Sometimes a talisman is linked to the story journey. Such a symbolic item can strengthen the therapeutic experience. A talisman is usually an object of mineral (e.g. a gemstone), vegetable (e.g. a four-leaf clover) or animal origin (e.g. a feather) that is believed to hold magical properties that provide particular power, energy and specific benefits to the possessor.

Most children, with their more open, spiritual relationship to the nature world, unquestioningly accept the connection with such objects. Some carry this through to adult life, and (myself included) may carry a shell, feather, stone, leaf, pearl, or several of these, in one's pocket, hand bag or travel bag at all times, and/or wear it as a piece of jewellery.

Both social and medical science have long correlated stressful conditions and situations with an increased relationship to magical thinking and symbolic objects. They can give a sense of control, comfort and reassurance in circumstances where it is lacking.[8]

A talisman may be gifted together with a therapeutic story. Some examples include:

- the amethyst ring connected to **'The Black Stone'** story (p. 170)
- the feathers in **'The Rainbow Dove'** story (p. 92)
- the painted stones in the story of **'The Rainbow Stone'** (p. 243)
- a little glass blue bird for the story of **'The Forester and the Bird'** (p. 129)

Sometimes a story journey can be constructed around, or include the idea of, a practical activity. For example, for those who have had a friend or family member recently die from illness or accident, the story of **'The Memory Treasure Box'** (p. 93) includes the activities of making and gathering special items, sharing memory stories about them, and keeping them in a special memory box.

Other examples include:

- a class of children in a town (recently threatened by bushfires) knitting memories of the year into different squares for a blanket (**'The Memory Blanket'** – p. 188)
- two sisters in Kenya weaving jasmine crowns to give them courage on the one-year memorial of their father's death (**'Taji La Upendo – The Crown of Love'** – p. 58)
- a tree-planting ritual, including a song, to commemorate the death of a beloved pet (**'Donna and Scruff'** – p. 132)
- compiling a photo album at the end of the story **'Time to Say Goodbye to Baby Roo'** (p. 137)
- weaving a nest of grasses and lavender for the dining table in the down-sized home (**'The Lavender Nest'** (p. 205).

Adjusting stories to different situations

Please feel welcome to use the stories in this collection in any way that may resonate with you and/or your child, family, client, class or community. Sometimes the sharing might need some slight changes to fit the situation. It may feel more appropriate to change the character or characters; or you may need to simplify the story journey, or make it more complex.

If you find any example in this book that speaks to your situation but needs some parts changed, I invite you to use 'poetic licence' but at the same time strive to retain the integrity of the story, and its positive intent, even if subtle.

When using story therapy in times of grief and loss, we must be sensitive with our stories – how to offer whispers of hope, but how to not be overbearing or presumptuous.

> Hope is important because it can make the present moment less difficult to bear. If we believe that tomorrow will be better, we can bear a hardship today.[9]

Thoughts on Metaphor

In simple terms, a metaphor shows us one thing as another, and in doing so extends the way we see the world, often refreshing and enlivening our perception. Succinctly described by Lakoff and Johnson as 'a fundamental mechanism of mind', metaphors allow us to use what we know about our physical and social experience to provide understanding of countless other subjects.[10]

In written and oral language, using the medium of picture imagery, metaphor speaks directly to our imaginative faculties, bypassing our rational brain. Such metaphoric byways and pathways enable us to explore the ideas, forces and powers that lie behind or beyond our rational thought. Overcoming the limitations of our fixed categories and often cumbersome or clumsy everyday human language, metaphor offers a form of 'higher' or more holistic cognition. Here is Ken DiBenedette:

> Metaphor juxtaposes familiar concepts to reveal higher, archetypal concepts. These higher concepts cannot be literally stated in familiar language. The higher concepts are 'unnamed'; no single definable word attaches to these 'thought beings', nor are they accessible to abstract, logical reasoning. They are poetical intuitions that incarnate into thought and language through the skilled manipulation of familiar concepts.[11]

Metaphoric language lives in the realm of the imagination, which is as valid for learning and knowing as the realm of cognition. Albert Einstein understood this only too well. He was famously known as saying: 'Logic will get you from A to B, imagination can take you anywhere.'

Metaphor is different from simile. While simile compares one thing with another and highlights its resemblance using the word 'like' ('Your smile is *like* the morning sun'), metaphor accomplishes the magical transformation of turning something into something else ('Your smile *is* my morning sun'). In simile, the process of comparison involves our more rational brain, our thinking processes, whereas metaphor reaches deep into our soul imagination and, simply stated, 'touches our heart'.

For this reason, metaphor has long been the language of mystics, spiritual teachers, poets, storytellers and other expressive artists. Metaphor is a heart-tool that helps us explore the ideas, forces and powers that lie behind our rational thought.

Margot Sunderland, Director of Education and Training at the Centre of Child Mental Health in London, argues that metaphor (picture language) and story are a vital part of a child's healthy emotional digestive system. She believes that the natural language of feeling for children is not literal everyday language – *a language of thinking* – but image, metaphor and story – *a language of imagining*.[12]

Story or picture language can be as simple as a single word or phrase in a sentence. A trip to the dentist for my son to have a tooth filled proved this. The dentist told my son, 'You need to have a silver star put in your tooth to keep it strong'. The previously reluctant child widely opened his mouth to receive the 'silver star' (despite the warning added by the dentist that it would hurt a bit to put the star in his tooth).

This was my first introduction to how powerful picture language could be. I then began to experiment with it in my parenting and teaching. Talking about shoes as 'friends together' was a much more effective approach than lecturing about the importance of being tidy and caring for your things. I found using picture language had a much higher success rate, resulting in children putting their shoes together at the door, instead of kicking them off and leaving them lying wherever they landed.

A Chinese parent in one of my online courses encouraged her eight-year old son to be a 'lightning rod' whenever he was feeling angry. He began to place his feet firmly on the floor and his arms stretched up high with palms together. This brought a new stillness to a usually aggressive and destructive time. Before the boy had this 'picture' to work with, he didn't know what to do with his anger and would often hit out at different family members or the furniture in the apartment.

Picture or story language can penetrate and enrich our daily life and work in so many ways – and not just with children! Psychologist Susan Laing[13] was consulting a new mother who had been grieving for six months. Her baby was healthy, but the mother was unhappy that she had to have a C-section, and not the planned natural birth. Susan asked her, 'If you were trapped in a room with the door stuck, what would you do?'. The woman answered immediately, 'I would have to climb out the window of course', and then she smiled. The picture language touched her deeply and helped her grief to slowly dissipate.

Another psychologist found a way to connect with a client in prison using a powerful set of metaphors. His client was a 17-year old boy who, while intoxicated, had been driving a car that crashed into a tree and killed three of his friends. The young man was the only survivor, and the psychologist was finding it difficult to connect with him, as he was in a seriously depressed state. After several visits with little progress, the psychologist began to talk about a captain that had led his soldiers into battle. All the soldiers had been killed – a consequence of poor decisions made by the captain. But the captain survived, with one wound so deep that no doctor could find the bullet. The captain returned home on a quest to find and transform the 'hidden bullet'. The psychologist left an empty journal for the young man, and on the next visit he saw many written pages in the journal. The young man let him read the pages. He had continued with the metaphors, listing many tasks for the captain to do that would complete the quest. These included different ways to help the families of the soldiers who had been killed.

A local doctor keeps on his desk a collection of figurines – including people, animals, trees, houses, fairy-tale characters. He uses it as a point of lateral reference for his patients to start connecting with their condition, physical and/or emotional, in a metaphorical way. In this way the patients are helped to find their own metaphors for their own unique situations. The doctor reports that this symbolic approach helps him understand his patients in a more effective way, and it also helps them to feel truly 'heard'.

Metaphor therapy

The above, consciously or unconsciously, intentionally or unintentionally, are examples of the modality of metaphor therapy, a kind of psychotherapy that uses metaphor as a tool to help people express their experiences symbolically. Metaphorical interpretation of life, rather than analogical, combines the past with what is new, the simple with the complex and the superficial with the deep.

In his book *Man and His Symbols*,[14] Carl Jung explains that there are many things beyond the range of human understanding. Therefore, a person naturally and constantly uses symbolic terms to represent concepts that they cannot fully comprehend or define.

Neuro-linguistic programmer and author David Gordon describes metaphors 'as our experience' (not just a way to talk about our experience), setting the filters through which we perceive and make sense out of the world. Because of this, metaphors can serve as powerful levers capable of moving perception, experience and behaviour. He argues that 'therapeutic metaphors' provide a depth of association and potential for insight that is often not available through more direct approaches. Metaphors do this by creating a shared language between therapist and client – a shared world within which communication about a problem and how to resolve it become easier and more impactful. Furthermore, once created, that metaphorical world can become one in which the person discovers his or her own resolution to the problem.[15]

Sometimes this shared metaphoric language can help between co-workers, or friends, or within families. Even if this effects just a tiny shift, it should be valued.

Metaphors in storytelling

The use of metaphor is a vital ingredient in crafting a therapeutic story. Metaphors help build the imaginative connection for the listener. They are responsible for delivering the story message in an indirect way, and this avoids any shaming, judgement or humiliation. The focus is on the character in the story, and the character's journey, thus taking the spotlight off the listener and the listener's situation. Herein, says Margot Sunderland, lies the story's power and safety and wisdom.[16]

As the journey moves from problem to crisis to solution (or open ending), the metaphors can play both negative and positive roles: they can be obstacles or hindrances, helpers or guides, shifters and/or bridge builders.

Integrated into storytelling, a metaphor or many metaphors can, as in spiritual writings and poetry, take on a mystery and magic that is sometimes subtle, sometimes powerfully medicinal. The metaphors seem to come alive and gain energy from each other in a vibrant interplay, and through this process they have the possibility of producing potent story medicine.

A 55-year old woman suffering from depression following several losses in her life (first her husband, then her job) wrote a story for herself at a therapeutic story seminar in Croatia. Here is a summary:

> ...a firefly had lost its light and was flying alone in a dark cave, not knowing who it was or where it was. Then it happened, just by chance, a silver ray of moonlight shone down through a tiny crack in the roof of the cave. The silver ray lit up the firefly and gave it back its light.

This little story helped the woman find her way out of the darkness of depression and encouraged her to take up bushwalking and to go camping. Apparently, her friends and family had been pushing her to go walking and get out into nature, but she had been ignoring their advice. It was the metaphors and the imaginative journey in the story that spoke deeply to her.

On one of my Eastern European tours I was in Bulgaria running therapeutic storytelling seminars for psychologists. One group worked on a story for a five-year old girl (mentioned earlier) who a month beforehand had tragically lost her father to a sudden illness. Because he had died at home in his sleep, the girl was extremely fearful of going to sleep, and she was also fearful of her mother going to sleep. She would do everything she could to try and stay awake – run around the house, scream and cry, refuse to lie down; and when out of sheer exhaustion she would fall asleep, she would wake up a few hours later and run to her mother and wake her up.

The grieving and sleep-deprived mother had tried several strategies – star charts, chocolate rewards, rationalization ('Your father is looking down on you and he'll be very happy to see you sleep so you can work better at school the next day'). But none of these strategies were working (the mother was using the 'language of thinking' referred to earlier). And so, the mother had visited a psychologist requesting help.

This psychologist happened to be attending my therapeutic storytelling seminar that weekend. Together with a small group of colleagues she worked on a story to hopefully help the little girl 'want to go to sleep'.

You may wonder where one begins with such a story. The girl's interests were ballet, music and dolls, so this was my recommended starting point.[17] The group wasn't getting very far, but then one of the participants had the idea of a ballerina that lived inside a music box. This was a perfect fit for the story journey. The opening and closing of the lid, with the subsequent dancing and resting of the ballerina, were a wonderful representation of the balance between waking and sleeping. The group introduced a four-legged table to represent the family. This was a most unusual metaphor, but they wanted to honour the mother's difficult position after the loss of her husband in keeping things 'balanced on three legs'.

You can read the completed story, entitled 'The Ballerina and the Music Box', on page 54. Three weeks later I received the following email from the mother's psychologist in Sophia:

This story did something amazing. The girl liked it very much and asked her mother to tell her the story several times, and then would fall deeply asleep. The story reduced the girl's tension and anxiety to a great extent. She asked a lot of questions about the Spirit of Dreams. We established contact with a young woman studying at The Academy of Arts in Sofia who painted the Dream Spirit on the wall over the girl's bed. The effect was just like in a fairy tale. The problem with the sleep seems to be solved.

    STORIES TO LIGHT THE NIGHT

In this situation, the choice of metaphors (ballerina, music box, table, storm, broken leg, dream spirit) worked together in a therapeutic story journey and created effective story medicine. This helped the girl overcome her fear and helped her 'want' to go to sleep each night.

A different choice of metaphors and story journey was used in a workshop in North America. The desired resolution was to find new strength and life following the suicide of a father. The group worked with a nature cycle theme, and the story was about a strong oak tree toppled over by a great storm. Where the roots had been torn out, a baby acorn was dropped into the earth. Cradled in the arms of the acorn shell, in the dark of the earth, all alone, the acorn slowly began to sprout.

This situation was quite different from the one in Bulgaria. The group felt it was important that the story should be written primarily for the mother, to encourage her to find strength to cradle and support her young child.

There are so many different situations where well-chosen metaphors can offer help – for children, teenagers and adults. A 22-year old Kenyan man was in the care of *Médecins Sans Frontières* in Nairobi. With only a few months left to live, he wrote a story about a family of rabbits to say honest and important things about his life, and quite shocking things about his father who had abused his mother and sister. It was a six-page cathartic story that his culture would not have allowed him to express as a factual account.

In Portugal, at a conference on 'Fairy Tale and Story Therapy', a group of six women wrote a story for their mutual situation of loss of respect and care. They were all feeling overwhelmed, overused and undervalued. They performed it for the group as a play, and felt quite empowered by their use of the harp as the central metaphor, an image they all agreed would stay with them for a long time. Here is the story summary:

There was once a beautiful harp that was the centre of a large home – the harp had been strongly built, and made wonderful music. All the family members and friends wanted to play it, even the dog wanted to play it. The harp was working overtime, and eventually some of the strings broke. The harp was then put out of the house and into the garden as it was no use any more. It sat there in all kinds of weather through the autumn and the winter. Then one day in the spring, a night-ingale flew down and landed on the top of the harp and began to sing a most beautiful song. Something deep in the harp resonated with the song and it began to play a soft tune again. The family and friends heard the music and brought the harp back inside, polished it and fixed all the strings. Now the harp was playing beautiful music once again, but this time the harp knew how to care for itself (the bird song contained wise secrets). Anyone who wanted to play it must ask first, and sometimes the harp would say 'No, not now', or 'Come back tomorrow', or 'Yes, but just for a little while', or 'Yes, but very carefully'.

There is such a need and a thirst today for story medicine, for all ages.

Thoughts on Imagination

A foundation for therapeutic story work calls for both an honouring of our imaginative 'way of knowing' and the exploration of the question, 'What is the imagination?'.

Stories speak to our imaginative intelligence – sometimes referred to as the right-hemisphere, right brain, or balanced and holistic mode of being. The ability to imagine was once celebrated as the *heart of our humanness*, but now, with the emergence of science as the dominant worldview, the significance of the imagination has sadly been diminished and devalued. Some educationalists and philosophers are concerned – and for good reason. In his book *Lost Knowledge of the Imagination*, Lachman argues that, for the sake of our future in the world, we must reclaim the ability to imagine and redress the balance of influence between imagination and science.[18]

McGilchrist,[19] in *The Master and His Emissary*, has used a poignant title to capture this imbalance. He contends that our society is suffering from the consequences of an over-dominant left hemisphere losing touch with its natural regulative 'master', the right hemisphere. From this, all sorts of difficulties can and have arisen, with implications for the Western cultural tradition as well as globally.

In my Masters of Education thesis,[20] completed at the turn of this century, I argued for storytelling modules to be included in teacher training courses. My justification was the need for balancing the curriculum with its overload of rational, logical subjects (what I like to refer to as the 'dominant siblings') by including more of the expressive, imaginative subjects – storytelling, of course, being one of these. My metaphorical intention? – a balanced family! I managed to convince my local university to include a storytelling module in their elective programme, and it is still running 20 years later.[21] Tiny steps, perhaps – but a small way of helping restore the imbalance, and of honouring imagination as a valid way of learning and knowing.

Every time a teacher brings oral storytelling into his or her classroom to teach different subject material, lighting up the children's imaginations, I like to picture that another grain of story-sand has been added to tip the scales of imaginative imbalance. Every time a therapeutic story is experienced with positive effect somewhere in the world, I like to picture that another grain of story-sand has been added to tip the scales of imaginative imbalance.

Dancing with the definition

Dictionary definitions of the word 'imagination' include: 'the faculty of forming mental images of what is not actually present to the senses; the ability to imagine things that are not real; the ability to think of new things'. However, these definitions can seem quite limiting and dry. They speak conceptually of something that is not conceptual. If one wants to understand a butterfly, one really needs to move and dance with it, not capture it in a net.

STORIES TO LIGHT THE NIGHT

From different cultural and poetic viewpoints, I want to dance with the question, 'What is the imagination?'. I won't try to capture definitive answers here, but instead I will attempt to build an imaginative picture of 'imagination'.

Cultural insights

I have been fortunate to travel widely since my therapeutic story collections have been translated into many languages, spending extensive time in Africa, China, Europe and North America. I have therefore had the opportunity to soak in different cultural understandings, and through this process I have found a deep reverence and respect in each country and culture for story and the imagination.

During my three years working in East Africa, often when I would meet someone new and tell them that I wrote stories, the Kiswahili response would be: *mawazo ni mwanga katika usiku* – 'imagination is a light in the night'. Or *hadithi mwanga usiku* – 'stories light the night'.

In my time in southern Africa, I discovered that the San people (Bushmen) have no word for imagination. For them 'story' is all encompassing. They have a saying: 'A story is like the wind. It comes from a far-off place and you feel it.' The Bushmen would 'story' their children on long treks across the desert and savannah. No literal and rational talk – 'just another thousand steps – let's count', or 'I promise you a treat when we get there'. The adults would carry the walk through the imagination – there would be stories of that rock, this bush, that lizard, those clouds, and much more!

Similarly, in my own country of Australia, 'story' in indigenous culture embraces and connects everything. Story and the imagination are one and the same thing, going back thousands of years to the Dream Time, which is the aboriginal understanding of the world, its creation and its stories.

In both Lakota and Ojibwe, two Native American languages, the word for 'imagine' is the same as the word for 'dream'. In these cultures, dreams are considered to have prophetic and healing power – an interesting link between imagination and healing.

In China when I have posed the question in my seminars, 'What is imagination?', a frequent reply has been that in Chinese culture, imagination is difficult to define but could most fittingly be compared to the Tao – the invisible force behind all things, the balance of all things, the heart force of nature. One Chinese scholar, on the connection of imagination to nature, claimed: 'If trees and flowers could talk, they would of course speak in stories!' Another, who had studied ancient Chinese paintings, talked of the empty spaces in each painting. He understood that the blank spaces were deliberately left to allow room for the imagination.

Poetic insights

Poets through the ages have worked to elevate the importance of imagination over logic, and have deeply respected the sacredness of image and metaphor. The English Romantic poet William Wordsworth believed that spiritual love could not exist without imagination, which is, he believed, 'reason in her most exalted mood'.

> This spiritual Love acts not nor can exist
> Without Imagination, which, in truth,
> Is but another name for absolute power
> And clearest insight, amplitude of mind,
> And Reason in her most exalted mood.[22]

One can feel bathed in love and wonder, and captivated by nature's beauty, while simply reading Wordsworth's classic poem 'I wandered lonely as a cloud'. His poetry seems to transport us out of the everyday to more spiritual, higher realms.

Another poet and philosopher who has helped me transcend the normal, the everyday, is Owen Barfield. In my quest for a poetic understanding of the imagination, reading Barfield led me to an exciting discovery. It shone out of his essay on 'Matter, imagination and spirit'[23] in which he depicts two realities – the spiritual and the physical, the 'hidden' and the 'everyday'. But he gives motivation to us as adults, for he suggests a bridge between the two, a way of travelling from one to the other. This bridge or connection between matter and the spirit is the 'imagination' – beautifully depicted by Barfield as 'a rainbow bridge of imaginative activity'. This is the realm of the story, the realm of metaphor, the realm of symbol.

With these poetic thoughts in mind, let us now examine the question 'Why does story language (story, poetry and song) seem to be such a natural language for children?'. Why does Sunderland[24] advocate its use for healthy emotional development? In the light of Barfield's thoughts, the answer seems quite simple: it is because our little ones have only recently crossed the rainbow bridge, they have only recently arrived in the 'everyday' world. For them this imaginative world is so near, is so real.

For a child, the imaginative and spirit world could be as real as the physical everyday world. Children seem to have the ability to cross back and forth like butterflies, while most adults struggle, like cumbersome many-legged caterpillars, from one realm to the other.

Imagination is an interesting phenomenon. In human development, we mostly grow stronger physically, socially and mentally, but often weaker in connection to the spirit, as well as weaker in our imagination. Most adults need to work hard to keep their imaginations flowering, tending their imaginative gardens through meditation ... poetry ... stories ... music ... and other artistic mediums.

Children have this naturally, but for many adults our connection has faded. We must strive to build this imagination bridge. Herein lies the challenge for us as teachers, therapists, parents: how do we re-develop, re-nourish and re-strengthen our imaginations so that we can work with children using the language most familiar to them?

How to nourish and strengthen our imaginations

As a long-time student of various spiritual practices, I have been particularly interested in the methods of spiritual science[25] on developing the organs of spiritual perception: Imagination, Inspiration, and Intuition – otherwise known as the three

'I's (spelt with a capital 'I'). But I can openly confess that I have not achieved these lofty stages of development. The practice comes with a warning – it is a long, hard and arduous task!

However, while one plods slowly along this path, I think it is important to be aware of and honour what I am going to refer to as the little 'i's – the imagination, inspiration and intuition belonging to our everyday life, to our everyday humanness. We sometimes get a sensing from somewhere. Sometimes we feel that something greater is working through us. Sometimes we receive gifts, grace from the spiritual world. We sometimes even say, 'I have an intuitive feeling about...' or 'an inspiration has come to me'.

I am sure that the little 'i's and big 'I's are connected, but from my personal experience this broader awareness has given me creative courage to write my stories. I was once confronted with, and surprised by, the question: 'If you have not developed your higher organs of perception, how can you claim to write therapeutic stories?' My response was, 'I dare to do it because our world needs stories, and more stories'.

I encourage you to contemplate your own experiences of the three little 'i's. You may be surprised to find, like I have, that they shine their sparks of light into your everyday life more often than you may have realised. But even if we find that these little 'i' gifts sometimes light up our life, how can we nourish and strengthen them? Particularly with our 'imagination', and particularly in reference to creating stories, how can we find ways to let it shine brighter and more often?

Here are seven tips that may help:

- **Read** – Read many stories. Immerse yourself in the images and motifs and rhythms of folk and fairy tales, myths and legends.
- **Listen and observe** – Let Mother Nature speak to you. Nature has so much to share. Walk in a forest, on a beach, in the park. Sit in a garden or on a balcony amongst the potted plants. Observation and research can help to inform our stories – how does a butterfly land on a flower? How does a turtle move across the sand? What does it eat? Where does it lay its eggs? Ideas for metaphors for stories can come from the most unusual places, e.g. a dustpan and brush as a metaphor for co-operation. It is surprising what we can pick up through our observation, both inside our homes and out in the garden, both in the city streets and in the forest.
- **Walk** – Poets and philosophers have attested to the positive effect that walking can have on our creative thinking. Bruce Chatwin[26] was a renowned travel writer from the last century who walked across Australia and up through Patagonia and South America. He believed that if you walked enough you would not need religion. In his writings there are many references to the creative attributes and spiritual benefits of walking. From my own experience, I find that most of my ideas for stories come to me while I am walking on my very long 'Seven Mile' local beach.

- **Explore imaginative ideas through different art forms** – Drawing, painting, sculpture, dance, music, drama. There are many ways of creative learning and knowing. Different art forms offer stimulating possibilities for diverse personalities and temperaments. In an ideal world, according to Abbs,[27] the 'six great arts' – visual art, drama, dance, music, film and literature – would be included in all education curricula. In an ideal world you wouldn't need to be reading these tips, as your educational experience would already have nurtured your imaginative intelligence!
- **Play with story-writing exercises** – These can encourage your imagination to flutter and fly, as they can give you helpful and playful structures to follow and can also help to bypass logical thinking. There are many to be found in my second book[28] and an extra one given in this book (see 'Random Story-Writing Exercise', page 175).
- **Give it time** – Allow time for your creative thoughts to develop and flow... sleep on your ideas... and sleep and dream, and sleep some more.
- **Give it a go** (an 'Aussie' saying) – When you have created a story, try to find a way to share it. Strive for it to be as polished as possible, but, at the same time, accept that nothing is ever perfect. Be encouraged by the chorus in Leonard Cohen's song, 'Anthem': 'There is a crack in everything. That's how the light gets in.'

Working with the above pointers can help us exercise and strengthen our imaginations. This will then help facilitate our creative choice of metaphors and the writing of imaginative journeys for therapeutic stories.

However, this genre of writing is not about recipes, it is not like a cooking class. I offer a framework and many tips and techniques that have helped me and helped the participants in my seminars. But most of the effort must come from you – playing, exploring, trying and re-trying, using your three little 'i's, slowly plodding along your own path of self-development.

There are so many circumstances and situations today that can be helped with a uniquely crafted story using an imaginative journey and specifically chosen metaphors. I believe it is our task as teachers, therapists, counsellors, parents and community workers to take up this challenge; and even if our writings may only be a 'stammer' compared to the beauty and depth of a folk or fairy tale, I encourage us all to 'stammer' away!

And as we stammer with our stories, we can be emboldened by the thoughts of Joseph Campbell, the great authority on comparative mythology. He gives us a courageous message to ponder, suggesting that our world needs new myths, new stories – ones that deeply empower us, that provide meaningful connections to nature and the universe, and at the same time give us hope and courage to manage our daily problems. He also emphasized the importance of our moral order having to 'catch up', to be appropriate for current times, for according to Campbell, 'living old myths is not fitting for today'.[29]

 STORIES TO LIGHT THE NIGHT

As a final thought, let me return to an image used in my introduction to this section. Take heart that every time you use your imagination to write a therapeutic story, or a story of any kind, another grain of story-sand is being added to tip the scales of imaginative imbalance.

The Story of Truth

I first heard this story told by a Chinese woman at a conference in Shenzhen (she had heard it from an Israeli teacher at a conference the previous year). As I have been unable to find the original story, I have rewritten it from my notes taken at the time. It is an anonymous tale that was calling to be shared in the introduction to this grief and loss collection.

There once was a land where everything seemed to happen in a perfect way. There was plenty to eat, plenty of sunshine and plenty of rain. All the people lived well and in peace.

But nothing good lasts for ever.

One day, a stranger came to this land and walked among the people. The stranger was old, with long white hair and a naked body. Every time this naked person came near, the people would run and hide in their homes. The stranger wandered everywhere across the land trying to meet the people, but they would always run in fear of the nakedness.

At the same time another stranger came to the land – beautifully dressed, wearing a flowing cloak covered in many birds, animals and flowers. When the people saw this beauty, they rushed out to be close, and sat and eagerly listened to this stranger's many stories. Everywhere this beautiful stranger wandered there were warm welcomes, and the people loved to hear the stories. They could point to any picture on the cloak and sure enough, there would be a story waiting to be told.

One day in the forest, the old naked one and the cloaked storyteller met on the path. The old one, who was called TRUTH, asked the beautifully dressed one how it was possible to be so well-liked and listened to by all the people. The storyteller smiled, took off the cloak, cut it in half and gave half to TRUTH to wear.

'If you wear my story cloak, people will want to hear what TRUTH has to say, but without it the TRUTH can often be too shocking, too strong, too scary to hear.'

From that day to this, TRUTH wandered the land sharing wisdom dressed up in stories.

Notes and References

1. See https://www.etymonline.com/word/therapy.

2. From 2019 Columbia University in the USA has offered a 'Master of Science in Narrative Medicine' that focuses on 'listening to the patient's story'. Narrative medicine is best defined as an interdisciplinary field that brings powerful narrative skills of radical listening and creativity from the humanities and the arts in order to address the needs of all who seek and deliver healthcare. Narrative medicine is a medical approach that utilizes people's narratives in clinical practice, research and education as a way to promote healing. It aims to address the relational and psychological dimensions that occur in tandem with physical illness, with an attempt to deal with the individual stories of patients. In doing this, narrative medicine aims not only to validate the experience of the patient, but also to encourage creativity and self-reflection in the physician.

3. In my first book, *Healing Stories for Challenging Behaviour*, I dedicated a full chapter (Chapter 6) to providing a detailed age-appropriate guide for story-making and storytelling.

4. Franz Kafka (1883–1924) was a Czech novelist and short-story writer.

5. In my books, *Healing Stories for Challenging Behaviour* and *Therapeutic Storytelling: 101 Healing Stories for Children*, I have explored this model in detail, including many charts and case-studies.

6. Most 3- to 4-year olds and some 5- to 7-year olds. There is no precise way of determining the right age for a story, and some sensitive or more imaginative older children will still be fully absorbed by stories originally intended for younger children.

7. You will find a detailed analysis of this story in 'Thoughts on Metaphor', p. 30.

8. Stuart Vyse, psychologist and author; *Believing in Magic: The Psychology of Superstition*, Oxford University Press, Oxford, 2013.

9. Thich Nhat Hanh, Vietnamese Buddhist monk, poet and peace activist.

10. George Lakoff and Mark Johnson, *Metaphors We Live By*, University of Chicago Press, Chicago, 2003. In this updated edition, the authors supply an afterword surveying how their theory of metaphor has developed within the cognitive sciences to become central to the contemporary understanding of how we think and how we express our thoughts in language.

11. Ken DiBenedette, 'Metaphor at the Threshold', 2005, available at http://moonchalice.com (accessed August 2020).

12. Margot Sunderland, *Using Storytelling as a Therapeutic Tool with Children*, Speechmark Publishing, Milton Keynes, 2016, pp. 2–6.

13. Susan Laing is an Australian psychologist well known for her creative work with children and families – see http://www.creativelivingwithchildren.com/.

14. Carl G. Jung, *Man and His Symbols*, Picador, London, 1964.

15. David Gordon, *Therapeutic Metaphors: Helping Others through the Looking Glass*, independently published, 2017.

16. Sunderland, note 12, pp. 16–18.

17. Different tips and techniques for choosing metaphors for stories have been explored extensively in my first and second books, so have not been repeated in this book.

18. Gary Lachman, *Lost Knowledge of the Imagination*, Floris Books, Edinburgh, 2017.

19. Iain McGilchrist, *The Master and His Emissary*, 2nd edition, Yale University Press, New Haven and London, 2019.

20. Susan Perrow, *Storytelling in African Teacher Training: A Cross-Cultural Study*, LAP Lambert Academic Publishing, 2009.

21. See https://www.scu.edu.au/study-at-scu/units/eng00355/.

22. William Wordsworth (1770–1850), from 'The Prelude' – Verse No. VII.

23. Owen Barfield, *The Rediscovery of Meaning and Other Essays*, Barfield Press, London, 1977, pp.143–54.

24. Sunderland, note 12.

25. Rudolf Steiner, *The Wisdom of Man, of the Soul, and of the Spirit*, Steiner Books, Hudson, NY, March 1972.

26. Charles Bruce Chatwin (1940–1989) was an English travel writer, novelist and journalist. His first book, *In Patagonia*, established Chatwin as a travel writer, although he considered himself instead to be a storyteller, interested in bringing to light unusual tales.

27. Peter Abbs, *Against the Flow: The Arts, Postmodern Culture and Education*, Routledge, London, 2003. In this book, Abbs puts the following arguments for the importance of the six great arts in school curricula: they form a family of related, if largely autonomous, practices; all work through the aesthetic; all address the imagination; and all are concerned with the symbolic embodiment of human meaning.

28. You will find many other exercises to get the 'imaginative juices' going in my second book, *Therapeutic Storytelling*, including 'story bone' exercises at the end of each story category section.

29. 'Joseph Campbell and the Power of Myth' – a six-part series with Joseph Campbell and Bill Moyers (available online as a free download).

3 LOSS OF A LOVED ONE

In this chapter you will find stories written for children who have lost a sibling or a twin or a parent or a grandparent; stories for families who have lost a new baby; stories for parents who have lost children; and stories for a school and/or community where someone has died from an illness or an accident.

Most of these stories, with respect and sensitivity, could be used for situations involving the opposite gender for whom it was created. For example, the first story, 'A Nest in the Stars', written about two male baby birds, could be changed to be about two female baby birds; 'Wolf Boy's Journey Home' could be changed to 'Wolf Girl's Journey Home'; 'Grandmother's Cloak of Light' could be changed to 'Grandfather's Cloak of Light'.

To help you find your way, I have summarized the background to each story as follows:

A Nest in the Stars – written for a five-year old boy after the death of his baby twin cousin (p. 46).

Wolf Boy's Journey Home – written for a three-year old boy, and his older siblings, to help carry the family through the process of the little boy's incurable illness (p. 48).

The Little Candle – written for a five-year old girl whose father had recently passed away (p. 52).

The Ballerina and the Music Box – written for a five-year old girl whose father died unexpectedly in his sleep (p. 54).

Heavenly Magic – written for a five-year old boy whose father died in a drowning accident (p. 56).

Taji La Upendo – The Crown Of Love – written for two girls (aged three and seven) whose father died suddenly of a heart attack a year earlier (p. 58).

A Doll for Sylvia – written for a five-year old girl in the SOS Children's Village in Nairobi who had lost her whole family in a tribal raid (p. 60).

Grandmother's Cloak of Light – a story for young children when a grandparent or elderly relative has died (p. 62).

THE TALE OF LITTLE FAWN AND DEAR FRIEND – written for a seven-year old girl grieving the recent loss of an uncle to a long-term cancer (p. 63).

THE BEAVERS AND THE OAK TREE – written to be told to two boys (ages six and nine years) after their grandfather and cousin both died in a car accident (p. 67).

SYLVIE AND THE STARS – written for children (ages 6–10 years) who have a mother with an incurable illness, or who have had a mother who has recently passed away (p. 69).

MISS BURBLE – written for twin brothers, eight years of age, whose aunt had passed away (p. 71).

THE ORIOLE AND THE CHERRY TREE – written for students at a primary school where one of the pupils had died in a car accident (p. 74).

PRINCESS ROSE AND THE GARDEN QUEEN – a story written for an older girl or teenager (8 years +) who has lost her mother to a difficult illness (p. 75).

THE ROSE AND THE THORN – written on request from a primary school in Norway, for children ages seven and upwards; its aim was to offer some hope after the traumatic event of the island massacre where many teenagers lost their lives (p. 77).

WHEN GRANDMA PASSED AWAY – suitable to use with older children and teenagers after the death of a grandparent or extended family member (p. 79).

THE FANTASTIC FLYING MACHINE – written for a ten-year old boy whose father was killed in a car accident (p. 82).

GOODBYE SHELLY – written for older children and families about the loss of a most precious treasure (p. 85).

THE LITTLE STAR WHO COULD NOT STAY – a story written for parents and their families who have lost a baby at birth (p. 89).

WHISPER SWEET DREAMS – some grandmother thoughts written for parents and their families who have lost a baby at birth (p. 90).

THE RAINBOW DOVE – written for use at memorial gatherings for dearly departed friends and family members; a story for all ages (p. 92).

THE MEMORY TREASURE BOX – a story for use with all ages who have someone in their family or community with a terminal illness (p. 93).

THE GARDEN – a story written for families / communities who have lost a precious child or beloved relation or friend (p. 96).

AND THUS CAME THE RESTFUL NIGHT – a mythological tale from the 'Rigveda', one of the ancient scriptures of India; the story of the death of a twin, Yama, and the creation of night that allows his sister, Yami, the passage of time and healing from grief (p. 98).

A Nest in the Stars

By Esther Moreno, mother and early childhood educator, Spain

Esther is a a teacher and a mother of two boys. This story was written when her twin nephews, Pablo and Tomás, were born prematurely. A few days after they were born, Tomás, who was the smaller of the twins and the second to be born, grew ill and died. It was, and still is, a very difficult experience for everyone in the family. Esther decided to write this story and illustrate it in a little book, so she could give it to Pablo and his family as a present in the future. She hopes the story will help her nephew build himself an image of everything that happened, an image that inspires love and acceptance.

Already the story has had a helpful outcome for Esther's oldest son, who was aged five at the time of hearing the sad news of his little cousin. After she shared the story with him, his immediate response was: 'Now Tomás will be able to see the stars from above, and Pablo from below.'

Esther also crafted a mobile to hang from the ceiling of the baby's room. In her words: 'When a baby dies during birth or a few days after, there's suddenly an emptiness both emotional and physical, you have barely any memories from the baby and at the same time a place in your home (a nest) that doesn't make any sense any more. There is also a need and a desire for the baby's memory to be kept alive in the family, so that he or she will always be remembered and somehow be present in their everyday lives. That's why I suggest this activity could have a double therapeutic function: the act itself of creating and filling up a physical void.'

There were once two little birds who lived in the highest nest in the forest. The tree was so tall that it reached all the way to the sky, and the nest rested on branches that stretched beyond the stars. From their nest the little birds could see beautiful landscapes filled with colourful flowers, a river flowing with crystal clear water and a meadow carpeted in fresh grass.

One morning, the bigger of the two birds, Pio Pio, said: 'Let's leave the nest! Let's fly down there to smell the flowers, bathe in the water and rest in the soft grass!' The other little bird, Cu Cut, was more cautious and preferred to stay in the nest.

However, one day at daybreak, the two little birds decided to go exploring. Pio Pio flew down to the field of poppies, flitting from one to the other, his heart filling with their sweet aroma. Cu Cut arrived more slowly, and tentatively sniffed at the flowers. He felt happy and content to be there.

The next day they decided to go down to the river. Pio Pio darted from stone to stone with great joy and excitement, plunging his head into the water. Cu Cut first wet his feet and then his beak. He felt happy, but for him the water was a little too cold, and he soon began to miss the warmth of the nest.

A few days later they flew back down, this time to the grassy meadow. Pio Pio had fun hiding between the plants and playing with the butterflies. Cu Cut found himself a peaceful corner where he could rest a while. 'This place is wonderful!', said Pio Pio excitedly. Cu Cut smiled: 'Yes, it is… but I miss the nest. I don't feel the cold wind there; everything is soft and warm.'

Pio Pio was saddened to hear that Cu Cut was not enjoying this new place as much as he was. Cu Cut, who loved his dear brother and knew him very well, said to him: 'Each of us has our own path to find. I'll be fine in the nest! From there I can see the flowers, the river and the meadow. And they'll always remind me of you.'

Cu Cut took to the air and soared up, up, up… all the way to the sky.

And that was how Cu Cut returned to his nest in the stars, and Pio Pio continued his journey through the world.

When night fell, Pio Pio looked up at the stars from the meadow, and Cu Cut gazed at the same stars from his nest. They both fell to sleep content and grateful in the knowledge that, on the other side of the sky, they each had a little bird that would always be with them.

Esther used a Mexican folk song to finish the story – in Spanish it is called De Colores *(In Colours).*

Wolf Boy's Journey Home

By Silke Rose West

Silke is co-author of *How to Tell Stories to Children*, a Kindergarten teacher and co-founder of the Taos Waldorf School. She has been supporting Golden Willow Grief Group in Taos, New Mexico, helping families to navigate through the loss of children and parents through storytelling and ceremony.

Introduction from Silke

Wolf Boy's story was given to us by the sad experience of a sudden incurable illness that a three-year old boy was diagnosed with. His family had just relocated, and had to navigate this challenging time with tremendous courage. To accompany a small child in a dying process requires us to be present in the day to day, and to find ways to celebrate this being. The story helped his family and our community to understand how powerful this little soul was, and how we could best honour him in his dying process.

The home death experience asks of us to engage and to face it. Heaven and Earth are still connected for our little ones, and statements like 'You are always one of us' are important and real. There is a part of us that travels with the being to the other side, and life will never be the same. But we will move on, and the star is an important connecting point.

Stars are not alone. We look up at the starry sky and can see Wolf Boy in the community, while he gazes down at us. Perhaps Wolf Boy can teach us about the precious days on Earth. If you have a family member who is ill, how can you bring joy to their heart? What can you do to help their spirit travel over the rainbow bridge? The animal council is often the community you need to call upon. The wise owl might be your doctor or hospice worker.

Papa Wolf walked about with his three pups. They frolicked under the warm summer sun and chased each other. Suddenly Wolf Boy ran into a tree. While everyone laughed, he shook his head and started to tumble. It was strange.

Papa Wolf called everyone to follow him to their new den, a place they had recently found. It was so beautiful. Mama Wolf was waiting with some yummy breakfast.

'I don't want to eat', said Wolf Boy, and he started banging his head on the floor. 'Stop it', shouted Papa Wolf. Little Wolf Boy started to cry. Mama Wolf scooped him up and said, 'I don't think he is well'.

This happened three days in a row.

On the third night, Papa Wolf decided to go and seek council with the wise old owl. He walked under the light of old Grandmother Moon to the Ancient Cedar Tree. There he offered his song, loud and clear, 'I need help, someone!'.

'WHO, WHOOO is calling for me?'

'I am. Papa Wolf. My son is acting strange. I don't know what to do.' 'What is his name?', asked Owl.

'We call him Wolf Boy. He is the only son we have.'

Owl looked up at the stars and went into stillness. 'Wolf Boy came only for a short time to this Earth. He must return to the stars before the winter is over.'

'NOOOO', howled Papa Wolf. It was the longest howl he ever made in his life. 'Not Wolf Boy. I don't want to let him go!'

'It is not in your hands', replied Owl. 'He has chosen to come for a short time. Your task will be hard, but you can do it. Go home to Mother Wolf and the other cubs and tell all your animal friends that you need to make Wolf Boy's life on Earth happy and joyous. Answer his questions. He knows how to help you prepare for when the rainbow comes down to mark his trail home. Sing his favourite songs. Tell him stories of his grandfather and grandmother that have returned home before him. Cry for him when he is gone. Celebrate him and know that every day of his life is a gift for you all.'

The owl hooted and flew away into the night sky towards Grandmother Moon.

Wolf Papa felt like his heart became a heavy stone, and every step was like walking a mile. He returned to his den and shared the news with Mama Wolf.

'We must listen to the wise owl, and we will celebrate Wolf Boy', she said, swallowing her tears. Inside her heart, she had felt that this message was coming.

After morning breakfast, the Wolf family walked out to the Ancient Cedar Tree. 'Sit down', called Papa Wolf. I have a message from owl to share, 'Wolf Boy is not well and will travel back over the rainbow bridge this winter to see his grandparents'.

'What are their names?', asked Wolf Boy.

'What does it mean that he is going over the rainbow bridge', asked little sister wolf.

Mama stroked all three pups. 'It is like being born, only it's the opposite way. You die and go home. We all will die one day and go home.'

'Can we go with Wolf Boy', asked big sister?

'No', said Papa Wolf, 'It's like being born. He has to make the journey alone, but his guiding star will lead him home. It's the wolf star!'

'Can we see the wolf star tonight?', asked Wolf Boy.

'Yes, we can, and we will all howl to old Grandmother Moon together.'

On the way home, Wolf Boy needed to be carried, as he could not walk the distance any more. At night they walked back outside to the moon. Mama Wolf carried Wolf Boy in his baby blanket. They sang their most beautiful song to the wolf star, and Wolf Boy fell asleep with a smile. It was a good night. The old owl hooted and wished strength and courage to the little family.

The next night Papa Wolf called the animal council together under the old cedar tree. He shared the news of his dying son. They all raised their voices to the moon and howled together. Even a little rabbit and mouse were with them. It was the saddest news they had heard in a long time.

'I need your help with something very important!', said Papa Wolf. 'You need to help me make Wolf Boy's life happy while he is with us on Earth. I need you to sing every night outside our den, the most beautiful songs you know. And if one of you can tell sweet stories, you can call for a visit. Soon he will not be able to leave the den any more.'

Rabbit hopped forward and offered to bring stories from the beautiful land beyond the rainbow. Mouse offered to call on all her relatives to drop food outside the door. Coyote offered his songs, and Fox said he would stand guard to protect the family and take the girl pups out to play.

The next day Papa Wolf awoke to a hard question from Wolf Boy.

'Papa, where will you bury my bones and my body?' Mama Wolf nodded towards Papa Wolf and spoke, 'What do you think about the old cedar tree, the place where you can look at the beautiful mountain?'.

'Yes', said Wolf Boy. 'Can we go there today so you can show me the place?'

Papa Wolf remembered that the owl had said that Wolf Boy would ask the right questions to get them ready. Once they got to the place, Wolf Boy said, 'This is my favourite spot in the whole wide world'.

The girl pups started to dig a hole. Wolf Boy requested that the hole would be so deep that he could talk to the root gnomes of the tree, deep down in the earth. 'They have good stories!', he said.

The following day Wolf Boy woke up and could not move any of his legs and had a hard time turning his head. 'Papa Wolf, will you carry me to the top of the mountain soon, so I can be close to my star?'

The time came closer, and Papa Wolf took Wolf Boy up the mountain with a special treat from Mama Wolf, who was at home with her girl pups. On that day, Fox came by to take the wolf girls to play. Hundreds of mice had brought food to be put into storage, and Mama Rabbit brought some of her soft fur, which she used for her nest to offer to Mama Wolf for a soft mattress.

That would be the last journey into the wild for Wolf Boy. Many moons passed. Wolf Boy started to sleep a lot.

Owl came flying by to call on Papa Wolf. 'The time is coming near!', he said.

For three nights and days, Mama Wolf and Papa Wolf and the wolf girls stayed with Wolf Boy. 'He is talking with his eyes', said little Wolf Girl. 'You will always be part of our family', shouted big sister.

Mama Wolf and Papa Wolf felt the last gentle breath of Wolf Boy. It was like the soft, gentle Spring Breeze. 'Go home, Wolf Boy', they said. 'Walk the rainbow bridge and follow your star! We will look for you every night!'

And so it was. All the animals had helped to dig a deep hole, so that Wolf Boy, who was wrapped in his baby blanket, could listen to the stories from the root gnomes deep in the Earth, while his spirit would travel home to the wolf star.

That night, there was a rainbow around the full moon. All the animals offered a song to Wolf Boy and thanked him for having come to Earth. 'We love you!', they sang, 'We will always remember you!'.

And to this day, they are honouring him whenever Grandmother Moon is full. The tree gnomes of the Ancient Cedar Tree are telling tales deep in the Earth, and wildflowers are starting to grow on Wolf Boy's resting place.

The Little Candle

By Suzette Ellison, early childhood teacher

This story was written in handmade picture book format for a five-year old girl whose father had recently passed away. The mother was very touched and grateful for the gesture. Suzette remembers that the act of writing the story and sharing it with the child was 'healing' in that she was able to acknowledge the little girl's tragic loss.

In Suzette's words: 'I believe that the simple act of acknowledgement has healing within itself. It is difficult to know for sure the impact such things really have on a person (how do we measure it?), but I feel it is important to find ways to connect with children and families and starting with letting them know, "I see you, I hear you and I care".'

There once was a little candle that had not yet been lit.

One very special day two big candles came to her. They hovered ever so closely, then together they touched her with a gentle kiss. The candle felt a ticklish sensation and a flow of warmth all through her. Right then, she realised that kiss had sparked a little light that shone brightly from the top of her head.

For many happy days she shone and sparkled. The flame of her love danced and sang and played. All the while, the two big candles stood behind her – watching and protecting her as their lights shone around her.

The little candle felt safe and warm, knowing that the two big candles were glowing right behind her.

However, one day the little candle felt a chill breeze brush beside her. Before she knew what was happening, the wind had snuffed the flame of one of the big candles – leaving behind just a smouldering wick.

All around seemed to grow darker. The little candle felt scared and cold. She moved closer to the other big candle for warmth.

After a while, the little candle began to get used to the strange new light with only one candle behind her. In fact, as her eyes adjusted to the strange new light, she noticed what appeared like little sparks in the distance that she had never noticed before. As she watched, the flickering sparks seemed to move closer and closer.

Soon, the little candle was surrounded by many beautiful shimmering lights. She wondered where they had all come from, and she turned her face upwards.

To her amazement, she saw the brightest shining lights. And she could hear the faint words of a song:

When your love light seems to fade, turn your eyes to see.
A thousand flickering candle lights that shine for you and me.
Every little candle, shining in the night,
Finds its glow in moon and stars,
That share with us their light.

The Ballerina and the Music Box

This story idea was crafted by a group of psychologists in a therapeutic story writing seminar in Sophia, Bulgaria. It was for a five-year-old girl who had, one month beforehand, lost her father to a sudden illness. Because he had died at home in his sleep, the girl was extremely fearful of going to sleep, and very fearful of her mother going to sleep. The story, together with a painting of the 'Dream Spirit' on the girl's bedroom wall, gave her confidence to sleep. There is a detailed account of the story writing process in the introductory section, 'Thoughts on Metaphor' (p. 34).

Here is the completed story, written from the outline that was sent to me translated from Bulgarian.

There was once a beautiful ballerina that lived inside a music box. The box sat on top of a strong table in a little coloured house at the edge of town. Every day the music box lid would open, and the ballerina would dance round and round and round. Oh, how she loved to dance. When she was tired the music box lid would close and she could rest.

And so, life went on, day after day – the ballerina would dance, then rest, then dance some more.

One evening, everything changed in the life of the beautiful ballerina. While she was resting in her music box, a terrible storm came in the night. It shook the coloured house so strongly that the table rocked backwards and forwards and almost fell over. One of the table legs cracked and fell off, and the music box lid flew open so wide that it couldn't close again. The ballerina woke up and began to dance, round and round and round – she danced all day and all night and all the next day – round and round and round – she danced and danced and could not stop.

One evening the Spirit of Dreams was passing by the window of the little coloured house. She looked in and saw the ballerina dancing round and round, and thought she could be of some help. So she slipped inside and sang a special song to help the music box lid find a way to close again. That night the ballerina was able to have a long, long rest.

The next morning the Spirit of Dreams was back again, this time to sing a different kind of song – a wake-up song. The music box lid opened, and the ballerina was able to dance round and round and round. Oh, how this ballerina loved to dance!

From this time onwards, with the help of the Dream Spirit, life could go on, day after day – the ballerina could dance, then rest, then dance some more.

HEAVENLY MAGIC

I wrote this story for a five-year old boy in Beijing whose father had died the previous year in a drowning accident. I met with the mother to find out more about the boy – his favourite things, toys, animals, things he liked to do. One of his most loved story books was about a bunny rabbit, and his favourite item, since he was a toddler, was his bunny blanket.

I also took time to observe the boy in kindergarten and could see that he had a very close connection to his 'bunny blanket'. He took it with him everywhere, and whenever the slightest thing upset him, he would wrap himself inside it.

His mother was planning to move to a new country where her son would be enrolled in a new school. She believed it was important for him to be able to start 'big' (primary/elementary) school without his blanket, to avoid him being teased; but to date, all her attempts to lessen the dependence on the blanket had been unsuccessful.

The intention of this story was two-fold – to aid metamorphosis of his security blanket into two special carry bags (one for him and one for his toy rabbits), and to help build a link between the boy and the place where the boy and his mother believed his father had passed on to (heaven). In a window of time when the boy had gone on an outing without the blanket, the mother planned for it to be sewn into the two bags, and some spare scraps of it used to make a blanket jacket for his toy rabbits. When the boy returned home, there was a gift wrapped in special 'starry' paper waiting on his bed, with the story rolled up in a scroll (tied with golden thread).

When the boy unwrapped the gift he was overjoyed. The mother reported that he accepted the transformation of the blanket into the bags without any question.

There was once a special blanket that belonged to a little boy called Tao Tao. This boy loved his blanket so much that he slept with it every night and took it with him everywhere he went. The blanket was his friend, and Tao Tao was the blanket's friend. They were happy together.

For many years the blanket liked this special friendship, but as Tao Tao grew older, it became quite difficult for the blanket to follow him everywhere. Tao Tao, like all growing boys, loved to climb trees and jump puddles and ride high on the swing, and the blanket was getting too old and too tired to do all these things. But the blanket still wanted to be Tao Tao's friend, and wanted to be a help to him as he was growing up into a tall strong boy.

Tao Tao's father looked down from high in heaven and wanted to find a way to help. At last he had an idea. He worked some heavenly magic to turn the blanket into a blanket bag, a bag that could easily travel with Tao Tao wherever he went. This new bag could carry Tao Tao's special things – his toys and his crayons and his books.

And, as an extra surprise, when Tao Tao's father worked his special magic, there was enough cloth left to make some tiny jackets for Tao Tao's new toy rabbits – a baby jacket for baby rabbit and a daddy jacket for daddy rabbit. The rabbits loved to live inside the blanket bag, and they all became friends together.

Taji La Upendo – The Crown of Love

By Tabitha Wangeci Gikingo, Kindergarten teacher and mentor, Nairobi

A story for two Kikuyu girls in Kenya (aged three and seven) written by their Aunty Tabitha. The girl's father had died suddenly of a heart attack a year before. Both girls loved birthdays and celebrations, and this helped guide the story journey. The story and the weaving of garlands, in loving memory, were shared with the girls on the first anniversary of their father's death. Tabitha reported that the gifts from the sun, the moon and the stars made such an impression on the two girls that 'they will forever be in their hearts'.

Once there was a man called Gitonga who lived by the slopes of Mt Kenya with his wife and two beautiful daughters. The daughters were called Makena (Happiness) and Nyambura (Rain). The mornings were icy and cold but Gitonga worked extremely hard. As soon as he heard the chaffinch birds singing, he would get ready for the day, kiss goodbye to his beautiful girls, and set off to take care of the coffee plantation where all the red berries had to be picked.

Every day was the same. The father would care for the coffee plantation and the daughters would go to school.

In the evening the father and his daughters loved to go biking. They would carefully ride down a path that led to the river. The father would fill his watering can, then water the tree seedlings with the help of his daughters. Then they would sit by the bank of the river and together loved to sing to the birds.

Kanyoni gakwa wee hitha hithe
My little bird little bird, kindly hide,
If you are seen, you don't belong to me. Fly, fly, fly up so high
Dance with the colours of the rainbow.

They would sing to the birds and then ride back home in time for dinner. Their Mama would prepare some delicious irio.* They would enjoy the meal together, then go out to watch the moon before they went to bed. This was a magical moment for the girls. They would sit on their father's lap listening to him tell a story while mama covered them all in a warm Maasai blanket.

One evening, as he narrated a new story, Gitonga placed a crown on each of his daughter's heads made from beautiful jasmine flower vines. The story was about a man who loved his daughters so dearly that he gave them everything they wished for, and now the time had come for them to receive very special gifts.

From the SUN they would receive warmth to warm their hearts every day;
From the MOON they would receive the courage to light up their world every night as they slept;
From the STARS, the gift of many friends and family, who would always love them for ever.

Gitonga then told Makena and Nyambura of a long-awaited journey for him to a beautiful place of no return. From here he would watch over them, unseen and unheard, and walk with them every step of their lives.

The girls needed to wear beautiful invisible crowns every time they needed their father, and he would always be there for them, on their birthdays and on their graduation and every other special day.

That night, when the father put them to sleep, he placed the crowns by their pillow as he kissed their forehead for the last time and went to bed.

That was the last kiss from papa.... His heart made of gold stopped to beat, and sadness filled their home.

Every new dawn the girls would wait for the warm sun to rise, in the evening for the moon to light up their bed and for the twinkling stars to shine down upon them.

From this time forward Makena and Nyambura forever cherished all the beautiful memories. With courage in their heart they faced every new day as Papa watched and protected his little girls from Heaven's Gate.

Kanyoni gakwa wee hitha hithe
My little bird little bird, kindly hide,
If you are seen, you don't belong to me. Fly, fly, fly up so high
Dance with the colours of the rainbow.

---

* Irio is a traditional Kikuyu dish made from maize, potato and greens.

A DOLL FOR SYLVIA

One of my storytelling students in Nairobi worked at the SOS Children's Village. Towards the end of one of my training modules, she asked if I could write a story to help with a newly arrived child called Sylvia who was having difficulty sleeping each night. This little girl was orphaned at the age of five after her whole family was killed in a raid on her village – she was adopted by the SOS Children's Village, where she will live until the age of 18.

After hearing the full account, my first reaction was to say, 'No, sorry, I can't possibly do this'. I then asked the student how she thought a story could make any difference to such a horrendous experience in a young child's life. The student pleaded, 'Perhaps a story could help a little, even if not heal?'.

Once back in Australia I worked on a simple story with this aim – to hopefully help the situation. I had been told that Sylvia's family were devout Christians. This information guided my choice of a story journey. Emailed back to Kenya, the story was told to Sylvia by her teacher, and followed up with Sylvia finding a doll, dressed in clothes embroidered in silver and gold threads, waiting in her bed the next morning. The doll became Sylvia's very special friend and sleeping companion. The teacher and the house mother later reported on her improved play and interaction with others.

This was a humbling experience, and one that has led me to realise that some stories may only help a situation in a tiny, tiny, way... and how wonderful if they can.

Sylvia's mother and father were safe in heaven. All their children were with them except for little Sylvia who had stayed behind on earth.

At night in the light of the twinkling stars they could see their little daughter asleep in her bed. They were so happy that she had a safe new home and a new mother to take care of her. But they could see that their daughter was sad and lonely, and they wanted to send down a gift from heaven – a gift of a little friend for Sylvia to play with and to sleep with at night.

With the help of heaven's angels, they gathered golden threads from the sun and silver threads from the moon, and on the heavenly weaving loom they wove a special cloth to make a little doll.

When the doll was ready, one of heaven's angels cradled it in her arms and travelled with it across the sky of twinkling stars and down to earth. When she arrived at Sylvia's new house she reached in through the window and tucked the doll into the bed next to Sylvia's sleeping head.

The next morning when Sylvia woke up, her new gift was waiting to greet her. The doll's dress sparkled gold and silver in the morning light and Sylvia was so happy to see her. She knew it was a heavenly gift.

She named it... and the doll became her special friend.

Grandmother's Cloak of Light

A story for use with young children when a grandparent or elderly relative has died. This was recently read out at an elderly person's funeral by her young granddaughter.

Grandmother was sitting in her favourite chair in the garden, thinking back to all the beautiful moments in her life. It was almost time for her to set off on the long path back to the starry heavens. Around her the butterflies and birds flitted in and out of the rays of golden sunlight, weaving a special cloak of light for Grandmother to wear on his journey.

By the end of the day the sun was ready to go to bed and let the moon take her turn in the sky. Grandmother was still outside. The garden chair was so comfortable that she had fallen asleep.

Mother Moon shone down her silver light and the night spirits wove some of the moonlight into Grandmother's cloak. Then all the little stars took a turn and shone down an extra sparkle and twinkle into the cloth.

When the cloak of light was ready, Grandmother woke up, wrapped it tightly around her tired old shoulders, and set off on her journey.

As she was crossing the sky, she remembered to stop, just for a moment, to blow a kiss back down to all her family. The dawn clouds caught the kiss in their early morning colours and when the family woke up, they could see it shimmering in the sunrise.

The Tale of Little Fawn and Dear Friend

By Annie Bryant, storyteller and songwriter (tales & songs)

Introduction from Annie

This story was written for a seven-year old girl grieving the recent loss of a very close and dear uncle to a long-term cancer journey. The girl and her mother and uncle, as well as her grandparents, were all very close, having lived together for much of the girl's life. Her uncle was first diagnosed just before she was born, so her uncle's condition had always been an ongoing presence in her life.

Because of her deep love and connection with animals, something she shared with her uncle also, I chose to base the story in the animal world, with a changing focus from deep within her forest-home sanctuary to a growing desire to explore the world beyond, reflecting her own journey out of early childhood. Her mother requested the story to reflect her daughter's growing interest in the world outside of her own family and property.

Her uncle and his close group of friends all had unusual nicknames such as 'Everything' and 'Dear Friend', which the little girl always loved to hear. For this reason I named the characters in a similar fashion. After reading the story of Little Fawn to her daughter, her mother noticed in time the little girl was seeing more signs of her uncle's continued presence in nature – in the bald Eagle family that showed up by their house and stream, or the rainbow emerging in the sky just as they were listening to his favourite music or talking about him. She writes, 'I really think this whole experience, grounded by the story, changed her perspective on death, and life after death, in a way I'd never be able to explain in words'.

Once in the heart of a great forest, on the edge of a light-filled clearing where the soft moss grew sweet upon the earth, there lived a little fawn. Her dappled fur was soft and wispy, her little hooves like tinkling bells on the forest floor, and her heart so full of golden goodness that every tree, animal and bird loved her dearly.

Little Fawn danced and played and dreamed and grew within the loving embrace of the gentle woods, and especially the beloved trees of the clearing. These tall, strong and magnificent trees grew beside Little Fawn, and they took special care of her.

On one side stood a beautiful young tree with graceful limbs and long flowing branches, each one filled with cascading leaves that danced in the breeze. Little Fawn loved to leap into those comforting limbs, tumbling and playing before cuddling in tight while happily falling to sleep each night. This tree she called 'Loved One'.

Not far away stood two old gnarled trees side by side. Their dark rough branches had grown so close over the years that it was impossible to tell which limb belonged to which, and each dent and furrow of their ancient bark was filled with wonderful stories. These trees she called 'The Wise Folk'.

And then there was 'Dear Friend'. His light slender trunk and fine branches grew at the very centre of the clearing, and although his limbs were thin and pale, he was by far the tallest of the trees. In fact, Dear Friend was so tall that Little Fawn was sure his branches reached all the way up to the heavens. Inside his trunk was a tiny hollow, just big enough for Little Fawn to fit perfectly, and it was here Little Fawn loved to hide away. Inside the hollow she sometimes felt sure she could hear Dear Friend's heartbeat, just like her own heartbeat, and every now and then she thought she could even see a magic kind of glow inside.

There was something else magical about Dear Friend. No matter how much she grew, bigger and bigger each day, the hollow seemed to magically grow bigger too, because it was always just the right size for her. Dear Friend sighed with happiness when Little Fawn crawled inside, filling his trunk with her chatter and songs, laughter and stories. And because she knew he was strong and a little magical, she trusted him with all of her secrets. Especially the ones cheeky wind whispered to her. That pesky wind was full of wild stories of faraway places and strange animals, places and things that all sounded terribly exciting, if not a little frightening, to Little Fawn. Only in the safety of the hollow did Little Fawn dare whisper wind's stories. Dear Friend listened to her excitement and listened to her fear, before finally laughing a kind sort of laugh, before replying, 'One day soon, when you hear your true name, you'll know you are ready to meet these strange friends in the lands beyond the forest'.

As he spoke, Dear Friend glowed brighter than ever.

'But how will I know my true name?', she asked.

'You will find it, Little Fawn, just after I take my big journey.'

Dear Friend often talked of his 'big journey'. In his dreams he practised, getting ready for the time when he really would fly above the forest, dancing in the clouds, beholding wondrous lands beyond their woody home, and soaring fast and free wherever he pleased. When Little Fawn heard of those far-away lands she wondered if they could be anything like the exciting and scary places from the wind's whisperings?

'Maybe I'll be coming on your big journey too?', she timidly suggested.

'Oh no, little one, you will indeed visit these far-off lands one day soon, but while I will fly high above, you will live among it all.'

 STORIES TO LIGHT THE NIGHT

Little Fawn felt excited to hear this, and for a moment it distracted her from the sadness that came every time she thought of Dear Friend leaving her for his magical journey.

A few days later, Little Fawn was out wildly chasing the wind once more when she tumbled into a part of the forest where she'd never been before. She stopped to explore, chatting with the birds perched among the trees and snacking on the delicious berries bursting from a nearby bush. Suddenly she froze. She heard voices close-by, strange voices, voices unlike anything she'd ever heard before. The noise grew louder as Little Fawn soundlessly sprang behind a fallen log, hardly daring to breathe as she watched from her hiding place.

Moments later, two of the strangest animals she had ever seen ran to the berry bush and started wildly munching. They laughed as juice ran down their odd-coloured skin, and she gasped in surprise as she realised they were standing on only two legs! Hearing her gasp, the creatures quickly turned before making their own gasping noise to discover Little Fawn looking back at them. Quick as a flash she darted off towards the safety of her forest home, her swift hooves springing over logs and streams, the wind carrying just the faintest shout of words behind her, '... wait... friend....'. But Little Fawn did not stop for a minute, not until she finally made it into the warm safe glow of Dear Friend's hollow. The words spilled out of her, each one filled with excitement, fear and wonder, before Dear Friend finally calmed her down, gently singing her frightened body off to sleep.

Little Fawn dreamt she was flying, just like Dear Friend did in his dreams, except it felt more wonderful than she ever imagined. She soared through the clouds looking down at her forest home, then across to rolling green hills and the endless sparkling water beyond. She never realised the forest and the lands that lay in the distance were so beautiful! She pranced and danced through the soft clouds, tumbling and gliding, as free as the wind, until finally the clouds began to gently guide her back to the forest. Just as she drew closer to the clearing, a familiar song filled her ears. The singing grew louder as she gradually floated down, down, down, back into Loved One's outstretched limbs and The Wise Folks' steady gaze, their voices carrying her all the way down on to the cool soft forest floor, where she snuggled into Loved One's mossy roots.

Not long after, Little Fawn woke with a smile on her face. But the smile soon turned to confusion when she realised the same sweet song of her dream was still all around her. Except now she was wide awake and the whole forest was singing. She looked up to Loved One for reassurance, and the beautiful young tree smiled deeply before returning her gaze to the centre of the clearing. Little Fawn looked too, and there, almost completely covered by soft glowing light, were the slender limbs of Dear Friend. He looked so beautiful! Joy bubbled up to her eyes and happy tears rushed down her cheeks, as Little Fawn joined in the singing. And just as she did, the solid bright cloud of warm light began to rise. Higher and higher the light moved, up up up through the clearing, lighting the grey dawn sky as it floated higher and higher and higher until, finally, it merged with the golden light of the rising sun. And only when the sun had risen way up high into the morning sky did the trees and animals finally quieten their song.

It was then that Little Fawn remembered. She dashed to the tree and the hollow where she knew Dear Friend no longer lived, and she began searching. There, sitting on the little patch of earth where Little Fawn had so often laid her head to rest, was a necklace. Hardly daring to breathe she slowly picked up the smooth long seedpod pendant attached to the vine. She rattled the tiny seed inside before turning it over to find the delicate writing carved into the wood.

Back in the golden light of the day she carefully read the inscription:

Thank you for flying with me, Brave Heart

From that day on, Little Fawn was known throughout the whole forest, as well as the many lands beyond, by her true name. She had many adventures and made many new friends with all kinds of strange and wondrous creatures. They took comfort in her kind words and sweet nature, even returning with her for healing or friendship in the hollow of the great sanctuary tree that was once Dear Friend's home.

And each night, curled up in Loved One's soft mossy roots, The Wise Folks' stories soothing her into sleep, she dreamt and flew, high in the sky, laughing and sharing secrets with Dear Friend.

The Beavers and the Oak Tree

By Mohini Frankel-Hutton and Stephen Sharpe, musician

This story was crafted at a Therapeutic Storytelling Seminar in Forres, Scotland. It was originally written to be told to two boys (ages six and nine years) who were going through a grieving process after their grandfather and cousin died together in a car accident.

The mother reported that the story gave the boys, above all else, a sense of hope around the cycles of life within the context of nature…. Trees grow, fall, and then find themselves lying on the ground in a forest, only to be re-born as a home to many other animals.

It has since been used in other situations of sudden loss, including the unexpected and tragic loss for parents of an unborn baby.

There once stood a tall and magnificent old oak tree in the middle of a beautiful forest. This tree was the home for many animals large and small. It housed a stunning red rose that climbed and intertwined around its trunk.

On the rose lived a caterpillar who was building his cocoon, safely nurtured by the strength and safe haven of the tree and the beauty and vulnerability of the rose.

One day, one hot sultry day, thunder clouds began to gather, then lightning struck, and the tree and the rose fell to the ground.

Squirrels, owls, spiders, ants; all of life large and small assembled in disbelief. How could this be? Where are we going to live now? What will happen to our tree? Why did no one warn us? Where will our young live now?

For three days and three nights, there was no bird song…. Squirrels fell silent, the ants stood still, and all was quiet.

Then along came two beavers…. They heard the silence and knew something was wrong. Chanting their song, they busily set to work:

The brave beavers we be, carving and gnawing this tree.
As night follows day, we beaver away,
Knowing life gives way to a brand new day.

After many days and many nights and many passing seasons, through sun, wind, rain and snow, finally what stood before them was a magnificent log home that sat proudly on the forest floor. There were perches for the owls, nests for the birds, tunnels for the rabbits, branches for the squirrels, and a safe haven for each and every animal to live together in the middle of the forest for years to come.

As the animals celebrated their first evening together, they heard a sound. They all looked up through the branches of the trees to see that the chrysalis stuck to the fallen rose had transformed into a beautiful butterfly and was flying high in the sky!

Sylvie and the Stars

By Yvonne Donohoe

Written for children (ages 6–10 years) who have a mother with an incurable illness, or who have had a mother who has recently passed away.

When one of her children died in a sudden accident, Yvonne Donohoe lost someone more precious to her than life itself. In the years that followed she came to deeply understand the healing power of grief. She shares her powerful story of living after profound loss in her book *Soul Stripped Bare – Growing through Grief*. Yvonne has generously contributed this and one other short story entitled 'Goodbye Shelly' to this collection.

Once there was a little girl called Sylvie. She lived with her mother and grandmother in a pretty cottage on the edge of a steep sea cliff.

Every night, Sylvie would look out of her bedroom window at the stars. They looked like a blanket of bright lights shining over the deep, dark ocean. She loved the patterns they made and would make up bedtime stories about them. Her favourite stars were the yellow star, the twinkling star and the bright star. Sylvie imagined that they were a star family, just like her family.

The yellow star was the grandmother, the twinkling star was the little girl, and the brightest star was the mother. As she nestled her sleepy head into her soft pillow, she would imagine her star family going on amazing adventures together. Soon, Sylvie would drift off into a deep, peaceful sleep.

One day, she woke to the soft sounds of someone crying. She wondered if it was just the sound of the gentle breeze. Listening closely, she could hear hushed voices. It was grandmother and mother talking. When she joined them, they told her that mother was very sick. Little Sylvie was so sad, she didn't want her mother to be sick. Perhaps if she tidied the house and washed the dishes mother would get better. Grandmother smiled a sad smile. 'Darling girl, if we could, we would do everything possible to make mother better, but sometimes all the love in the world and all the wishing and all of the tidying won't change things.'

Her mother agreed. She hugged Sylvie tightly and said, 'We will spend the next months making wonderful memories together'.

And that is what they did.

Mother taught Sylvie her favourite recipes. They sewed a beautiful blanket which was covered in satin hearts. It was soft and snuggly just like mother. They made a photo book filled with their special photos and mother wrote stories and made up sweet poems, just for Sylvie.

As the wintry days passed mother became weaker and weaker. Sylvie knew that she would be leaving soon, and as big salty tears slid down her cheeks, mother hugged her and tried to cheer her.

She said she would be going to live in the stars and that she would watch down on Sylvie every night. She explained that Sylvie would feel very sad at first but over time, she would be able to be happy again. 'And', said mother 'you will always have my love in your heart.'

With those words, she gave Sylvie a beautiful heart-shaped necklace. 'Whenever you're feeling sad, just hold this little heart in your fingers, close your eyes and smile, knowing that I am sending you love and kisses from the stars. You won't see me, but you will be able to feel my love.

That night, as Sylvie lay looking out of her bedroom window at her little star family, the bright 'mother' star began to flicker and glow. Suddenly, it became a shooting star. It shone ever so brightly as it flashed across the night sky before disappearing into the darkness. As it disappeared, Sylvie heard her mother saying, 'Goodbye darling. I will love you for ever'.

Sylvie was lying there feeling very sad when the door gently opened. Grandmother came in and quietly snuggled into bed next to Sylvie. As they both lay there with soft tears falling, something magical appeared in the night sky. There, in front of Sylvie's window, appeared a new star. She knew in her heart it was her mother watching over her.

Sylvie smiled a sad smile. As she felt her heart necklace, she whispered to the night sky, 'Thank you, mumma, I will love you for ever'.

Miss Burble

By Ana Barišić, M.Sc., writer, Croatia

By Ana Barišić, M.Sc., writer, Croatia

Introduction from Ana

I wrote this story at the request of a teacher who attended my workshop. It was written for twin brothers in the second grade, eight years of age. Their aunt, to whom they were very close, had recently passed away.

While talking to their mum on the phone, I found out that they always had so much fun with their aunt. She took them for walks and played with them a lot in the yard. Sometimes she played a video game with them in which they were supposed to shoot bubbles in the air. They ate pizza together and they talked with her about everything.

She let them do all the things that most parents tend to limit: a bit more playing video games, a bit more fun, and long walks. And then she became ill.

She had been fighting cancer for a long time. The boys were by her side until the last moment. They would cuddle up to her in bed, as close as they could, even when she could no longer speak. The boys asked their mother, 'Who will replace their aunt?'.

I wrote the story and sent it to the boys' teacher. She read it out loud in front of the entire class. After that the children wrote about how the story left them feeling. This is what Twin A wrote about the paragraph with tears: 'Lovely and sad.' He also drew a picture of himself (not of the story character, but of himself!) jumping into Miss Burble. Twin B wrote a whole paragraph about playing with Miss Burble and drew a picture of the story characters playing with her. He drew a big smile on the rock from where the boys were jumping.

After a few months, the mother sent a thank-you letter to the teacher. She said that the teacher's engagement, together with reading the story in front of the class and the attention she had given to the children, helped her and her sons tremendously.

I n the magical land of Geyseria, in a small cabin by the shore, lived the Waters family: the mother's name was Waterine, the father's name was Waterford, and they had two twin sons, Waterly and Waterby. They had their beloved grandparents and a circle of good family friends.

Waterly and Waterby were just like any other boys of Geyseria. Their skin was pale blue, they wore a blueish crown, and between their hands and torso there was a thin folded shroud. If they wanted to fly, the shroud would spread like wings, and as soon as they dove into clear water, it would help them swim and dive faster.

Geyseria is a land full of sunny green hills. There is a stream coming from each and every hill, forming little rivers that run across cascades of waterfalls. Numerous Geyserian families live in their little cottages built alongside these waterfalls. Each Geyserian family has its own little cottage, and next to it flows a beautiful stream of white-blueish water, emerging from underground. Each spring is special and alive. Whenever a family swims in it, the spring rejoices with them and bursts with joy. The Geyserians themselves are made of water on the inside, so they can easily communicate with the spring. They understand its burbling perfectly.

The Waters family spring was right behind their home and its name was Miss Burble. Every morning, right out of bed, Waterly and Waterby would run there to play. It was like a celebration, every time. Crystal-clear Miss Burble flowed over a slope covered in soft moss. The twins would climb up to the top of the hill and slide down this soft water slide. Since they could also fly, they would go up in the air, make a couple of loops, and then plummet into crystal-clear water. They would then come up to the surface and laugh so hard.

Miss Burble would laugh along with them and make water balloons to bring the boys even more joy. The boys' favourite game was 'hit the water balloon'. From the top of their hill they would wait until they saw a water balloon, and then jump on to it. Sometimes it would lift them up so high that their cabin seemed so tiny. Throughout their play, Miss Burble would sing a joyful melody. Sometimes the boys would start to dance; they couldn't resist the music, and they would bounce happily along to the rhythm.

When they tired of playing, the brothers would sit next to their Miss Burble and talk to her about whatever they had in mind. Miss Burble loved talking to them. Sometimes Waterly was sitting there alone, and he would share some of his secrets. Miss Burble would listen carefully, and then hug him with her magical hands of water. Sometimes Waterby would share his secrets and secret joys with Miss Burble, too. Waterly and Waterby, and the whole Waters family, loved Miss Burble very much, and she loved them.

But one day in Geyseria there was a huge earthquake. It shook the ground so severely that it disrupted the groundwater flows. Miss Burble's wellspring cracked in one place, so there was less and less water in her stream.

When Waterly and Waterby came to visit her that day, they could tell she grew quieter and more tired. The water kept flowing out of the green hill, but each day it was retreating more and more. The twins could no longer jump from the top of the hill. They could no longer dive into Miss Burble. All they could do was talk to her,

   STORIES TO LIGHT THE NIGHT

lie next to her on the shore and listen to her dwindling burbling. And then one day when they woke up and ran to their beloved Miss Burble, there was no more water. Not a single drop.

That made Waterly and Waterby and the entire Waters family very sad. They missed their Miss Burble. They were so overwhelmed with grief that their tears were falling down their cheeks and soaking the dry ground. After a while the soil whispered: 'Thank you for your tears.'

Time passed by. Waterly and Waterby played with their parents, grandparents, family friends and other children in Geyseria. One time, mum hugged Waterly so hard that he was overwhelmed with happiness to such an extent that his eyes welled up with tears, and one tear of joy fell down on to the ground.

The ground whispered:

Thank you for your tears of joy. And now I can share with you the biggest secret of all. Remember that day when the earthquake hit, and Miss Burble disappeared? Do you wonder where her water is now? Well her water moved to another magical place. Many groundwaters flow inside of me. After they pass through dark ground, they resurface again, on a far away, sunny green hill. Missing someone is the love that stays behind. Each time you start to cry because you love someone so much that it makes you sad they're gone, and each time your eyes well up with tears because you love someone so much that you're so grateful for having them near, your tears of love become a part of my underground waters.

Therefore, your tears of love become a part of Miss Burble, too. The more you love each other, so much that your eyes tear up with love, Miss Burble will be happier, because your tears of love are reaching her. And when you look into the eyes of a person you love very much, you will be able to see a glimpse of your dear Miss Burble in the reflection of your tears of joy or sadness.

The Oriole and the Cherry Tree

This story was written in a workshop in Singapore for an all-girls school where one of the pupils had died tragically one week beforehand. The story was told at assembly to all the children as part of the memorial service; the school had a cherry tree in the garden – hence the choice of this tree in the story. The girl who had died was very popular with all the students, and a leader figure in the school.

The children then returned to class to help their teacher write words for a song that connected them to the story; then at the next assembly, each class sang its song for the rest of the school.

There was once a beautiful cherry tree that grew in the middle of a large garden where many birds and insects flew and fluttered and flitted. Children loved to play in the shade of the cherry tree. They especially loved it in the summer when the branches were laden with ripe, red, juicy cherries.

The cherry tree enjoyed all the birds and insects and children who played around it, but it had one special friend, a golden oriole bird. This beautiful bird had its nest on one of the tree's top branches, and from here it sang sweetly all day.

But it happened one night, without any warning, that a violent storm passed over the garden. There was lightning and thunder and strong winds and rain. One of the lightning flashes hit the top branch of the cherry tree and killed the golden oriole bird in an instant.

The storm passed over, leaving the cherry tree and all the garden friends mourning the death of the golden bird. The cherry tree was so upset at the loss of its friend that it refused to flower the next spring – and without any flowers there would be no cherries in the summer.

The bees that liked to get pollen from the cherry tree flowers circled the tree and hummed a special song to the tree. Soon all the other friends from the garden joined in the song... the ants, dragonflies, butterflies, birds and children.

The song helped the cherry tree find the strength to grow its flowers once again, and the following summer it was covered with ripe, red, juicy cherries.

Princess Rose and the Garden Queen

A story written for a young girl (8–12 years) who has lost her mother to a long and difficult illness. This story has also helped me as an adult come to terms with the loss of my mother (who died when I was much younger) and 'find a way forward, find a way onward'.

This story could have two possible endings, depending on the situation and who it is being shared with. Either it could end with 'And her beautiful rose perfume filled the air'. Or the additional sentence could be added: 'Princess Rose had now become the new Garden Queen.'

Little Pink Rose lived in a warm earth bed next to her mother, Red Rose. The rose bed was at the centre of a large circular garden, surrounded by flowers of every colour of the rainbow.

What a beautiful place this was. The air smelt of sweet perfume, birds sang merry songs, butterflies fluttered, and bees buzzed in and around the petals.

The garden was cared for every day by an old gardener. She had lived there for longer than anyone could remember. As her favourite flowers were roses, she had built herself a wooden bench close to the rose bed. Every day she would sit and linger, enjoying the sweet perfume from the many rose blooms.

The gardener called the magnificent red rose in the centre of the garden her Garden Queen. The little pink rose next to her she named Princess Rose.

Life in the garden continued in a happy peaceful way for a long time. The gardener tended the flowers with loving care, and the perfume of the roses and many other flowers filled the air.

But then, one day, everything changed. Princess Rose looked up at her mother and noticed some strange spots. The gardener also noticed these spots on her Garden Queen, and straight away mixed up a special healing oil to rub into her leaves.

There were just a few spots at first, but every day they were growing larger and larger. Soon they had spread over most of the leafy branches. The oil wasn't helping and the gardener was so upset – she didn't know what else to do.

Princess Rose could see that her mother looked very sick. Her leaves were starting to fall to the ground and her branches, that were once straight and strong, were now hanging limply down. And the worst thing of all, the deep red petals were slowly falling off some of the red roses on Queen Rose, even before her blooms had opened.

Princess Rose was confused. She had always thought her mother would last for ever. After all, she was the Garden Queen!

She bent her rose leaves in sadness.

Then she heard a soft song from above.

Look up Princess Rose - breathe in the last perfume of my deep red roses.
Look up Princess Rose and soak in the last beauty of my red blooms.
These will be the memories to help carry you forward.
These will be the memories to help carry you onward.

Princess Rose tried to follow the words of the soft song, even though it was not an easy thing to do. She breathed in the last of her mother's beautiful perfume and soaked in the last of her red beauty.

Soon, all too soon, the gardener knew it was time to come and dig up the Garden Queen and take her to her resting place.

Princess Rose was left alone.

But not for long. The gardener returned to tend this small delicate rose with loving care. She watered her every day and carefully weeded and mulched around her roots.

Slowly, oh so slowly, Princess Rose grew tall, stretching her branches wide – some reached into the empty space where her mother used to live, others grew out in different directions.

Eventually, with help and care by the loving gardener, she was covered in large pink buds that slowly opened for all the world to see. And her beautiful rose perfume filled the air.

Princess Rose had now become the new Garden Queen.

   STORIES TO LIGHT THE NIGHT

The Rose and the Thorn

A story written on request from a primary school in Norway, for children ages seven and upwards. Its aim was to offer some kind of hope after the traumatic event of the island massacre in July 2011, where 77 people lost their lives, the majority of whom were teenagers.

The images in the story were inspired by the Rose March Tribute that was organized in Oslo to help bring solidarity and hope back to a shocked nation. Norwegian's Prime Minister Stoltenberg, addressing the rose-holding crowd, said: 'Evil can kill a human being but never defeat a people.'

There was once a prince and a princess who lived in a castle surrounded by a beautiful garden. In this garden grew many kinds of flowers, but the most beautiful of all was the rose bush. This rose bush was like no other – it had one perfect red rose that never seemed to grow old. And it had a smooth green stem and smooth green branches without any thorns.

People came from far and wide to look at such perfection... a rose without thorns that never seemed to die! Every day the prince and princess would walk through their garden and stop to give thanks for the wonder and beauty of this rose.

However, deep in the rose bush, hiding far down inside the stem, there was a long sharp thorn that was bursting to find its way out. It had been living in the rose bush for a very long time and slowly, slowly, slowly, it was making its way to the top. As it travelled up through the green stem it knocked against the woody edges, but these were too strong for the thorn to push through.

Then one day the long sharp thorn reached the top of the bush, where the soft red rose sat shining in the sun. Here was an easy doorway for the long sharp thorn! It pierced right through the heart of the red rose and came out into the daylight.

As the thorn broke through the heart of the rose, all the red petals fell off and fluttered to the ground. When the prince and princess were walking in their garden later that day they were shocked with what they found. Their beautiful red rose had died, all its petals had been blown across the garden and the stem and branches were withered and brown. The only thing left shining in the late afternoon light was one silver thorn, pointing high to the sky.

The prince and princess quickly called for the castle gardeners to come and dig out the dead rose bush. Then they returned to the castle to mourn the loss of the beautiful red rose. That night a heavy fog settled down upon the gardens.

Many days and nights passed. Summer merged into autumn and then autumn merged into winter. The castle and the gardens seemed to disappear under the weight of the heavy fog.

But then came the spring sunshine, and the wintry fog slowly melted away in the bright new light. One fine spring morning the prince and princess looked out of their castle window and a most wondrous sight met their eyes. Everywhere that a rose petal had landed in the garden a rose bush had taken root, had grown tall and strong and was budding with rose flowers.

As the sun climbed across the sky, each of the new rose buds opened their petals to the light. There were many different roses of many different perfumes and many different colours – yellow, orange, blue, purple, pink, red and white. The prince and princess walked out into the garden with joy and hope in their hearts, and people came from far and wide to give thanks for the wonder and beauty of the roses.

When Grandma Passed Away

By Diana Petrova, Bulgaria

This story is suitable to use with older children and teenagers. It is part of an award-winning Bulgarian Collection of Therapeutic Storytelling for Children and Parents: *Tales for the Whole Family* by Diana Petrova.

These stories are used by Psychological Centres for Child Development, Foundations for Social Education and the Association of the Adopted and Adopters. They may be used as pieces to introduce difficult topics or as grounds for discussion between parents and children.

When Grandma left this world for good, I was just going out with my sled. As soon as Mother told me what had happened, I put on my jacket and left the house. I didn't take my sled with me. I walked down the street. Several icicles, sparkling in the sun, hung under a window pane on one of the houses. The snow was melting, and water droplets trickled down from them. I watched how they slowly grew heavier before they fell. Like tears.

I broke off one of the icicles, and then another and one more. I gathered them in my hands and went back home. I came inside and left them in the freezer.

Mother was sitting at the kitchen table and crying. I decided that I wouldn't, because if she saw me crying too, that would only make it worse. She started to say something to me, but when she saw that I wasn't up for talking, she laid her face in her hands once more.

I went to my room and lay on my bed. I tried reading my book, but it was no use. Only one thought was spinning through my head: What would Grandma look like now? I heard my aunt and uncle arrive, but I didn't get up to greet them. I just left my door slightly ajar and looked on as my uncle embraced his sister, my own mother. Later, she and my aunt spoke softly as my uncle sat on a chair, staring into the painted curves of the table. Mother gave my aunt a key to the house. Then she came into my room and kissed me. She drew me into her tightly – so much that for a moment I stopped breathing. Afterwards, she backed away without looking at me and left the room with Father.

Soon my uncle left, and I was left with my aunt. She suggested we play a board game, but I didn't want to.

'If you like, we could talk about her', she offered, after pausing to think for a bit.

'Yes.'

We were silent for a while, and then we were remembering lots of different things about Grandma. First her cooking, then the shirts and tablecloths she used to crochet. Flowers and various shapes, a little wrinkled but very beautiful, sprung forth from her hands. We remembered how she used to iron them, and then how we would bring them to a shop to sell them.

Grandma was quite talkative. She knew what everyone in the neighbourhood was doing, who had gone to the shop and what they had bought. I wondered how she managed to learn all those details, since she always looked busy with her knitting. It was only at the end, when she grew ill, that she ever rested.

We kept telling stories. Meanwhile, my stomach started to hurt. My aunt told me not to worry and that it was normal, and then she asked if I wanted to go to the bathroom. I went several times and got tired. She made me some cheese on toast with tomato – my favourite meal.

I ate, drank some water and felt sleepy. I lay down and she sat next to me. She looked through the window and didn't say another thing.

I awoke to her hand stroking my hair. It was time to get up and change clothes. Unlike before, I felt happy upon waking up. But soon enough, all at once, I was overcome with sadness over Grandma.

It was late now, but Mother hadn't come back. My aunt explained that my mother was staying the night with Grandma at her house, and that we'd see her there the next day. We did some drawing together and then my aunt made us dinner. We went to bed early. She pulled out the folding bed and laid it next to mine. She held my hand as I slept. I didn't sleep well. I awoke several times, asking for water. My aunt got up and brought me some, and then she rubbed my back and I fell back to sleep.

In the morning I didn't want to get out of bed. My stomach still hurt. My aunt said she was going to make me some rosehip tea before we had to leave, and I begged her to put exactly three lumps of sugar in it. I heard her talking to my mother on the phone – they were discussing whether I should even go. That's when I flew into the kitchen to tell them straightaway that I wanted to see Grandma one last time. My aunt relaxed her phone hand and nodded her head in agreement.

There were lots of people in front of Grandma's house. Her friends, various relatives. And all of them wanted to pat me on the head. It started to really annoy me, and I wished they would disappear.

When I went inside, I saw Father first. He kissed my forehead. Right then, his phone rang, and he pulled away to answer it. We went ahead to Grandma's room. Nothing about her house was the same any more. Unfamiliar people were coming and going without taking off their shoes. The hallway cupboard had been removed and the coat rack was overburdened. On top of all that, the whole place smelled of candlewax. I entered the room in the middle of which Grandma had been laid to rest. She looked a bit thin, but there was such a calm expression on her face that she appeared to be only sleeping. I don't remember from where my mother appeared. She took me by the hand, and we went closer to Grandma together. Mother started talking about how Grandma was supposed to be in heaven now. I didn't understand that at all. How could she manage to stay up there without falling down?

She was dressed in one of the shirts she had herself embroidered with roses. I rested a hand over hers. They were very cold. They had never been so cold before. And then I looked into her face again. There was no way Grandma hadn't known where she was going. Grandma always knew everything. Well, by now I was really crying. I didn't even care if Mother saw me. She hugged me, drawing me in tightly again, like the day before.

It wasn't long until my aunt took me away, which was a good thing because I don't think I could have stood there for much longer. We decided to take a walk on the way home because the weather was getting warmer. We talked about school and whether I would return the next day. My aunt didn't waste her breath asking me too many questions. She let me speak only as much as I wanted to. I was feeling better now because everything was over and done with. I even felt like congratulating myself for holding up so well. My stomach didn't hurt any more, either.

We stopped so my aunt could buy me a notebook from the bookshop. She said that it would be good for me to write down whatever I was thinking.

As soon as we came back I took the icicles out of the freezer. I went back to my room, opened the window and left them outside. I closed it and sat behind my desk. I turned the pages of my new gift, which smelled nice. I looked out at the windowsill. The icicles were starting to melt and drip. I watched the small puddle of water forming underneath them. They didn't disappear, but rather only changed form. Just like Grandma.

I leaned forward and wrote in my notebook: 'Grandma isn't in heaven. Grandma is in my heart.'

Then I closed it. I decided to go and see what my aunt was doing. She hadn't come to see me in my room for about an hour. When I went into the kitchen, I saw her standing there by the oven. She was crying without making a sound. The tears rolled down her cheeks as silently as my melting icicles. I hugged her and her body heaved in my arms.

It was time for Mother to come back home.

THE FANTASTIC FLYING MACHINE

A story written for a ten-year old boy whose father was tragically killed in a car accident. The aim of the story was to help, in any small way, to rechannel the boy's anger for what had happened – anger that he was directing at his mother – into something productive for his future. The story focused on what the boy most loved doing with his father, which was flying drones.

The story was given to the grandfather who passed it on to the mother in Holland to read to her son. After he had heard the story, the grandfather back in Australia received a very enthusiastic call from his grandson. The boy interpreted the story that his father was an inventor (which he was, in a way) and built a Flying Machine and they all had a lot of fun with that. Then the Flying Machine crashed.… The boy said that was the accident dad had, and this is what had killed him… (this is an interesting interpretation, very different to what I had imagined in choosing the story metaphors and journey).

The grandfather found these words 'brutally honest and moving'.

'I want to be an inventor too! Just like my father', he said. His grandfather told him that he had packed up all his father's tools to send to him so they will be all his to work with and he can use them for his inventions.

The grandfather reported that he loved hearing his grandson's interpretation and that the boy was now inspired to be an inventor just like his father! His attitude had changed from anger to motivation.

There was once, in a land far away, a tinkering, toiling inventor. This inventor, with a helpful young apprentice by his side, spent many hours in his workshop, tinkering and toiling with sheets of metal and bits of wire and pieces of wood. He especially loved to make things that moved – small and large, slow and fast. For the paths and roads he had built electric bicycles and cars; for the snow and ice, sleds with runners and solar heaters. And for the canals and rivers, wind-powered boats to use on sunny summer days.

But his prize invention, the best of all his creations, was what he affectionately called the FFM – *the Fantastic Flying Machine*. The inventor had spent years with its planning and designing, and now it was under construction. His apprentice would arrive early each day and set to work – cutting bits of wire, drilling holes here and there, and sorting and re-arranging pieces of metal to achieve the perfectly balanced machine. Once completed, it was sent out on many test runs to ensure it could fly up high and return safely home. One of the special features of the FFM was that it carried a high-powered camera which gave wonderful possibility to take photos from far above the earth.

Finally, after various intricate adjustments, the FFM was able to fly so high, it could reach above the clouds; the FFM was able to fly so wide, it could cross the valleys and hills and travel out over the sea. As it flew, its many parts whirred and ticked and spun. Meanwhile the camera clicked away, taking photos of such beauty to bring back home. How the inventor and his apprentice loved to sit together in front of the viewing screen at the end of each day – looking at the photos taken from on high – feathery clouds, arching rainbows, ocean patterns, long golden beaches and winding rivers glinting in the sun.

But one day the FFM was high up in the clouds and, without any warning, it was caught in the middle of a terrible storm. Lightning flashed so strongly that it cracked the machine apart, and the bits came falling, down, down, into the sea below.

Some of the pieces of the FFM sank deep below the waves. But other parts floated and eventually were carried by the waves to the shore. Here they were picked up by a friend of the inventor who just happened to be out walking on the beach that morning.

The day the rescued parts were returned to him, the inventor was still feeling so upset and angry by what had happened to his precious FFM that he did not even want to look at them. He put them in his work shed on the highest shelf of a dark cupboard. He shut the door of the cupboard and then shut the door on his workshop.

Many weeks passed by and the once-busy workspace remained silent and still. Dust slowly settled on the benches and the tools, and the bits and pieces of metal and wood sat untouched in the dark cupboard.

The inventor stayed in his house and his young helper had no work.

But after some months, the apprentice was growing bored with nothing to do each day. He was missing the tinkering and toiling and busy work. So, early one morning he returned to the workshop and quietly pushed open the door. Once inside he climbed up to reach the bits and pieces of the old FFM, and carefully lifted them down on to the workbench. Then he set to work, trying to build a new flying machine. Every day he returned and kept working – cutting bits of wire, drilling holes here and there and sorting and re-arranging pieces of metal. He was not exactly sure what he was doing, but he strongly knew he wanted to give it a try. When he thought the machine was ready, he inserted a new camera. Then he carried it out into the garden behind the work shed to give a first test-run.

At this time the inventor was sitting in his kitchen, enjoying a quiet cup of tea. He heard a noise and looked out to see what appeared to be a version of the FFM rising high above the workshop roof. He watched in surprise as it went up a little higher, then slowly began to come back down.

By the time the inventor had reached the garden on the other side of the workshop, the little FFM was back on the ground. His apprentice was busy with a spanner trying to adjust bits here and there. 'I am so sorry', he said, 'I just can't get it working like your old one.'

The inventor smiled a warm smile. 'But you have tried!', he said. 'This is wonderful. This is important. Keep tinkering and toiling and next time your new FFM may fly a little higher.'

Then the inventor returned to the workshop, pulled out a key from his pocket and opened a storage room that was full of many new materials. 'Please make use of anything here', he said, and handed the apprentice the key.

With a whole range of new materials to choose from, the apprentice continued working on his new project. Each time he gave it a test-run it lifted higher and higher into the sky and was able to travel further and further away. First, it cleared the trees, then it crossed over the town, then over the hills, then out over the sea. And always it found its way back home.

Time passed, and with every new season the apprentice worked to improve his design of the FFM, to the pride and joy of his master. After many years it was flying so high and so far, and the images caught by the camera were so exceptional, they were now being shared with many people all around the world – feathery clouds, arching rainbows, ocean patterns, long golden beaches and winding rivers glinting in the sun.

STORIES TO LIGHT THE NIGHT

GOODBYE SHELLY

By Yvonne Donohoe

A story for older children and families about the loss of a most precious treasure.

When her son died in a sudden accident, Yvonne Donohoe lost someone more precious to her than life itself. In the years that followed she came to deeply understand the healing power of grief. She shares her powerful story of living after profound loss in her book *Soul Stripped Bare – Growing through Grief*. Yvonne generously contributed her short story to this collection.

Jenny loved the beach.

There was nothing better than feeling the warm sand between her toes and the salty spray on her face. She loved the sound of the gulls and loved exploring the rock pools. And whenever Jenny saw the sunlight dancing on the water, she always imagined it was mermaids scattering millions of diamonds.

If possible, Jenny would visit the beach every day, but she lived on a farm a long, long way from the coast. Looking through her bedroom window Jenny could see paddocks and horses, not sand dunes and dolphins. Right now, she could see their new farm dog, Bluey, jumping up and barking excitedly at her dad on the tractor. Dad had been planting water melons down by the river. That thought made her heart sing because she knew that in a few months' time, when the melons ripened, it would be summer. And summer meant going to visit her grandparents who lived at the beach.

Jenny was supposed to be doing her homework, but she was staring at her most precious possession – a large shell she had found last summer. Jenny loved combing the beach for treasures and could hardly believe her eyes when she saw it. It had washed up on the morning tide and was pink and pearly, and the most beautiful thing she had ever seen. Grandma was always strict about what Jenny could take from the beach. Normally she had to leave her treasures there because that was their home. Grandma taught Jenny about habitats and eco-systems, and Jenny loved caring for the environment too; but when her grandmother saw how much she loved the shell, she let Jenny keep it – *just this once.*

When the holidays ended and Jenny returned to the farm, she took the shell with her. She found a small box and filled it with soft, shiny satin left over from when mum had made her ballet dress. She carefully placed her shell on the nest of satin and placed it on her desk. Every afternoon when she did her homework Jenny would look at her shell and smile. She even talked to her shell, asking it things like, 'What is 7 times 8?'. The shell couldn't answer, of course, but it always seemed to help her work out the answer.

Every night Jenny would carry the box to her bedside table and before going to sleep, she would hold the shell up to her ear and listen to the sound of the sea. Closing her eyes, she would imagine she was at the beach and that her shell was telling her stories about its adventures in the ocean. Jenny wondered about all of the places it had been to before she found it. Had it been to tropical islands? Had it been used by a mermaid to hold her beautiful pearls? Perhaps it had been on adventures with pirates!

Jenny drew pictures of her shell and made a book of short stories called *The Adventures of Shelly* (the name she had given her shell). Jenny even told Shelly her secrets, and she always felt better when she did. Her worries seemed to disappear, and her fears would fall away after she had shared them. Shelly was like her best friend.

Soon it was summer, and Jenny was packing to go on her holiday to the beach. She had made a list: swimmers, hat, flippers, clothes, toothbrush and in BIG letters she had written 'SHELLY'. Her mum questioned whether she really needed to take a shell on a holiday to the seaside.

'Please mum, please? Shelly will be lonely here without me for six whole weeks', she pleaded. When her mum gave that special look that meant 'Okay, but I think you're being a bit silly', Jenny jumped up and gave her a huge hug.

The very next day, after a long trip Jenny's grandparents met her at the train station. Soon she was running into the ocean and splashing in the waves. She was so happy to be back at the seaside. A new family had moved into the house next door. They had a girl the same age as Jenny. Her name was Maddy and soon the two were inseparable.

One particular day the surf was too rough to go swimming, so the girls spent ages creating THE best sandcastle ever. It had lots of rooms with connecting tunnels and a massive moat that went all the way around it. Jenny had carefully placed Shelly in one of the rooms and pretended she was *Shelly, Queen of the Sea*. She collected lots of small shells and placed them around Shelly, as if they were sitting listening, mesmerized by her adventures.

The girls decided to explore the rock pools. Grandma was lounging in her favourite beach chair. Looking up from her book she checked that the girls had their hats on before waving them goodbye. With a shout they raced to the other end of the beach. The rock pools were full of interesting sea creatures.

   STORIES TO LIGHT THE NIGHT

They spent ages exploring the rock pools. Jenny found some spiky sea urchins, Maddy found some interesting sea cucumbers and there were hundreds of periwinkles. They were Jenny's favourite sea creatures; she loved watching them close their shell with their tiny door. Jenny always made sure she replaced them carefully after observing them (like a real scientist). The girls were so absorbed in looking at the sea animals they lost track of the time. They didn't realise that the tide was coming in.

When Jenny turned, she could see that the waves were washing in really quickly. Right along the beach, back to where Grandma was sitting, people were hurrying to move their towels and bags away from the rising tide line. In an instant Jenny realised what this meant – their castle could be washed away.

'Run Maddy, run. We have to rescue Shelly before the waves take her out to sea.'

Both girls took off like the wind. They ran as fast as their legs would carry them, but Jenny feared that they'd be too late. They were about 100 metres from the castle when a huge wave washed up on to the beach and completely flattened it.

'Noooooo!', cried Jenny as she kept running. By the time she arrived at the spot where the castle had been, the sand was flat and small air bubbles were popping at her feet. Shelly was nowhere to be seen.

'Oh no, oh no', she kept repeating as she dug frantically in the sand. Then she ran to the water's edge. Jenny looked and looked, but couldn't see Shelly anywhere. The incoming tide kept pushing her back until eventually she had to give up her search. With tears streaming down her face, she walked back to Grandma.

'Whatever is the matter?', Grandma asked. Through loud sobs, Jenny explained what had happened. Grandma knew how special Shelly was to Jenny. 'I didn't realise she was in the castle. I would have rescued her for you.'

Jenny climbed into Grandma's lap. She didn't care that she was ten years old and about to go into the fifth grade. She didn't care who saw her sobbing. She felt numb, and her heart felt like it had been shattered into a hundred pieces.

Grandma soothed her. She hummed a little lullaby as she rocked Jenny from side to side. It felt good to be rocked, but Jenny still felt sadder than she had ever felt before. The last time she felt this sad was when their old dog Honey had died.

Grandma began to talk very calmly. 'Oh Jenny. I am so sorry darling. I know how much Shelly meant to you. You know you will always have beautiful memories of Shelly.' She even promised to get a frame for Jenny's special picture – the one that Jenny had drawn when she first found Shelly last summer. 'You can hang it on your wall and every time you look at it, it will remind you of all the fun times you had with Shelly.' Then Grandma said something really unexpected. 'You know, Jenny, even though Shelly's not actually with you, she is somewhere, so you can always send her love and happy thoughts.'

'Do you think she is happy being back in the ocean?', Jenny asked quietly.

'I'm sure she misses you, but I think she would be very happy to be starting a new adventure. She came for a little visit with you, but the ocean is her real home', explained Grandma.

Jenny began to imagine Shelly off on a new adventure. She smiled to think of her riding on the back of a turtle or playing with the colourful sea anemones. She even imagined her back with the mermaids; perhaps she was storing their jewellery or their special hair combs. Jenny knew that she would really miss her, but thinking that Shelly was happy left her feeling a bit better. She would always be glad for the time they had had together.

The one thing Grandma *didn't* say was, 'You can always find another shell'. Jenny was so glad that her Grandma was wise, and knew that saying that would not have helped. Jenny didn't want any other shell – she wanted her shell, her beautiful Shelly. There would be other shells, but Shelly would always be special.

The Little Star Who Could Not Stay

By Pamela Celestine Perkins, M.Ed.

This story was written for parents (and their families) who have lost their baby at birth. It is dedicated to Norah and all the other little stars who now shine down upon us. The story is used as part of a care package in NICU in a hospital in the USA.

Volunteers make wool-knitted shrouds to hold the child in, plus tiny felted star babies (if a mother wishes to take one) plus flannel 'lovies'.

When you look up at night at the thousands upon thousands of stars shining and shimmering in the darkness, do you know that some of them have lived briefly among us here on the Earth?

It is said that a very few special stars are entrusted with a delicate and important task: they plant seeds of Love within human hearts. This Love is so deep, so profound, that countless human lives are forever changed by its Light.

This Light, though exquisitely beautiful, is so bright that it is deeply painful as well as joyous to behold; people sometimes describe the experience as having been touched by an Angel.

You see, for a few brief moments in time these unique stars take the form of a tiny human baby, leave their gift of Light, then must return to the deep, infinite blue once more. But the gift of Light they leave behind shines for all Eternity.

When you are outside on a clear night, gaze upwards with awe and reverence. Know that in the mysteries beyond our Mother Earth shines a little star who once briefly came to an earthly mother, and to a family, but who could not stay, and now shines its Love and Light as a gift for all open hearts.

Craft Activity

Sew a golden felt star to fit inside a mauve felt moon pocket (or any other colour of your choice). The felt pocket is a circle with a half-moon shape stitched on the front to create the pocket part. See Patterns and Templates, p. 277.

Whisper Sweet Dreams

Words and images by Lyn McCormick and Charles Kingsley, *The Water Babies**

These words and story-images were spoken by Lyn, the grandmother, at the gathering to celebrate the birth and the death of a perfect and yet still, little one.

When I think of him now – I see him in the red blanket which I had knitted for him and he is being held by my father, and around them both are other members of my family who died just before him, and those who have died since... all looking after each other, and looking after our little one, and all around them is the most wonderful golden light....

My heart goes out to you... his mum and his dad, so unprepared for this and yet warriors of hope and love.

I have no words that express my love and my care of the child, for his mother and his father, and so I have paraphrased words of Charles Kingsley from *The Water Babies*:

The Queen of the Water Babies was asked... where had she been? She explained that she had been smoothing sick folks' pillows and whispering sweet dreams into their ears and then she said... 'but I have brought you a new little brother and watched him safe all the way here'. Then all the fairies laughed for joy at the thought that they had a little brother coming.

Now the little one, who was so hot and thirsty and unwell, tumbled himself as quickly as he could into the clear cool stream. And he had not been in it two minutes before he fell fast asleep, into the quietest, sunniest, cosiest sleep that ever he had in his life; and he dreamt of everything and nothing at all.

And why did he fall asleep?... it is very simple... it was merely that the fairies took him.

Some people think there are no fairies. But it is a wide world and plenty of room in it for fairies without people seeing them, unless of course they look in the right place. The most wonderful and the strangest things in the world you know are just the things that no one can see. There is life in you; and it is the life in you which makes you grow, and move, and think: and yet you can't see it; and so there may be fairies in the world, and they may be just what makes the world go round, and yet no one may be able to see them except those whose hearts are going round to the same tune.

Ah, now comes the most wonderful part of this wonderful story. The little one then awoke, for of course he woke – children always wake after they have slept exactly as long as is good for them.... He found that his whole husk and shell had been washed quite off him and the beautiful little one was washed out of the inside of it and swam away, just as a butterfly flies away out of its cocoon....

* Charles Kingsley, *The Water Babies*, Puffin Books, 1863, pp. 42–3.

The Rainbow Dove

A story for a special friend who tragically lost her daughter in a fire. Her daughter was an exceptional young woman dedicated to helping others and exploring the deeper, spiritual aspects of life. I used the image of the 'rainbow dove' to capture her beautiful qualities.

The story has since been used at memorial gatherings for some of my dearly departed friends and family members – on one occasion, beautifully coloured feathers were given out to everyone present.

There was once a beautiful white dove who always wanted to fly up high. Instead of spending her time foraging for food and playing in and out of the branches of the forest with all the other doves, she was more interested in exploring the secrets of the sky.

Eventually the white dove flew so high that she reached the top of the rainbow. There she met the rainbow spirit who taught her the wisdom of the colours. Using this new wisdom, the white dove was able to change all her white wing feathers to rainbow ones. She was so happy!

The white dove flew back down to the forest and in and out of the trees, leaving some of her new, bright feathers for family and friends to find colourful treasure-feathers that would last for ever.

Then the white dove flapped her rainbow wings and flew up high in the sky to meet the sun.

Craft Activity
Collect feathers from the garden, park, forest – hang each one separately to make a mobile, or use as tassels at the bottom of a 'dream-catcher', or keep in a special jar or vase – keep adding feathers as you find them and/or think of more special memories.

THE MEMORY TREASURE BOX

A story for all ages of family / community members who have someone in their family / community with a terminal illness. It was written also as a help for families / communities who have had a grandparent, parent, friend or relative recently die from illness or accident.

Death is not often talked about, particularly in Western culture, and this can be very isolating. A story that gets friends and family sharing memories can be of some help in the weeks and months and years following the loss. It has prompted some families / communities to create a memory book as well as having a box for memory treasures.

I have made such a book for my two nieces whose father (my brother) died when they were quite young — the book, using pictures and text, has helped give them a broader, richer picture of his life. As my brother had been quite a wanderer in his younger years, with no record of what he had done and where he had been, it was hard to cover everything, so I called the book *A Patchwork of Memories.*

Keeping memories is a deeply human trait. From cave art to murals to modern photo collages for our home, it is important to find ways to value and preserve our memory treasures. In some cultures, quilters have used needle, thread and material to capture family stories and memories. Traditional rug makers have woven wool stories into their carpets, and embroiderers have stitched family memories with coloured threads. No matter how the memories may be preserved, stories such as this one can hopefully help to encourage memory conversations in a potentially isolating time. The 'queen' can be changed to 'king', the boy to girl, etc., to suit the situation.

The queen was very ill.

The king called all his family to the castle. He had been told by the best doctors in the land that the queen didn't have long to live.

Children and grandchildren travelled from all corners of the kingdom. The adults sat by their mother's bed while the grandchildren filled the days and hours playing inside and outside the castle.

However, the youngest grandchild soon tired of these games and went to a corner of the garden to sit by herself. She was feeling too sad and confused to play. She loved his grandmother and wished she wasn't ill. But she had been told that there was nothing that could be done.

While she was sitting in the garden, a golden feather fluttered to the ground and landed at her feet. She picked it up and held it in her hand. The feather helped her remember a walk that she had shared with her grandmother when she was well. They had been in the forest together and a bird with wings the colour of golden sunlight had flown across their path.

As she was holding the feather the gardener came by. The girl told him about her special memory. The gardener asked the girl to follow him. He led the girl to his work shed and lifted down a large wooden box. It had a strong lid and a shiny brass latch. 'Take this box', said the gardener, 'and fill it with memories of your grandmother. It will help keep her close to your heart, even when she is gone.'

The girl thanked the gardener and put the golden feather in the box. She carried it carefully back to the castle. The other children saw the girl with the box and wondered what she was doing. When they heard that the box was for keeping memory treasures, they started to think of their own memories of their grandmother. Soon the box was filling up with all kinds of special things. One grandchild found a shiny blue stone – 'This reminds me of the colour of grandmother's twinkly eyes', she said as she put it in the box. Another grandchild took some crayons and a large piece of paper and drew a picture of his favourite memory – paddling with his grandmother in the castle pond. The oldest grandchild, who had many years of memories, made a folding collage to put inside the box.

After some time, the adults were curious to know about this box. They began to add their special memory treasures... a bracelet, a teacup, a diary, a book, a painted stone. The box was filling up.

For many days and weeks and months after the queen passed away, the whole family would sit together around the treasure box. With tears in their eyes they would share their stories of each and every special memory.

CRAFT ACTIVITY 1
- Make a wooden treasure box as a family wood-working project
- Or look for one in second-hand stores or markets
- Or use a cardboard shoe box and paste pictures on it for decoration – see list overleaf for ideas

CRAFT ACTIVITY 2
Make a memory collage. You will need all or most of the following materials:

- firm cardboard or construction board or heavy paper
- scissors and glue
- coloured paper of all kinds – tissue, cellophane, origami paper
- magazines and photos (that can be cut up and used)
- scraps of fabric, ribbons, buttons
- small-sized natural objects – leaves, feathers, pressed flowers
- crayons, coloured pens and pencils and/or felt markers

The Garden

By Paula Bowles, psychologist

A therapeutic story written for families who have lost a precious child or beloved relation or friend. A person to whom they devoted their love and care.

Paula reported the following heartfelt response: 'Through the pain and heartbreak of loss, this story has helped me connect with the idea of one day rebuilding a life. It is a life which grows organically and gradually – in a time that is right. It is a life made with support, love and devotion to precious memories.'

Once there was a garden – it was a beautiful garden. It was a big garden. The flowers were always bright and gave hope to people who walked in there. The perfume from the flowers was strong and emotive. The garden was carefully looked after by a gardener. She kept it in perfect condition. Birds would live in the surrounding trees, and all through the day they would sing to each other. Often, in the evening the flowers and trees would be bathed in the light of the setting sun.

The flowers in springtime were the best in the land.

The garden was so beautiful that people would travel a long way just to walk through it. Each year more people visited. The gardener lived right opposite, and she was the first to visit in the morning and the last one to visit at night. Everyone loved it, but the gardener loved it most of all.

The years passed, the seasons followed, one after the other. Then, one winter's day a cyclone started forming out to sea. Throughout the day the cyclone gained in intensity as it headed towards the mainland. A cyclone warning was given out. Everyone was advised to be extremely cautious.

The cyclone hit the mainland and debris flew everywhere and trees fell down, blocking roads and causing extreme damage.

Then the cyclone hit the garden. Some of the surrounding trees were ripped out and fell down on to the flowers. The rain was so strong it caused flooding, and the birds and animals fled to find shelter. The storm continued for days, and caused devastation wherever it went.

After the storm had gone and the water had subsided, the gardener went to see what was left of the perfect garden.

There was nothing left.

The gardener was heartbroken. All the joy had gone. She felt that all her care and love was for nothing. She felt that the hours of work were wasted and had all been for nothing. The dead trees were impossible to move. The strong water had washed away the plants and the soil – only rocky ground remained. The gardener locked the wooden gate to the garden and never wanted to look in there again.

When people heard this they felt incredibly sad, and they felt deeply sorry for the gardener. They visited, and some offered to help move some of the fallen trees. The gardener did not want to do anything, because the ground was now desolate.

A year went by.

One winter day, the gardener went out to buy some food and as she walked, she noticed a little field that used to have animals grazing on it. It was overgrown and uncared for. She walked up to the fence and looked at the ground. It was full of weeds. She asked about the field and who it belonged to. She heard that the owner of the field had moved away.

The gardener went back a few days later and removed some of the large weeds in the field and planted a few bulbs. It was still winter.

A month or two went by and she visited the field. The bulbs had turned into lovely spring flowers and they looked so pretty amongst the weeds. After this, the gardener contacted the man who owned the field and, to her surprise, he said he was happy to donate the field to the people who lived in the town.

The gardener planted a few more flowers. She planted some herbs. The flowers and herbs didn't need much attention as they looked after each other – the scent of the herbs prevented many of the insects from eating the flowers.

The local people came to help the gardener. They thanked her for everything that she had done. They were very happy to hear of the kind donation of the land. Many of them didn't have a garden, and they were so glad to have somewhere to grow their food.

The gardener was happy to see the people joining in and caring for the plants.

A year later when spring came around again, the gardener was looking out of her window when she saw some children climbing over the fence into her old desolate garden. It brought back memories that she had not had for a long time. Several minutes later, the children climbed back over the fence and happily went on their way.

The gardener walked across the road and looked over the old gate. She smiled as she saw, amongst the rocks and debris, a few beautiful wildflowers.

And Thus Came the Restful Night

Translated and transcribed by Bandana Basu, B.Ed. Co-founder of
'Shishyaa School', Navi Mumbai, India

INTRODUCTION FROM BANDANA
This is a mythological story from the 'Rigveda', one of the ancient scriptures of India, which is a collection of Vedic Sanskrit hymns, stories and commentaries that explain the presence or existence of the elements of this earth.

Rig-Veda, meaning 'praises of knowledge', is the first of the Four Vedas or sacred Indo-Aryan scriptures of the ancient Indian traditions. These stories gently bring wisdom and consciousness to everyone. Here, the original story has been revised to suit the needs of older children and teenagers.

It is the original story of 'Coping with Death'; Yama and Yami are twins who were the first-borns on this earth. They were siblings, and were the first two mortal humans to be born upon this world. Also, Yama was the first mortal to die. Having experienced death as a portal to immortality, he attained the divine status of a god in his own right, becoming the 'Lord of Death'.

This story speaks of the time of the eternal present, and the eventual creation of night that allows the passage of time and healing from grief.

Long time ago there was a boy and a girl who were the first-borns upon the earth. They were twins called Yama and Yami, and were the only humans living on this earth. They loved each other very much and played with each other happily.

The whole earth was available to them for play. The river, the trees, forests, animals, birds, insects and flowers – they loved to be with all of them. Back then the day never ended, and so the fun was unending. They ate what they wished, played as much as they wanted and sang happy songs. The sun shone on them brightly all the time and it was eternally day time. The moon and stars never had a chance to peep out from behind the brightly lit sky.

One day, when they had finished playing with the animals and had eaten the fruits, they thought they would climb a tree and sit there and sing songs. Just as Yama began climbing the tree, Yami saw a beautiful little bird sitting on the same tree. It was very colourful and sang the most beautiful song. Yami was so fascinated with it

STORIES TO LIGHT THE NIGHT

that she wanted to hear her sing a little longer. But as soon as Yama climbed the tree the bird began to fly away.

'Stop Yama! Don't climb!', she exclaimed. But by then the bird had flown off.

'Look now, that little birdie flew away!', she said with disappointment. 'I wish I could play with it for longer.'

'I can see it perched on the other tree', said Yama. Why don't you go over and play with it?' 'Will you come with me, then?', Yami asked her brother.

'I don't have to', he said. 'You can go and be by yourself for some time. I will sing on this tree and you can watch the bird on that tree. We could come back and play together after that.'

Yami liked the suggestion. She trailed the little bird that went from one tree to the other. She loved the sound of the bird and sang the song it sang. It was so melodious. She kept following it for a long while until it flew far away, and she couldn't see it any longer. She sighed and looked around, and realised that she had come far away from where her brother was. So she began her journey back to meet Yama. She was happy and decided she would sing this lovely bird song to her brother.

When she arrived at the spot where she had left Yama, she saw him lying down below the tree as if he was asleep. She whispered his name but he did not answer. She sat down next to him and sang him the melodious song. But Yama did not stir. She gently shook him, calling his name, and still there was no response. She shook him more vigorously to try to wake him up. That's when she noticed that his breathing had stopped, and his body felt cold and still.

Yami was deeply grieved. Her brother Yama was dead! She looked around and wondered what she would do now. She began to realise how lonely she was, and it left her feeling even more sad. Her grief only increased with time and she cried out loudly, 'Yama has died today! Yama has died today!'

The birds, flowers, insects and animals all looked on, but none could help in easing her grief.

Her sorrow was as deep as the ocean, and as she grieved tears welled up in her eyes and ran down her cheeks. She could not stop herself from crying, and her tears started to fill up all the land, and slowly flooded the earth. All the creatures of the earth began running helter-skelter. Trees got uprooted and animals washed away in the flood. There was no way to stop Yami's tears from flowing, and so there was no way the flood could end.

The gods and the angels taking care of the earth were now worried for both Yami and the earth, and wanted to protect them both. They came down to her and hugged her. They tried to comfort her in many ways, yet her grief was unending. Yami could not imagine how to live without her brother, and all she kept saying was, 'Yama has died today!'.

In despair, the gods and angels began wondering how they could help Yami. They longed for her to forget about what had happened so that she could begin living happily again. Suddenly one of the angels said, 'I wish this day could end so her grief could end, and she could begin to feel better'.

That's when it occurred to the gods that until then, the day on earth was eternal and it never ended. Yami had only known today. There had been no yesterday, nor was there a tomorrow. And for Yami's pain to ease, today had to end and tomorrow had to begin. So they decided that they needed to begin by ending the present day. This they began by creating the sunset. And just as the sun began to crawl out of the sky, a gentle blue settled in and revealed the beautiful moon and stars that were hidden behind the bright sky.

Yami was taken aback by what she saw. She gazed at the sky and was transfixed by the beauty that the evening brought in. The moon played with the clouds, and the clouds played with the stars and the wind was cooler now. Yami felt the cool night wind caress her face, and slowly she felt her eyelids grow heavy. She did not know what was happening to her, but it did feel good. Slowly, before she knew it, for the first time Yami had fallen asleep. The dark sky enveloped her, and she curled up in the gentle embrace of the night. It felt good to sleep.

As she slept her tears stopped and the flood upon the earth eased. The animals and birds, and bees and insects, all calmed down and fell asleep.

Next morning, Yami felt the warmth of the sunshine on her face. She heard the chirping of the birds and the buzzing of the bees. She opened her eyes and looked around. She felt a little different. She realised that this was a new day and she remembered, 'Yama had died yesterday'. She still felt sad about it, but thankfully it wasn't as painful as yesterday and things seemed a little lighter. She wandered around, busying herself doing things, and later looked up to the sky waiting for the day to end. The restful nights gently eased away her grief, and with each passing day she felt better than before.

Since then, a day upon the earth is always followed by a peaceful and restful night that can slowly help to heal all sorrow and grief.

     STORIES TO LIGHT THE NIGHT

4   LOSS OF FAMILY CONNECTION

This chapter includes stories for children whose parents have separated, stories for adopted and foster children, and stories for family members who for various reasons can only have limited time with other members of their family.

To help you find your way, I have summarized the background to each story as follows:

TWO HOMES FOR SPARKLE – written for a young child (three to five years) living in a separated family situation (p. 103).

MAMA ROO AND LITTLE ROO – written for a three-and-a-half-year old girl to help her 'accept' constant change and separation; her mother was regularly on the move to escape domestic violence (p. 105).

THREE BEARS AND TWO BOATS – written for a three-and-a-half-year old boy who had never met his father (he had disappeared from the family scene before the child was born). The boy was now beginning to ask, 'Where is my father?' (p. 107).

THREE BEDS FOR KOALA – a story to help a young child with separation anxiety about leaving the parental bed and/or room, and sleeping in their own bed and room (p. 109).

THE LITTLE YELLOW TRAIN – written for a four-year old girl to help her re-connect with her big brother (p. 111).

LITTLE BIRD AND FATHER BIRD – a story for a five-year old boy whose father was in prison (p. 114).

THE FAMILY SHIP – written for a family who had adopted a baby boy from another country. At the age of five the boy found out his family story, and he wanted to return to his original home, which was not possible (p. 116).

THE CRACK – a story written by a mother to tell her adopted twin boys when they were five and six years old, and still having tantrums of anger (and fear of their past experience) (p. 118).

THE SEED THAT DREAMT A FLOWER – written for a couple who had adopted a little girl at five months old; now the girl was six, and demanding to know the facts of her birth and early years. As well as slowly sharing this, her mother requested a story to help deliver the truth in an imaginative way (p. 120).

THE CUP TOWER – a story for an eight-year old girl with separated parents (p. 122).

THE GANNAN ORANGE – written for a 14-year old girl who was left in the care of a boarding school after her parents had separated (p. 125).

THE WHALE AND THE PEARL – a story for a fostered teenager who was in unstable living circumstances (p. 127).

THE FORESTER AND THE BIRD – written to give hope and strength to a father who was unable to live close to his daughter during her early years (p. 129).

Two Homes for Sparkle

A story for a young child (three to five years) living in a separated family situation. The song at the end of the story could be used by both parents to help consistency for the child.

Once upon a time, in a large rock pool by the beach, there was a family of little fish who lived together. All day long they would play happily, twisting and diving and slipping and sliding in their rock-pool home.

One small shimmering fish was called Sparkle. She was learning from her brothers and sisters how to make a night-time bed in the coral rocks at the edge of the pool. They showed her how to gather seaweed to make her bed soft, so that she could sleep in it as cosy as can be.

Shimmering swish, Sparkle the Fish
Plays and rests with her fishy family,
Shimmering swish, Sparkle the Fish
Has a seaweed bed as cosy as can be.

One morning, Sparkle was playing with her brothers and sisters when there was a rumbling sound in the sky. At first Sparkle took no notice, but soon she joined the others as they swam to the top of the rock pool to see what was happening.

Dark clouds had begun to gather in the sky. Soon the thunder rumbled, and the lightning crashed. Rain began to fall, and the wind began to blow. The fish all huddled together in the middle of the pool to wait for the storm to pass. They were very quiet.

Suddenly there was great movement in their pool as giant waves crashed in, one after the other. For a long time, the waves tumbled into the rock pool. They were so strong that they washed half of the coral rocks away.

Eventually, the waves died down and the pool water cleared. Now the family of little fish could see what had happened.

Because many of the coral rocks had been smashed, some of the fish family had to go and make their night-time beds in another rock pool close by. Fortunately, the storm had made a long tunnel through the side of the rock wall that led out of the first pool and into another one.

Sparkle thought it was rather exciting to travel through this rock tunnel and go and visit some of her family in the other pool. She gathered seaweed and made a soft bed there too, just in case she decided to sleep over.

Shimmering swish, Sparkle the Fish
Has a seaweed bed as cosy as can be,
Shimmering swish, Sparkle the Fish
Shares two homes with her fishy family.

Now the fish family lives in two rock pools, and little Sparkle has beds in two places, so that no matter which pool she stays in, she always has a cosy place to sleep. And every time she travels through the rock tunnel, she always sings her cosy sleeping song.

Shimmering swish, Sparkle the Fish
Has a seaweed bed as cosy as can be,
Shimmering swish, Sparkle the Fish
Shares two homes with her fishy family.

CRAFT ACTIVITY
Make a Felt Fish. See Patterns and Templates, p. 279.

MAMA ROO AND LITTLE ROO

A rhyming story written for a three-and-a-half-year old girl to help her 'accept' constant change and separation. Her mother was regularly on the move to escape domestic violence and also needing to work, so her child was often with different carers. The feedback from the mother was that before even sharing it with her daughter, she herself felt soothed and strengthened by the story. This is an example of a therapeutic story that, although written for a child, can also help an adult.

Mama Roo loved Little Roo so much! Sometimes she thought she would burst because her love was so great. But of course she knew this would never happen! She needed to stay strong. She needed to carry Little Roo in her pouch as she bounced along – over the hills, across the plains and far away, together whatever, whatever together, every day.

Mama Roo was always looking for the best place to live with Little Roo – a sheltered home with grass to eat and water so sweet.

Sometimes the wind would swirl and whirl and too much dust would be around. So away to find a new home they would go, Mama Roo and Little Roo. And as Mama Roo bounced along, she would sing to Roo this little song:

> *Over the hills, across the plains and far away,*
> *Together whatever, whatever the weather, every day.*

Sometimes the storms would bring too much rain, making slippery mud all around. So away to find a new home they would go, Mama Roo and Little Roo. And as Mama Roo bounced along, she would sing to Roo this little song:

Sometimes Mama Roo had busy things to do. So with other Roo friends she would leave Little Roo. Together with new friends Little Roo would play. Oh, how Little Roo loved to play all day!

And later in the day, when Mama Roo would come back to the play, they would bounce around together and sing this little song:

THREE BEARS AND TWO BOATS

This story was written in Chengdu at a Therapeutic Story Seminar. It was for a mother of a three-and-a-half-year old boy who had never met his father (he had disappeared from the scene before the child was born). The boy was now beginning to ask, 'Where is my father?'.

The mother had explained to me that she believed she had created 'an island of harmony' for her son, and to keep this harmony protected she had been tempted to tell her son that the father was no longer alive, even though she knew that he was. I encouraged an open-ended story that captured the truth but helped protect 'the island of harmony'.

The boy's favourite toy, one that he slept with every night, was a cuddly brown bear.

There were once three Bears – mother bear, father bear and baby bear. They lived together in a forest that used to be rich with food... crunchy nuts, juicy fruit and sweet honey. However, this food was growing very sparse, so one day the Bears decided to leave the forest and search for another place to live where once again there would be plenty to eat... crunchy nuts, juicy fruit and sweet honey.

They walked and walked and walked, and after a long time they reached a sandy shore. Sitting by the edge of the water were two small boats. Father bear climbed into one boat and mother bear, together with baby bear, climbed into the other boat.

The waves gently lifted the boats and began to rock them backwards and forwards, backwards and forwards, away from the shore. The wind blew and the waves rocked, and the boats journeyed further and further across the sea. Father bear's boat was carried far away in one direction. Mother bear and baby bear's boat was carried in another direction, with the waves rocking it backwards and forwards, backwards and forwards, through the day and through the night and through another day.

Eventually the boat with mother bear and baby bear reached the shore of an island and came to rest on the golden sands. Mother bear and baby bear climbed out of the boat and walked across the sand into a thick forest. They soon saw that here was plenty of food to eat... crunchy nuts, juicy fruit and sweet honey.

This forest was so rich with food. It also provided warm and comfortable shelter amongst the large rocks and tree roots, so mother bear and baby bear decided to make this forested island their new home....

And as far as I know, they are living there still.

Three Beds for Koala

A story to help young children with separation anxiety about leaving the parental bed and/or room and sleeping in their own bed and room.

When Koala was very tiny, his first bed was in his mother's pouch. It was so warm and cosy inside.

He slept and he grew. He grew and he slept.

After many months of sleeping and growing, he became too big for his pouch home. But he was still too small to sleep by himself. What was Koala to do?

Then he heard his mother whispering to him. 'Climb on my back little one – this will be your next cosy bed.'

Little Koala crawled up on to his mother's back and held on tightly to her soft fur. What a wonderful new bed this was! He especially loved looking out at the world as his mother climbed up and down the eucalypt tree. She was always searching for new gum leaves to eat. Sometimes he could even reach out to pick his own crunchy leaves for dinner.

When his mother slept in a curved branch of the tree, little Koala slept on her back. Together they would sleep most of the day and most of the night. When they were not eating, they were sleeping.

However, after many more months of sleeping and growing, Koala became too big to ride on his mother's back. She wasn't strong enough to carry him. He was not a little Koala any more!

Koala now needed to climb by himself. Koala now needed to pick his own leaves for his dinner. Koala now needed to find his own sleeping branch.

He managed just fine climbing by himself. He managed just fine picking his own leaves to eat... but Koala was not managing sleeping by himself. There seemed to be so many uncomfortable distractions! The branch was too hard; the light was too bright; the air was too hot.

He had never noticed such things when he was inside his mother's pouch. He had never noticed such things when he was cuddled into his mother's soft furry back. It had seemed so easy to fall asleep when he was smaller.

What was Koala to do? He was growing more and more tired each and every passing day. He wanted so much to sleep! But he couldn't find a way to fall asleep.

Then he heard the eucalypt tree whisper to him, 'I can give you a comfortable bed, Koala. Find a curve in my branches. I will soften my bark for you. I will use my leaves to shade against the strong light. I will call on the wind to blow cool breezes around you.'

Koala was so happy. He wondered why he hadn't listened to the tree before this time. He found a curve in the branches, and felt the tree soften its bark under him to make a bed. Then the tree gathered its green leaves above him to keep out the light, both in the daytime and in the night. And soon the wind was blowing cool air around him.

Koala fell into a long deep sleep. And from that time onwards, the eucalypt tree continued to be his bed and his home and his friend.

Koala Sleeping Lullabye

Sleep Koala sleep,

Rest your weary head

Let my branches hold you In a soft bark bed.

Sleep Koala sleep,

Close your eyes so tight,

Let my green leaves shade you, From the strong sunlight.

Let my green leaves shade you, From the bright moonlight.

THE LITTLE YELLOW TRAIN

This story was written for a four-year old girl to help her re-connect with her big brother. The request came from a Pakistani mother living in London, who was struggling with her daughter's challenging behaviour. The older brother was wheelchair-bound with cerebral palsy, and the little girl, who used to be his best friend, had decided to not have anything more to do with him. Instead of coming home from school and telling him stories of her day and playing with him, she was now ignoring him. She was also starting to compete for attention by pretending to have aches and pains.

The mother requested a story to help the daughter accept and empathize with the brother's disability and stop pretending to have aches and pains.

I asked her for some information on her daughter's likes and interests – she replied with a list that included 'playing with trains' and yellow as her favourite colour.

The previous year my husband and I were travelling in the Pyrenees and went for a ride through the mountains on the famous 'Le Petit Train Jaune' – this experience inspired the setting for the story, and I used the interaction of the yellow and blue train to reflect the desired outcome.

Two weeks after sending it I received an email with a picture of the little girl pushing her brother in his wheelchair. The text said the following: 'We are all doing well. Just wanted to share this photo with you. The story has really worked.... She is engaging well with my son now and is very willing to help him. I told the story many times using a kind of a puppet show with her wooden train that I painted yellow. She has a blue wooden block that we used as the blue engine, an empty box as a train yard, a cushion with a cloth over it as a mountain, and small model wooden houses as shops and town houses. Then afterwards I told it out of my head using hands as puppets.'

Far away and across the sea there was a country that had a little yellow train that was loved by all the people. This country had many mountains that were too steep for cars and roads, so the only way people could travel from one place to another was in the little yellow train. Families that lived in the city would use the yellow train to go on holidays into the mountains. Families that lived in the mountains would travel in the yellow train to go shopping in the city.

The little train loved its daily journeys, giving rides to many different passengers inside its bright yellow carriages. It especially loved the adventure of going through the dark cool mountain tunnels, crossing high bridges and travelling past the fields of hillside flowers. Its shiny whistle would blow, and its black wheels would sing with joy as it travelled along...

Clickety clack, clickety clack, along the track we spin each day,
Clickety clack, clickety clack, across the land we make our way.

Each night the little yellow train would return to the rail yards to be cleaned and polished, and there it would rest till morning.

Also living in the rail yards was a big blue engine. It was not working very well so was not able to leave the tracks where it stood. Train mechanics were continually tinkering with its engine bits, and the children who lived in the rail yard sometimes played inside and on top of it. The big blue engine was very patient through all of this, and loved it when the children came to play. And at night, it especially loved to listen to the adventure stories of the little yellow train.

The big blue engine hoped that one day it could have such adventures... travelling through the dark cool mountain tunnels, crossing high bridges and passing fields of hillside flowers.

One evening the little yellow train had an idea. It had to hold this idea all through the night until the driver came on duty the next morning. As soon as the driver climbed into his cabin, the little yellow train excitedly whispered to him. Within minutes, the smiling driver had backed up the little yellow engine behind the big blue engine and was slowly, ever so slowly, pushing the big blue engine out of the rail yards.

What a wonderful sight this was. The people cheered and waved as the little yellow train pushed the big blue engine along the tracks, out of the city and into the countryside. The big blue engine felt so happy, it could burst. Its whistle, that hadn't ever been used before, began to splutter and crackle out tiny sounds of joy, and its creaky wheels tried hard to hum along with the little yellow train...

Clickety clack, clickety clack, along the track we spin each day,
Clickety clack, clickety clack, across the land we make our way.

They didn't travel very far this first time. It was a hard task for the little yellow train to push such a big blue engine! And the little yellow train still had other journeys to go on that day. After going through one short tunnel, across one high bridge

       STORIES TO LIGHT THE NIGHT

and past a lovely bright field of flowers, its driver turned it round at the next station and the little yellow train slowly pushed the big blue engine back to the rail yard.

The big blue engine was the happiest it had ever been. And the little yellow train also felt happy that it was able to share some of its adventures with its friend. From that time on, whenever the little yellow train had some spare time, it would push the big blue engine out of the rail yards and go for a small adventure somewhere. And as they travelled along, the people of the land could hear the wheels singing...

Clickety clack, clickety clack, along the track we spin each day,
Clickety clack, clickety clack, across the land we make our way.

LITTLE BIRD AND FATHER BIRD

A story for a young child (five years old) whose father was in prison – the child was so upset he didn't want to do anything or get involved in anything at school. The aim of the story was to bring some light and motivation into the child's life.

Little Bird sat on a branch of a bush with his head tucked into his wing. He didn't want to fly; he didn't want to sing. He just wanted to sit and do nothing.

The bush was right outside a big grey house. Little Bird knew his father was inside that big grey house. If he lifted his head out of his wing he could see through the window to where a bamboo cage was hanging on a hook. How he wished his father could be out of that cage and with him!

Father Bird was sitting on a perch in that cage. He couldn't fly anywhere, even if he wanted to. He could sing but he didn't want to – he felt too sad to sing. He knew he had taken one risk too many. This is why he had been caught and put in this cage.

Many days, and many nights, and many more days passed by. Little Bird kept sitting on the branch of the bush.... Father Bird kept sitting on a perch in the cage.

Then one day, Father Bird happened to look up and out through the window. He saw Little Bird sitting in the bush. Father Bird was shocked to see Little Bird so still. At first he didn't know what he could do – he was trapped in his cage so he couldn't fly out to greet him. Then, slowly, ever so slowly, a memory of birdsong rose in him, and Father Bird began to sing... softly at first, then stronger, and louder.

If you can fly, fly high; fly high, touch the sky.
If you can sing, sing strong; strong and sweet, all day long.

Father Bird's song travelled from the cage, through the window, and out to the world. Little Bird lifted his head from his wing and listened. Then he too began to sing, joining with his Father's song... softly at first, then stronger, and louder.

After some time, Little Bird spread and fluttered his wings and lifted himself out of the bush. He then flew past the window, over the roof of the grey building and up to touch the sky.

If you can fly, fly high; fly high, touch the sky.
If you can sing, sing strong; strong and sweet, all day long.

THE FAMILY SHIP

This story was written for a family in Australia who had adopted a baby boy from Columbia. At the age of five the boy found out his family story, and he wanted to return to his original home.

The adoptive parents were bound by a legal agreement with the boy's family in Columbia that no contact was allowed until he was 18 years old. The story attempted to reflect the limits of this situation. I used the metaphor of 'the family ship' to help the boy accept his current situation and slowly process the grief and loss that came with this new awareness.

The mother reported that the story assisted the family to find a way forward together, and that it was 'good medicine' for them all.

There was once a beautiful ship with coloured silken sails and a golden yellow hull. The golden ship was travelling on a long family journey across a very wide sea, visiting many islands on the way.

Mama and Papa were the captains of the ship, and the children were the crew members. Mama and Papa took turns steering and guiding the ship on its journey, following the light of the sun by day, and the light of the moon and stars by night.

Sometimes the children had to help with tasks, and sometimes they could play. There were so many exciting things to do... climbing the masts, swinging on the sail ropes, paddling in the lifeboat and, when the sea was calm, swimming around the golden hull.

It was a wonderful adventure that they were sharing together. Every day the family would chant and sing:

Ahoy ahi aho,
Adventuring we go
Following the light, day and night,
Ahoy ahi aho.

Ahoy ahi aho,
Adventuring we go
Whatever the weather, we'll weather the weather,
Ahoy ahi aho.

On the long journey all kinds of things happened. Some were good and some not so good. There were beautiful islands to explore. But there were also tricky reefs to navigate, and care to be taken close to high cliffs and rocky coastlines.

There were silver dolphins that swam with the boat, and sometimes gave the children rides on their backs. But there were also slippery sea snakes that liked to slither and slide on board, and needed to be caught and put back in their ocean home.

Seagulls sometimes landed on the masts and squawked loud songs. On other days, beautiful songbirds would visit and sing sweet songs and share sweet stories.

On the long journey the family had to face all kinds of weather. There were storms with wild winds, strong thunder and cracking bolts of lightning. Other days were calm and sunny, with beautiful sunrises and clear starry nights. Every day the family would chant and sing:

Ahoy ahi aho,
Adventuring we go
Following the light, day and night,
Ahoy ahi aho.
Ahoy ahi aho,
Adventuring we go
Whatever the weather, we'll weather the weather,
Ahoy ahi aho.

With the help of the song the captains and the crew stayed strong. They steered a balanced course forward, and together they weathered the weather.

After a very, very, long journey, the golden ship reached the land on the other side of the sea.

THE CRACK

By Ninna Nygaard, storyteller, teacher, architect

Ninna wrote this story to tell at bedtime to her adopted twin boys when they were five and six years old, and still having tantrums of anger and fear. The boys had grown up in a foster home with very few nannies, and hundreds of children. They were three-and-a-half years of age when they reached their 'home' in Denmark.

For several years Ninna and her husband had to hold the boys, and rock them to calm them down, for one hour every night. In Ninna's words, 'It felt like they again and again had to go back to the feeling they had when they were left alone in the foster home, or in some dark and hopeless place. The boys were asking a lot of questions about the beginning of their life at the age of five to six years. So the story, I think, helped them settle down with the thought that there was a long, and not-so-nice journey before they finally got home – and this was okay! The two mice holding each other's tales was such a good picture of their relationship. So the story was really just about accepting the way things were. It is okay to feel afraid, to have dark tantrums, to find yourself in mother's (and father's) arms – it is all okay!'

Another comment from Ninna: 'In a way the story also worked for the storyteller – to get into a very patient place of – no matter what, it is okay! And of course, the mouse that couldn't count to more than 10 made them laugh and start counting – to more than ten!'

Note that in this story, some humour and lightness were used to balance the dark and hopeless times – apparently the twins loved hearing the part about the mouse-mother who had so many mouse children, she didn't even know how many babies she had, as she couldn't count to more than ten.

There once was a mouse-mother who had a lot of mouse children – more than 20! In fact, the mouse-mother couldn't even count to more than ten, and so she didn't know how many babies she had.

One day she was driving all the mouse babies in a big baby carriage. And all the little mouse babies were playing in the pillows in the wagon. It was such fun – and everybody was laughing loudly. So when two of the little ones fell over the edge of the baby carriage, the mouse-mother didn't notice.

The two little mouse babies fell into a crack in the ground, and suddenly everything was very dark, and all they could feel was cold dirt. Fortunately for the two babies, they both held on to each other's tails. And in the darkness, they rolled up against each other, shaking with fear.

The two babies were in the crack for a long time! A mole who was living nearby found them, and thought they were very cute. She fed them when she came by almost every day, and for a little while she held them – and the mouse babies loved that. Every day she brought some roots for the babies to eat. When the mole left the babies, they were so lonely and afraid. They held on to each other's tails and looked into the darkness.

This continued for a very long time, until one day in spring, the farmer who lived there was planting apple trees. He set his shovel in the ground, just next to the crack. And when he turned the earth around, he saw the two little mouse children, holding each other's tails. He took them to his barn, and put them outside a mouse-hole in the wall, where he had seen a mouse couple running in and out.

The mouse-mother found the little ones shortly after. She called the mouse-father and they both fell in love with the beautiful little mouse children. How fortunate! The mouse couple were so happy! They so much wanted more children! They lived in a cozy house and had a lot of food – much better than roots to eat!

They gave the mouse children names, Bo and Morten. They were both boys. And they all lived happily – almost. Because sometimes Bo and Morten could not believe that they were out of the dark crack. They would sleep and dream they were still in the crack. Or they would go to a place where the smell of dirt would remind them of the smell in the crack. But then the mouse-mother and the mouse-father would hold them and comfort them – and tell them, 'It's all over baby, mum and dad aren't going anywhere'.

One day they went to the place where the crack once was, and there was growing an apple tree. It had its roots firmly planted in the crack. Next to the apple tree there was a molehill.

Mouse-mother had baked a sweet pie and written a letter to the mole.

Dear Mole
Thank you for taking care of my beautiful boys when they were lost in the crack.
I hope you will enjoy the pie.
Loving greetings,
Mouse-mother

The Seed that Dreamt a Flower

This story was written for an Indian couple in their mid-forties who had adopted a little girl at five months old (the couple had no other children). They named her Sayuri (in Japanese it means 'little lily') because when they saw her for the first time, she was so small and she looked so delicate, like a lily.

The family lives in an apartment on the 7th floor with windows but no balcony. The windows have a wide ledge protected by grills where Sayuri sits out to feed the birds each morning, and the family also grows plants there. Sayuri loves being outdoors, and talks of wanting to live on a farm to grow mulberries, blueberries and all possible fruits.

At six years old Sayuri was demanding to know the facts of her birth and early years. As well as slowly sharing this (she was born to a minor and put in the care of a foster family for five months), her mother requested for me to write a story to help deliver the truth in an imaginative way. The wind in the story represents the foster family and adoption process that helped connect Sayuri with her family. For the idea of using the wind, I acknowledge two young men, Chinese twins, Morgan and Orlando, whom I was fortunate to meet in Denmark and hear their self-narrated adoption story that used the wind as the change-maker. (The twin's mother has her own story included in this book – 'The Crack', see p. 118.)

At the same time as this story was shared, Sayuri had become very attached to the Little Gnome story (see p. 145), especially to the character of the Little Gnome, and the flower story became intertwined with it. For her, it was not about a little girl and the plant but about the Little Gnome and the plant. But with the merging of the stories, the mother reported, the little seed's journey has been 'sown' into her, and, at some level, she now knows she is adopted, and a productive conversation has begun.

Other versions are possible. My husband was adopted, and when he looked at this story he connected straight away with the theme of the seed and the wind. But he wanted his story to be 'The Seed that Dreamt a Tree' – about a seed that was carried by the wind to grow into a tree in another garden, not a flower seed in a pot. There could be many different seeds for many different situations.

Little Seed was all alone, lying between grass and rocks, longing for warm earth to surround her and golden sunshine above. Eventually she shivered herself into a deep sleep.

While she was sleeping, Little Seed dreamt that she had turned into a shiny green plant cradling the most beautiful flower that had ever been seen.

When she woke up there was movement around her. At first it felt strange, but then she heard a whispering – 'I am the wind, your friend. Please trust me to carry you to a place where your dream can come true.'

Little Seed was happy to know she had a friend. She let the wind lift her up and away from the rocks and the grasses.

The wind carried her far away... over green hills and through valleys... on and on. Over rivers and forests... on and on. Past farms where red and blue berries were growing in the sunshine... on and on.

Little Seed was amazed to discover such a beautiful world. She was shivering with excitement now (not cold!), and wondered where her friend was taking her.

Soon the wind reached a city and passed over the tops of tall buildings. It swirled around and around, then blew down to a window in one of the buildings. A mother and father together were holding an earthen pot just inside the open window... could they be waiting for Little Seed?

Ever so softly, the wind blew inside and around the top of the pot, making a little hollow in the soil for Little Seed to nestle into like a bed. Then with a gentle kiss goodbye, her friend continued his journey, promising to return from time to time for special visits.

Little Seed snuggled into the rich brown earth in the pot and fell fast asleep. After such a long adventure she was very tired. The mother and father carefully placed the pot on the windowsill in the warm sunshine. As Little Seed slept, her earthen bed was warmed by the sun and watered lovingly by her new family.

After many days she woke up, feeling strong and happy to be alive. She slowly pushed roots down into the soil and reached her arms up towards the sun. As she stretched up and out of the top of the pot, Little Seed could see that she was turning into the shining green of the plant in her dream.

The sun continued to shine down, and the family continued to water her soil. Very soon Little Seed's green leaves were cradling the most beautiful flower ever seen.

Many birds flew down to sit on the windowsill to sing to the world of the new beauty that had come to live there. The family cared for their flower treasure, and every day the world rejoiced in her loveliness, charm and grace.

The Cup Tower

By Petra Kapović Vidmar, teacher, Croatia

This story was written for an eight-year old girl with separated parents.

NOTE FROM PETRA
I wrote this story after attending your Therapeutic Story Seminar in Opatija this year. In my class there are 24 pupils. Some 13 of them live with separated parents. I wanted to write a story for all of them, but the cases were so different. One of my pupil's mother talked to me recently about getting a divorce. This gave me an idea for the story, and I wrote one for her daughter, hoping it would help her and maybe some other pupils facing separation.

I told it as a 'motivation story' before art class. After hearing the story, all the children made an artwork, drawing and designing cups. I especially hoped that the story would help prepare this one particular girl, who is very tidy and likes things to be in order, for the new changes in her life. This pupil knows about her parents getting separated. She is an only child, and for the past eight years has lived with her parents in a small house, but the father is now moving to his own apartment.

I also met with the mother and gave her a copy of the story to read to her daughter during the summer break. I suggested that after reading the story, to buy with her daughter some cups for the father's new kitchen and/or to give her artwork to her father as a gift. I explained to her how this story could help. I am sure on one thing – it helped the mother (and maybe the father, too); and sometimes that is a good start!

In the middle of the bay there is a little colourful house. It is a perfect house with a red roof, white walls, green windows with yellow curtains and a small balcony full of colourful flowers. All the rooms are small but nicely decorated and very neat.

The kitchen is tiny and full of sunlight. The kitchen cupboards, table and chairs are white, but details like dish cloths and vases with flowers are full of bright colours which bring joy to the room.

Six brightly coloured cups live in that kitchen. They are neatly stacked in one of the kitchen cupboards. You can see them through the glass doors of the cupboard. And they can see you. They look like they are watching what is going on in the kitchen. Six of them don't fit in the small cupboard separately each on its saucer, so they are nested on each other. In that way they form a group together – a small cup-tower.

From these cups, family members drink hot tea every morning, coffee with milk in the afternoons and milk every evening. So each cup goes on a journey every day.

The journey begins in the morning when they are placed on the dining table to serve tea. They feel hot because of the hot water with a teabag inside that colours the water red, yellow or orange. When they serve tea, their cheeks get rosy and hot. Family members drink their tea very carefully. When cups are emptied and cold, they are moved into the kitchen sink where they enjoy their bubble bath. After they are washed up and dried, they soon get back to their kitchen cupboard to rest until afternoon coffee time.

While serving coffee the cups listen to the neighbours' stories and also some compliments on their brightly coloured look. Coffee gets the cups very dirty, so they enjoy their bubble bath in the sink a little bit longer. Now the cups are shiny and clean, ready for their evening milky look.

Tired but pleased after a long hard-working day, the cups are happy. They are all together in their kitchen cupboard, forming a small cup-tower.

One day, instead of their usual morning journey the cups are shut into a big box. Terrified and surprised inside the darkness of the box, they await their destiny. A few days pass until the box opens. They are blinded by the daylight but happy to get out of the box. Soon they notice that their kitchen cupboard isn't where it used to be, or anywhere else in the kitchen. Instead, there are completely different cupboards and shelves. Three cups are placed on a saucer in one kitchen cupboard and the other three in another kitchen cupboard, new and bigger than the old one.

This is the first time ever that the cups are separated in this way. It is a very strange place for each cup although there is a lot more space for them now. Also, they miss their glass doors. Now they can't see what goes on in the kitchen any more.

Three cups in one cupboard wonder what the other three cups do in the other cupboard. They miss each other very much.

However, during the next few days they realise that they leave their cupboard as before and meet with the separated cups on the kitchen table or in the sink. Oh, how happy they are again! Separation isn't so bad because nothing has changed except their place in the cupboard. And that isn't so bad because they all have more space sitting each on its saucer and still close to the others.

The separated cups meet the other ones almost every day on their journey. Just before their favourite bubble baths they make a cup-tower just like before.

New things are so exciting!

THE GANNAN ORANGE

By Bai Chun Yan
English translation by Scarlet Cheng

This story was written for a 14-year old girl who was left in the care of a boarding school as her parents had separated, and neither of them wanted their daughter back – the girl was a very intelligent and diligent student. The story was written by the school counsellor and given to the girl to help deliver the truth in a different kind of way – the parents tasked the counsellor to inform her of this difficult news. The counsellor shared the news and also gave the girl a copy of the story. The counsellor reported that the story gave the girl something small to hold on to, to give her strength.

In China there is a kind of fruit called Gannan orange. It is renowned for its juiciness and sweetness, and in the harvest season merchants from all directions come to Gannan and transport the oranges out of the mountain area to every corner of the world. This is what every Gannan orange is proud of.

One beautiful Gannan orange was picked up on her way being transported on a train by a fruit merchant. It was taken out of its box to give as a treat to one of the train crew. But all of a sudden, with an abrupt rocking of the train, the orange tumbled out of his hand and out of the window.

The orange bounced and rolled into a broad patch of weeds far away from the railway line. Listening to the train chugging away, the orange cried in despair. She knew that she would not have the chance to see the view beyond the mountains and enjoy the praise of the people. She knew she would stay in the loneliness and coldness of the weed patch. 'This is so unfair!', she thought. How she longed to be taken away from here, even if by a shepherd who might peel off her beautiful coat and enjoy her sweetness....

Day after day, the orange lived with a mixture of hope and disappointment, and slowly she felt herself being dried up by the sunshine in the day and by the cold wind in the night. At last, the orange split on one side and a seed fell out and into a small crevice in the ground. There was no quilt of fallen leaves from the mother tree covering her, and home was now just a memory.

In her loneliness in the ground, she often recalled the orchard of oranges in her home town. In deep autumn, layers of falling leaves covered the foot of mother trees, and the seed sisters under the leaves were kept very warm. The farmer and his family working around the trees would tramp on the leaves, crackling, crackling, stepping the seeds into the depth of the soil, in the familiar fragrance of orange.

Although this seed was not cared for with tenderness and comfort, she found herself embedded in the soil mingled with gravels and weeds roots, after some rains. It seemed that the earth had some kind of appealing force that she couldn't resist, and she began squeezing deep down into the soil.

She felt a kind of new freedom while she endeavoured to stretch downward with her newborn roots digging their way into the soil. New hope was burning inside her, what in her mind were only two words: Rooted! Rooted!

The seed spent the following winter in the hope of growth. Grudge, resentment and sadness had been thrown behind, and she was absorbed in the process of growing and transformation. She was realising that relying on her own strength was the true path for her!

She tried to take care in every minute, every day, in the silent soil, never giving up one chance of stretching her roots. She now believed that one day she would sprout, and no one could hinder that.

Ah! The spring eventually came back to the deserted land, and large patches of grass sprouted tender leaves! The sun melted the remaining ice and snow, which produced enough water for the seed to drink. She had stayed a long time under the ground, and the energy reserved for all this time exploded, and a tender orange seedling sprouted in the desert land!

It seemed that the sun caressed the seedling specially, bringing her warmth and light. She sprang up little by little with the support of the earth and the summons of the sun.

When the hot summer arrived, she grew to the height of a man, and after two years she fruited five oranges, picked by a shepherd boy for a fresh taste.

Three years later she was not only full of fruits, but also surrounded by many orange seedlings in the desert land, thanks to the shepherd boy spitting out the orange seeds while eating on the ground, and thus her offspring grew up.

By and by, the shepherd boy grew up and turned into a fruit merchant himself, because only he knew that there was an orchard of sweet orange trees in the desert land.

The orchard of this orange and her offspring became bigger and bigger, and eventually the oranges were being freighted on the train and transported to every part of the country.

There are no more sad sighs here, but the proudness and boldness and the sense of accomplishment!

The Whale and the Pearl

By Kaitlyn Tighe, child safety officer, Queensland, Australia

A story written for a fostered teenager who was in very unstable living circumstances.

Note from Kaitlyn
The 15-year old girl I wrote the story for loved it. Not long after I gave her the story she was kicked out of her home, and was only able to grab a few of her belongings before she left…. When I was trying to find her a new home, I saw in her bag the typed copy of the therapeutic story. I pointed this out to her, and she said, 'Yeah, I take it everywhere!'.

There once was a whale who lived deep, deep, deep down in the blue ocean. It was very dark at the bottom of the ocean where the whale lived, and this meant that she could not see very well. At times the whale had great difficulty finding her way across the vast dark waters.

One day, the whale was swimming along the ocean floor happily – when all of a sudden, she swam into an old fishing net and became tangled. The whale was very scared as she struggled against the strong netting ropes. As the whale struggled, she thought perhaps she was not strong enough to break free.

'Maybe I will be stuck in this net at the bottom of the ocean for ever', she thought. But she did not give up. She fought and fought against the net ropes, until finally… she was free. The whale swam upwards in the dark, dark water until it started to get a little bit lighter. Now the whale could see some fish next to her in the water because it was not as dark.

Sometime after this, the whale was swimming happily with her fish friends when, all of a sudden, she swam into a strange black liquid in the ocean. The whale quickly realised it was oil! The oil made her feel very sick as she swam through it. She could no longer see her fish friends through the thick blackness. She felt scared because she was alone. It seemed like she was swimming through the black oil for days and days and days. It felt like she would never see the clean blue water again.

'Maybe I will be stuck in this black oil for ever and never able to see my friends again', thought the whale. She thought about giving up and not swimming any more.

Then the whale saw a small bright light up ahead through the thick oil. The light looked like it was very far away. The whale swam towards the light because she was curious about what was brightly shining through the oil. She swam and swam for days, weeks, months – it felt like a long, long time.

Slowly she grew closer to the light – it became bigger and bigger and the oil in the water became thinner and thinner, until finally she was swimming in the clean ocean water once again and... there on a sand bank in the middle of the ocean was a beautiful pearl!

The whale knew the pearl was hers and had been waiting for her all this time. The whale saw that the pearl was attached to a long strand of seaweed. She wrapped the seaweed around her neck, so the pearl sat proudly on her chest with its light shining in front of her.

From then on, the whale wore the pearl with her wherever she went. She now had a white light guiding her through the dark, dark ocean.

The Forester and the Bird

A story written to give hope and strength to one of my sons, working as a forest scientist who, for personal and practical reasons, couldn't live close to his daughter during her early years, but could visit on a regular and consistent schedule. Each visit involved many hours of driving, there and back. The story was rolled up and given as a birthday gift, together with a little glass blue bird.

In a follow-up message to me, he was thankful for both the imagery in the story and the talisman of the little glass bird.

There was once a kind and good man who worked with the trees. His home was in a forest surrounded by fields and farms and not too far from the sea. Every day the forester would do what tasks needed to be done to keep the forest alive and healthy – planting, weeding, watering, protecting.

In this forest grew many kinds of trees, short and tall and thick and thin. When he had some time to spare, the forester enjoyed climbing one of the trees and sitting in the branches. So much could be seen from up high, and it was very peaceful listening to the birds and watching the sunlight sparkling on the leaves.

Right in the middle of the forest, up on a high hill, was a tree so tall that the forester couldn't even see the top branches – it looked like it truly disappeared into the heavens above. This grand tree was so difficult to climb that for many years the forester left it alone – its trunk was too gnarly, and its branches were prickly and rough. It was not a comfortable choice as a place to relax.

However, one day, while walking up the hill in the middle of his forest, the forester heard a beautiful bell-like song. He looked up and noticed a new bird's nest high up in the tallest tree, and he could see the pearly blue head of a little bird peeking out above the top of the nest.

Oh, how the forester longed to get closer to this beautiful little bird! As he watched, it stretched out its wings and they seemed to shine like two small rainbows high up amongst the branches. He had never seen such a beautiful bird, and he had never heard such a beautiful song. He knew he had to find a way to get closer to this heavenly bird.

He began the difficult climb up the trunk. It seemed to take for ever, but finally he was close enough to the nest to see and hear the little bird clearly, and he sat for hours on a branch enjoying this new beauty in his life. He had once heard of a 'blue bird of happiness' and thought it was just a line from a song, but now he knew that such a bird did truly exist.

From this time on, whenever the forester had some hours to spare he would visit the hill in the forest, hoping to see the beauty of the little blue bird and hear its song. It was always such a long climb up the tall tree, and an even trickier and longer climb back down, but his new-found treasure at the top of the tree was worth it.

After many visits, the forester found that the little blue bird was feeling more comfortable with his presence and let him come closer and closer. Soon the forester was able to sit right on the branch next to the nest.

Then one day, the most amazing thing happened. The pearly blue bird stretched its wings, fluttered up and out of the nest and came to land down on the forester's shoulder. And there it sat, singing its bell-like song right into his ear. The forester thought that he must have reached heaven!

From this time on, the little blue bird began to look out for its new friend as he climbed the tree, and it started to fly down to meet him halfway. And soon the bird was strong and brave enough to fly all the way to the ground.

Oh what special adventures these two friends could now have!

There was so much to do and see and explore.

The blue bird would sit on the forester's shoulder as he strode out along the paths – through the forest, across the fields and farms, sometimes all the way to the sea. When the little bird needed to stretch its wings, it would fly up and down, and flitter around. When the little bird needed to rest, it would enjoy riding with the forester, singing its bell-like song as they went along.

What happy adventures these two friends could now have, the forester and the pearly blue bird.

    STORIES TO LIGHT THE NIGHT

5   LOSS OF A PET

There are only three stories in this short chapter, but each of these, and the suggestions in them, can be adjusted to use for a variety of situations concerning the death of a beloved pet, or situations of having to say 'goodbye' to a bird or animal that has been nursed back to health

DONNA AND SCRUFF – written to encourage conversation and ritual with a child (and the whole family) following the death of a beloved pet (p. 132).

A NEW DAWN – a story to help a nine-year old boy who was missing his connection to a stray dog in his neighbourhood (p. 134).

TIME TO SAY GOODBYE TO BABY ROO – written for a seven-year old boy to help him say goodbye to a little kangaroo he had taken care of for many months (p. 137).

Donna and Scruff

This story was written to encourage ritual and conversation with a child (and the whole family) following the death of their beloved pet. The story could be adapted to be about a cat, or a rabbit, or a bird – indeed, any kind of pet.

Here is feedback from a friend who recently shared the story with her grandchildren after the death of their family dog: 'After reading the story we went for a walk and gathered pine cones and wild flowers, and made a circle around the vase of flowers on her grave – like Donna did in the story – and it really helped to "normalize" a new experience for them. They liked the little song at the end. This is something I will focus on in the days ahead to consolidate the concept.'

Donna and Scruff had been friends since Donna was a baby. When Donna first walked, Scruff walked next to her. When Donna first ran, Scruff ran with her. They did everything together. They played in the back garden, they played in the park, and they played on the beach. At night Scruff slept in his dog basket on the veranda right outside Donna's window. He was the first friend Donna would greet each morning when she awoke.

As Donna grew older, she would help her mother scrub out Scruff's drinking bowl and fill it with fresh water. Best of all, she would help her father on dog-washing day. Donna would stand on a stool next to the big round tub... what fun it was, rubbing soapy bubbles into Scruff's brown coat. After his bath, when Scruff had shaken out all the drops of water and dried himself in the sun, Donna loved to bury her face in the warm softness of his fur.

But dogs don't live as long as people. The years passed, and as Donna grew taller and her running grew faster, Scruff seemed to grow slower and sleep for longer. He didn't want to run and play chasing games with Donna any more. He mostly wanted to lie on his bed on the veranda. His legs had grown old and tired, and his bones were stiff and sore.

One day, when Donna woke up she called out 'Good Morning' to Scruff. But he didn't respond as usual. He didn't bark, he didn't move, he didn't even open his eyes. Donna called for her father and mother to come out on the veranda. Her father knelt next to the dog basket and sadly shook his head. 'It looks like Scruff said "goodbye" to the world while we were all sleeping. Now he is at peace and in no more pain, it's time to make him a resting bed in the garden.'

Donna could hardly see for the tears welling up in her eyes, but she followed her father as he carried Scruff down the back steps. Together they made their way to the arbour of trees at the bottom of the garden. Donna's mother followed with a big spade in one hand and a small potted tree in the other. They all took turns digging the hole. When it was ready, Donna gave Scruff a last loving pat, and then her father carefully lowered him into his new earth bed.

Donna's father filled in the hole, leaving space at the top for the little tree. While he was doing this, Donna and her mother collected some smooth round stones and built a circle around the tree. Then the family stood together at the grave, each one taking a turn to share their favourite Scruff memories. There were so many!

While they were sharing their memory stories, a little wind began to blow through the garden. As it blew, it seemed to be whispering a song in Donna's ears:

In the circle of life, we dance and flow; in the circle of life, we come and go.

Donna picked up the words and began to sing as well:

In the circle of life, we dance and flow; in the circle of life, we come and go.

Soon her father and mother were singing too:

In the circle of life, we dance and flow; in the circle of life, we come and go.

After a while, the little wind blew out of the garden and up high into the sky. It blew rain clouds down from the mountains and across the town. After Donna and her parents had returned to the house, misty rain began to fall on the little tree.

The family fell asleep that night to the soft sound of raindrops on their roof.

Over time Donna's tears dried up, and the little tree grew strong. Memories of Scruff sometimes left Donna feeling sad, and sometimes feeling happy. She knew she would never have a dog again that was quite like Scruff. But perhaps... somewhere... there was a new kind of friend waiting to come and live at her house.

And whenever Donna was playing in the garden, the leaves of the new tree would dance in the breeze and Donna would sing:

In the circle of life, we dance and flow; in the circle of life, we come and go.

ACTIVITY
Plant a tree or a flowering bush – in the garden or in a pot on the balcony or on the windowsill.

A New Dawn

By Bandana Basu, M.Com., B.Ed., teacher and co-founder of Shishyaa School, Navi Mumbai, India

Bandana created this story to help a nine-year old boy with separation and loss. This child had shifted to a new apartment, but his heart longed for, and terribly missed, a stray dog that lived near his older residence building. The boy had befriended the dog and was used to feeding it, and in return the dog had become his playtime companion. He was having a hard time settling down in his new home as he missed his friend very much.

His mother, a single parent, had shared the situation with Bandana. This story worked beautifully with the child. He later asked his mother to take him to a garden.

What came as an outcome of this story and his visit to the garden was that the boy, who now lived on the seventh floor of an apartment house, asked his mother if they could have 'birds' (even though the story is more about butterflies).* She brought home a few lovebirds whom he caringly tended. Later they started to leave bird food on their balcony that attracted parrots residing on neighbouring trees. Eventually these parrots started to claim food by calling out to this family. The boy had healed. Bird watching continues to be his hobby even today.

Bandana writes: 'It was remarkable that this story helped the mother and son connect as he reached out to his mother and, together, they worked at rebuilding their life. What is also wonderful is how they found a way to fulfil their wish. In Mumbai city, due to paucity of space it is very difficult to imagine having a garden to oneself. However, most people have a balcony which they fill with potted plants. Theirs became one such home, with a wholesome green balcony, full of life and cheer.'

---

*According to Hindu legends, the butterfly symbolizes a new beginning, or the promise of a new beginning. Although this is often interpreted as marriage, it is also associated with moving into a new phase in life.

It was a summer afternoon. Aryan was sitting at the doorstep of his cottage looking out at the far distant roads, his eyes searching for his dear little friend, Sunshine. Aryan's puffed eyes revealed the tears he had shed for the past twelve days, when he realised that Sunshine had gone missing for good.

Aryan lived with his grandparents, while his parents worked abroad. He called his grandpa 'Dadu' and his grandma 'Thamma'. Two months ago, Sunshine had popped out of a gift box right on to Aryan's lap and licked his face. The 18-days old pup had a golden yellow coat. Aryan received this soft, fluffy and endearing gift from his Dadu, with a squeal and utmost delight.

Since then Aryan had been the sole caretaker of Sunshine. He fed, bathed and walked Sunshine. Although Aryan was just eight years old, he was remarkably capable of caring for this little dog. What he enjoyed the most was their playtime. Sunshine loved to nibble on hard things, holding on to them tightly as he chewed. And Aryan loved to tug upon the objects that Sunshine nibbled upon. Their tug-of-war was hilarious, with both rolling on the floor and Sunshine baby-barking at Aryan angrily. Aryan couldn't get enough of it and teased him further. At the end of each day, both cuddled each other and drifted off to sleep. They were each other's best companions and almost inseparable.

On the fateful Sunday, Aryan had insisted on taking Sunshine along to the shop to buy a loaf of bread for Thamma. While he was paying the shopkeeper, Sunshine began barking at a street dog across the road. The dog teased Sunshine to follow him, and before Aryan could do anything, Sunshine lunged at the other dog and right in front of his eyes both the dogs disappeared into the streets one after the other. Aryan shouted out after Sunshine but all he could hear was his barks, which too eventually faded away.

Aryan sat on the steps of the shop for a long time with the most worried look on his face, hoping and praying that Sunshine would return. It was a long while before Dadu walked up to the shop looking for them. Aryan leapt up and hugged Dadu and started to cry. In between his sobs Aryan managed to tell Dadu what had happened. Together, hand-in-hand they walked the streets until late into the evening looking for Sunshine, but there was no trace of him. At night they finally returned home with a heavy heart.

It had been twelve days now, and Aryan still sat at his cottage door, hoping that Sunshine would come leaping and barking out of somewhere. He hardly spoke or ate. Both Dadu and Thamma worried, and hoped there would be some way by which Aryan could overcome his grief.

The following week, Aryan's class teacher announced a nature trail on the weekend. Although disinterested, Aryan packed his backpack on Saturday morning. Dadu dropped him off at school and bid him goodbye. The group of 23 students and their teacher walked through the dense garden. Aryan noticed that although right in the city, it felt like a different place altogether. It was much quieter and cheerful than the outer world. The teacher divided the children into three groups, and asked them to go to different parts of the garden and look for all the different flowers and other living creatures around.

Aryan walked with his group. They went to the guided spot and started looking around. The beautiful flowers that were all around the garden made the place smell wonderful. Slender beams of sunlight passed through the branches of the tall trees and lit up the ground. Birds played hide and seek as they chirped, flew across from one end to the other and disappeared into the branches of the trees. Gentle little butterflies fluttered upon the flowers and shrubs. Some of them played with each other as they fluttered together from flower to flower. Some hovered above Aryan's head for a while before they flew away into the distance.

Aryan's eyes followed each of them, and before he realised it he was smiling. He quickly took out his notebook and started to write all that he saw. He then pulled out his colour box and began to draw the things he saw. Sitting on the ground in the middle of the dense garden, he was completely absorbed by what he saw. Dragonflies fluttered around him and a delicate little butterfly settled on his knee. He slowly raised his hand towards it and touched its delicate wings with his fingers. This was the first time that he realised how dainty they were, and it amazed him further. Aryan was mesmerized by the beauty of the butterflies.

At the end of the trip, he returned to school and showed his work to his teacher. She loved it. When Dadu came to pick him up after school he was shocked to see a broad smile on Aryan's face and the excitement in his eyes. Aryan was back to his happy little self after a long time!

Next morning, as Dadu watered the plants around the house, Aryan asked him whether they could create a garden in the backyard, so that butterflies could visit their home too. Dadu was delighted to hear that and asked if Aryan would help. That way it would happen faster. Aryan shouted 'yes'...!! – and waved his arms up and down as he fluttered around the house like a butterfly.

In a few months, the backyard had transformed into a little garden. One morning as Aryan tended to a flower tree, a little butterfly fluttered by and settled on Aryan's arm. He remained steady and watched it with twinkling eyes. How he loved butterflies!

ACTIVITY
Create a butterfly garden with pots and plant boxes – for your balcony or your garden – or do it together with other families at the Community Garden.

TIME TO SAY GOODBYE TO BABY ROO

This story was written for a seven-year old boy to help him say goodbye to a little kangaroo he had taken care of for many months. It could be modified to suit many situations with different animals or birds that children have been involved with short-term – either helping nurse them back to health or caring for them when they were orphaned. The photograph album mentioned at the end is a good compliment to the story – the child could help compile the album, or it may be a surprise gift, as in this ending.

Jarrah lived on a farm surrounded by bushland. Many kangaroos lived in the bush, and Jarrah could often see them through the farm fence. He loved to watch them hopping here and hopping there, seeking the fresh green shoots of the bushland grasses. Jarrah especially loved seeing the little Joeys peeking out of their mothers' pouches, sometimes daring to jump away and explore a little, then jumping back into their cosy homes.

One side of Jarrah's farm was close to a busy highway. Usually the kangaroos stayed away from the speeding cars and kept safe in the bushland. But one summer was unusually hot and dry, and the bushland grasses had turned brittle and brown. So the kangaroos began to seek food elsewhere. On the sides of the highway there was still green grass to be found, and this is how the terrible accident happened.

Jarrah heard the screeching of wheels and the loud bang. He ran up his driveway to see what had caused the noise, and an awful sight awaited him. A mother kangaroo had been nibbling grass too close to the edge of the busy road, and she had been hit on the head and killed instantly by a speeding car.

Jarrah called his father to help remove the kangaroo's body from the road. His father then fetched his big spade to dig a hole to bury it near the fence.

Jarrah was watching all this, and to his surprise, as the dead kangaroo was lying near the hole he noticed a tiny movement in the mother's pouch.

Jarrah took off his cotton T-shirt and lay it on the ground. Then he slowly reached his hands inside the pouch. He carefully pulled out a tiny Roo, talking in soft comforting words, trying not to frighten him. Fortunately, the little Roo stayed very still, probably out of shock and fear, and let Jarrah wrap him in the soft cotton shirt. I will call you 'Joey', he whispered, 'because this means "little animal". Please trust that I will not hurt you.'

With Joey now safely bundled in this new human pouch, Jarrah was able to carry him back to the farmhouse. Once inside, Jarrah found a small basket and put the little bundle inside it. He carried it into his room and put it next to his bed. The bundle had stopped wriggling because Joey had fallen fast asleep.

Jarrah lay on his bed reading his books, with one eye on the basket. Meanwhile his mother drove into town to visit the vet. She arrived back one hour later with some special milk formula, a feeding bottle, and an information sheet on how to feed and care for a baby kangaroo.

For the next few weeks Jarrah was in charge of nursing and feeding Joey, even through the night! Fortunately, the night feedings didn't last long and little Joey began to sleep through till morning.

Jarrah's mother used her sewing machine to make a little pouch for Joey, with flannelette from some old pyjamas as the inside lining and some heavy cotton calico for the outside. There was a special seam on the top to thread a wooden rod through, and this rod hung on two hooks from the end of Jarrah's bed. Of course, over the next months, as Joey grew and grew, new and bigger pouches had to be made.

Also, as Joey grew he needed to be introduced to some solid food, so Jarrah would walk with him across the lawn and around the garden. Jarrah would hold the wooden rod with Joey in the pouch in front of him, so Joey could reach his little head out and nibble fresh green shoots of grass and leaves.

By this time Joey had grown big enough to hop out and have adventures. Fortunately, the farmhouse had a high fence around the garden so the little Roo couldn't hop too far away!

Jarrah and Joey shared many wonderful play times on the wide lawn in front of the house. Jarrah didn't want these moments to ever come to an end.

But Joey was growing... and growing... and growing! Eventually he reached the stage where he needed to be set free.

Jarrah was dreading this moment. 'Why can't he stay with us for ever?', he pleaded to his parents.

Jarrah's parents were grateful that the information sheet from the vet had clear guidelines on this. Once a baby Roo had grown big enough to live outside the pouch and feed himself, it was time to let him go back to join the kangaroo mob. They repeatedly explained to their son, 'If you love your new friend, you need to let him go.

It would be cruel to keep him from his own kind any longer.'

Fortunately, it had been a year of good rain, and there was plenty to eat in the bushland. On the chosen day, after Jarrah patted and hugged Joey goodbye many times, he opened the garden gate and watched his friend hop away. Across the paddock Joey hopped, all the way to the farm gate that led to the forest. Jarrah's father was waiting there to open the gate to let him through to freedom.

Within minutes Joey had joined his mob in the bush.

It was difficult for Jarrah to get used to life without Joey. For many weeks, every afternoon after school he would sit on the farm fence and watch the mob of kangaroos in the distant forest feeding on the bushland grasses.

Joey never left the mob to come close, but Jarrah was sure that Joey knew he was there and was watching him from a distance.

A few months after Joey's release into freedom, it was Jarrah's birthday. When he woke up on this special morning there was a present on the table next to his bed. It was wrapped up in one of Joey's old pouches.

Jarrah carefully undid the folds of cloth, and to his great surprise he found a photograph album, filled with memories. There were photos of the first day that he had brought Joey home, all the way through to the last hugs on the day of the goodbye.

It was the best present that Jarrah had ever been given.

'I will keep this for the rest of my life', he said to his parents. And he did!

CRAFT ACTIVITY
Making Joey Pouches: Wildcare Australia have patterns online for making pouches for baby kangaroos and wallabies – search for 'Making Joey Pouches' on https://wildcare.org.au/

6 LOSS OF HEALTH AND WELL-BEING

This chapter includes stories for extended illness, anxiety about germs, the loss of mobility, the loss of voice (including selective mutism) and the loss of sight.

To help you find your way, I have summarized the background to each story as follows:

LITTLE ROSE – a story for a young child about the importance of rest when one is ill (p. 142).

A BOX OF HANKIE FRIENDS – an activity story for a child who needs to spend extended periods of time in bed (p. 143).

THE LITTLE GNOME WHO HAD TO STAY HOME – a story written for use with young children (suggested ages, 3–7 years of age) who were required to stay home during the Covid-19 pandemic (p. 145).

A HANDKERCHIEF FOR LITTLE POSSUM – written for the Covid-19 pandemic to help young children (ages 4–8) who were overly anxious about 'germs' and getting ill (p. 148).

LITTLE SINGING BUNNY – a story for a very shy two-and-a-half-year old boy (p. 151).

THE CHILDREN AND THE RIVER – an East African cultural story for situational mutism (p. 154).

THE PRINCESS AND THE PEARL – a story for a six-year old girl with selective mutism (p. 156).

A FISHER OF WORDS – a story to encourage patience and perseverance in children (and the elderly) with speech apraxia and speech delays (p. 159).

BRIGHT LIGHT – written for an eight-year old girl with a degenerative eye disease (p. 161).

HEALING WITH WORDS – Poems from 'Our Kids' – three poems from young people living with chronic and serious illness (p. 165).

THE FROG AND THE PAIL OF CREAM – a short Russian tale to encourage strength and determination in fighting illness and adversity; suitable for children and families (p. 167).

HEALING BONES – a story for an older child or teenager who has become temporarily immobile because of a broken ankle or leg (p. 168).

THE BLACK STONE – written to help a 17-year old girl accept the use of a wheelchair (p. 170).

LITTLE SHELL AND THE DANCING PEARLS – a personal story written about a woman's growth through suffering the loss of an eye from childhood and living with a skin disease (p. 172).

LITTLE ROSE

A simple story with a simple message for
a young child – when a little person is
unwell, he or she needs to rest.

A golden butterfly flew into the garden early one morning to visit her flower friends. But when she reached Little Rose in the middle of the garden, she could see that something was not as it should be.

Instead of holding her arms of pink buds up to the sun, Little Rose was droopy and weak and needing to sleep.

The golden butterfly fluttered across the garden, whispering to all the flowers:

'Little Rose is tired and weak.
Little Rose needs to sleep.'

The flowers opened their bright petals and whispered to the trees above:

'Little Rose is tired and weak.
Little Rose needs to sleep.'

The trees swayed their green branches from side to side and whispered to the breeze:

'Little Rose is tired and weak.
Little Rose needs to sleep.'

The breeze whirled and swirled and swirled and whirled. After some time, it swirled into a wind that could fly up high. And high in the sky it whispered to the morning sun:

'Little Rose is tired and weak.
Little Rose needs to sleep.'

The sun smiled a warming smile. Then it sent its golden sunbeams across the sky and down into the garden to gently shine on Little Rose.

A Box of Hankie Friends

The idea for this story comes from my own childhood. There was a time when I was sick for many weeks, and my best memory (which seems to override the throat pain and other uncomfortable aspects of my illness) was a book given to me by my mother. The book came together with a box of coloured handkerchiefs, together with instructions on how to turn the handkerchiefs into knotted dolls. I am sure it was this family of hankie friends that helped nurse me back to health!

This book, which gave me hours and hours of enjoyment, is unfortunately now out of print and only available in antique bookstores... or if you are lucky, you might find it in a second-hand book shop. It is called *Araminta, Arabella and Aristide*, written by Lorna North and illustrated by Phyllis Harrap (P.G. Gawthorn Ltd, London, 1955).

There was once a box that lived in a drawer next to a little girl's bed.

If an adult was to open this box, all they would see was a neat pile of folded coloured handkerchiefs.

The little girl was the only one who knew the hidden truth to this box. She had been taught a secret craft that turned all the handkerchiefs inside the box into her bedside friends. The little girl only used this secret when she was sick and in bed for days, sometimes weeks, at a time.

There were ten handkerchiefs in the box, which meant ten bedside friends. All the little girl had to do was lift out each hanky, one at a time, and tie a knot in the middle of the hanky for the head, and a knot on each of two corners for the hands. With some of the handkerchiefs she had worked out a way to twirl and knot all four corners to make dolls with long arms and legs. The other ones without legs just had long flowing dresses.

The little girl would spend most of her waking hours each day playing with her different coloured hankie friends. She would use the sheets and blankets to make hills and valleys, and little caves, and long tunnels, and houses and bedrooms. There was a whole world waiting to be explored.

Sometimes the other toys in the room would be invited to join in. Teddy and Tiger and Little Red Car and The Flowered Tea Set would wait on the toy shelf, hoping to be chosen. They knew they couldn't all be part of the bedtime play, as there wasn't enough room on the bed for everyone to join in.

But if they weren't chosen, at least they could watch from the shelf.

And so the days passed by.... with hours of play, in a cosy restful way, and many hours of sleep... and more play and more sleep and more play and more sleep.... Just exactly the amount of time that this little child needed to recover.

Craft Activity
Making Knotted Dolls from handkerchiefs: Silk scarves, handkerchiefs and/or plain cotton squares can easily be turned into dolls for creative play – even paper serviettes could be used to make short lived ones. All you need are some small balls of wool or other stuffing for the heads and some yarn or string for tying. Place a ball of stuffing in the middle of each square and tie for the head, then knot two corners to make the hands.
Alternatively, you can just do a large knot for the head and two smaller knots for the hands.
See Patterns and Templates, p. 281.

The Little Gnome Who Had to Stay Home

This story was written for use with young children (suggested ages, 3–7 years of age) who were required to stay home during the Covid-19 pandemic, or who had their freedom severely modified (e.g. perhaps they could attend school, but couldn't attend special assemblies, festivals, parties or events). The song at the end was left open for teachers and parents to create more verses with ideas from the children. The story can be changed/edited to suit different situations – e.g. mother tree could be father tree or grandmother or grandfather tree, or you may want to omit the part about 'gnome school'. The main character could also be changed (e.g. instead of using a gnome, the story could be about a mouse stuck in his little house, or a bird that must stay and rest in the nest).

I chose to write this story with a 'mirroring' structure – the story simply reflects the situation and expands upon it, with images that help share a message that is too strong to state directly with little children. I didn't promise any timeline because that would have been irresponsible, as no one knew it at the time of writing. The story's aim was to encourage acceptance of the current 'social distancing' situation, and to help motivate the children to find and enjoy activities that they can do within the home.

I put the story on my website and posted links to it on social media, and within one week the story had travelled the world, translated into 27 languages, and turned into puppet shows, plays, short films, and even a crochet cartoon. I was overwhelmed by the response – it proved to me how much our world today needs story language in troubled times. Although this story was written for young children, there were many comments from adults on how the message helped them to have a more positive attitude about being 'stuck' at home. One 80-year old male friend contacted me to say, 'This story is for me'!

Little gnome was confused.

Why did he have to stay home?

Didn't everyone know how little gnomes love to roam!

He couldn't go to gnome school, he couldn't play with his friends in the forest, and his friends couldn't visit him.

Little gnome was stuck all alone in his tree-roots home.

At least he could look out of his window through the roots of the tree. He was surprised that there was so much to see. Little ants were scurrying by, and brightly coloured beetles caught his eye. Floppy-eared rabbits hopped up and down, in and out the bushes and round and around.

But even with all these things to watch, little gnome was growing impatient. Why did he have to keep on staying home? It didn't make sense to him why he could not roam.

Then Mother Tree whispered to him: 'Things are not as they used to be – but trust me, soon you will be free – trust me, trust me.'

Little gnome knew in his heart that he could always trust Mother Tree.

Mother tree was as wise as wise could be.

Mother Tree carried the wisdom of the whole forest!

Mother Tree knew all about everything. The birds and the wind were her friends. They visited her each day, bringing messages from far away.

Little gnome could hear when the birds came by. He could hear them singing with glee high up in the branches of Mother Tree.

Little gnome could see when the wind was blowing past. He could see the branches swaying this way and that, sometimes slowly, sometimes fast. Often, he had to close his window to keep out the dust and leaves stirred from the ground by this windy friend whooshing around.

Every day Mother Tree continued to whisper: 'Things are not as they used to be – but trust me, soon you will be free – trust me, trust me.'

So little gnome had to trust, and little gnome had to wait. Soon he knew he would be free to leave his home amongst the roots of the tree. Soon he knew he would be free to roam the forest once again – oh how little gnomes loved to roam!

And while he waited, he was surprised how many things he could find to do, on his own, in his tree-roots home.

Little gnome can dance
Little gnome can sing
Little gnome can paint and draw
And do somersaults across the floor.
Little gnome can dance
Little gnome can sing
Little gnome can clean and cook
And curl up with a picture book.

Little gnome can dance
Little gnome can sing
Little gnome can weave and sew,
And knead and bake some sourdough.
Little gnome can dance
Little gnome can sing
Little gnome can hammer and screw,
cut and glue,
make a stew,
And if feeling blue,
Look out the window at the view,
So many things for a gnome to do!
So many things for a gnome to do!
So many things for a gnome to do!

CRAFT ACTIVITIES
Make an illustrated book of the story, create a puppet show, dance and/or act the story, make music for the poem.
You can also write more verses for the poem (what other activities can you think of to do at home?)
Little gnome can…
Little gnome can…
Little gnome can…
And…

A Handkerchief for Little Possum

A rhyming story written for the Covid-19 pandemic to help young children who were overly anxious about 'germs' and getting ill.

The story includes a 'handkerchief chorus' that can be sung to the tune of 'Here we go 'round the Mulberry Bush' – or you may make up your own song!

Important note: Please do not share this with children who are too young to even know about germs and viruses.

Note: a possum is an Australian marsupial, and like the kangaroo the mother carries her baby in a pouch.

Little Possum was so worried.
 All the day and through the night.
The forest news and chatter,
Had given him quite a fright.

Every trunk of every tree,
Had a sign that said: 'Watch out!'
In big letters on the bark –
'Nasty germs are all about'.

Little Possum was so worried,
All this germ-talk everywhere,
How could he even dare
To breathe the forest air!

Mother Possum told him:
'It's safe to be in our tree,
If you're playing close to me,
You'll be as safe as safe can be.

But still Little Possum worried,
And stayed inside his pouch.
If nasty germs were about,
Why would he want to come out?

Every day his mother begged,
'Come out and play in our tree,
Jump from branch to branch,
Be as free as free can be'.

But Little Possum still worried
And refused to play in the tree.
Little possum could only think,
'What if the germs get me!'.

Then a breeze blew round the tree,
With a whispered song so clear.
Mother Possum heard the message,
And let out a happy cheer!

She called out to her spider friends
That lived in all the trees.
'What we need to keep us safe,
Are many handkerchiefs!'

Handkerchiefs to catch the germs,
Handkerchiefs for every day.
Helping to make the forest safe,
And keep the worries away.

So, the spiders in the forest
Set to work in all the trees,
A-spinning and a-weaving,
Making many silk hankies.

Next morning from the pouch,
Little Possum poked his head.
He saw a precious gift
Woven from the spiders' thread.

Soon every possum had a gift,
There were fewer germs about,
At last our Little Possum
Could climb safely from his pouch.

Now all the forest possums
Could play up and down their trees.
With hankies in their pockets,
To use... so easily.

Handkerchiefs to catch the germs,
Handkerchiefs for every day.
Helping to make the forest safe,
And keep the worries away.

When the handkerchiefs were finished,
The spiders had another chore.
Weaving soft and silky wash cloths
For each little possum's paw.

If you visit Possum forest,
Look for washing in the trees,
Many little cloths and hankies
May be drying in the breeze!

Handkerchiefs to catch the germs,
Handkerchiefs for every day.
Helping to make the forest safe,
And keep the worries away.

     STORIES TO LIGHT THE NIGHT

LITTLE SINGING BUNNY

By Becky Whitcombe, early childhood educator

This story was written for a two-and-a-half-year old boy who had great shyness in talking and making any eye contact with anyone in his community besides his parents, brother and grandmother. Two languages are spoken at home, which could be a reason for this behaviour. His mother was concerned that he was very closed towards his teachers and playgroup leaders, and wished he could find a voice and feel comfortable to communicate with them in some form... and so this story was born.

COMMENTS FROM BECKY: 'I was really trying to hone in, to send the boy a message that his voice was important and worthy of being heard, no matter what volume. And that magic can happen when he does speak... that others care to listen, and they love to hear his voice. Although the story is quite long, this little boy is story bound.'

COMMENTS FROM THE MOTHER: 'I found the whole process incredibly rich and rewarding, and helpful for both of us. My son now offers a few special words to others besides the immediate family. He now communicates a lot more – making gestures with smiles, nods, eye contact, and giving people things more than before. He also speaks to family members in front of others, which was minimal before the story. There have been subtle but powerful changes. When he first heard the story he seemed to really respond, and it seemed to help him open up to the outside world and use non-verbal communication with others. He sang it with me once!'

COMMENTS FROM THE TEACHER: 'The next time I saw the child after he had heard the story, he made eye contact with me for the first time ever. And this alone was huge. It was like he offered this gift as a gesture of trust. It was beautiful! He had barely talked at playgroup to his mother in front of anyone. He would whisper in his second language. Now he speaks with no fear and with volume!'

There once was a Bunny family who lived in a very cozy warm burrow. There was a mother and father bunny and two small bunnies. They all had the softest fur of golden brown and fluffy white, so clean and bright, with shiny pink noses.

The youngest bunny loved singing, and he would start to sing the moment he woke up.

He especially loved singing to his family. Only his family. It would bring so much fun and joy.

La la I sing my song
Every day I sing along
La da da, La di di
Singing along so happily.

When they left their burrow to find food, Little Bunny would stay close and softly sing his song as they all hopped along.

La la I sing my song
Every day I sing along
La da da, La di di
Singing along so happily.

But whenever the Bunny family would pass another animal in the forest Little Bunny would look down and stop singing. Only once the animal had moved on and was far away in the distance, Little Bunny would look up and start to sing his song as he hopped along.

La la I sing my song
Every day I sing along
La da da, La di di
Singing along so happily.

One day, as the Bunny family was out looking for the new berries of the season, everyone else was around. Little Bunny tried to sing his song very quietly to his family, but there were too many animals nearby, also searching for berries. It was all too much for Little Bunny, so he simply stopping singing.

But Little Bunny did not know he had the magic voice that made the forest glow in all the colours of the rainbow. His song was heard and seemed to travel across the forest floor and the forest sky. To all the animals that crawl, walk or fly.

All the birds and the bees, all the flowers and the trees had been listening to his song. And it was his voice that had made the forest glow in the most beautiful colours. All the colours! So when Little Bunny stopped singing, the forest started to lose its shine and to lose its colour.

All the animals that crawled, walked and flew turned grey.

All the birds and bees, flowers and trees turned grey.

And then the Bunny Family looked at each other and saw they too had lost their shine and colour. They too were now grey.

Nothing had colour.

The Bunny Family were very tired from berry picking (the berries were also grey), so they returned to their burrow to sleep through the night.

When they all woke, Little Bunny started to sing his song –

La la I sing my song
Every day I sing along
La da da, La di di
Singing along so happily.

All of a sudden, the Mumma Bunny started to turn into the brown and white so clean and bright fur again. And a nice shiny pink nose appeared too. She was amazed. She looked at little Bunny and said, 'Keep singing! Keep singing!'.

And as he continued to sing, *all* the family turned back into their fur of brown and white so clean and bright, with shiny pink noses.

Then Mumma Bunny took Little Bunny to the entrance of the burrow and saw that as the bunny was singing his song, the colour of the forest began to reappear again. The grey began to disappear, and the grass turned a lovely spring green, and the flowers bloomed in all their glory of red, purple and pink. As the song was spread across the forest, the birds flapped their coloured wings and the sky turned the brightest blue.

Mummy Bunny turned and said to Little Bunny, 'This is you, this is you! It is your voice and your song that gives the forest all its colour.'

From that day on, the Little Bunny was very proud of his song and it made him happy to sing to all. And the forest was more pretty and colourful than ever before.

If you listen very carefully, you can hear all the birds and the bees hum along, and the flowers and the trees sway and dance to his sweet song.

La la I sing my song
Every day I sing along
La da da, La di di
Singing along so happily.

THE CHILDREN AND THE RIVER

Narrated by Annet Mukyala

This is a Banyoro story from Uganda, East Africa, narrated by Annet Mukyala and transcribed by the author. It is an example of a cultural story for situational mutism.

Once upon a time there lived a man and his wife with their five children, four girls and one boy.

The parents took good care of their children, and they worked hard in their garden to grow enough maize and vegetables to feed their family.

However, it happened that the boy in the family would not speak. The parents and the boy's sisters tried all they could to get him to talk, but to no avail.

One day when the parents had gone to the garden to work, the children decided on their own to go to the well and fetch water. But when they were about to reach the well, they came across a great river that they had never noticed before, and they had nowhere to pass.

The eldest sister moved closer to the river and started singing:

Maama na taata bakampakana ntaligenda haiziba
mbere amaizi gate keire nyanja iwe mpikiza ndabeho.
(Mother and father wanted me to go to the well where the waters are still.
River, please give way so I can pass.)

The river divided itself into two and there was a path for her, and when she had crossed over, the river closed again.

Then the second sister came and sang the same song:

Maama na taata bakampakana ntaligenda haiziba

Once again, the river divided and there was a path for her, and when she crossed over, the river closed again.

Then the third sister had her turn and then the fourth. They all sang the same song, and it happened that the river divided and there was a path for each one, and when they crossed over, the river closed again.

But when it came to the brother, who up to this point had never spoken, he tried to sing as his sisters had done before him, but the words would not come out. So the water covered him up to the knees. He tried the second time but still he could not make any sound, so the water covered him up to the waist. He tried the third time but still he could not sing, so the water covered him up to his neck.

Then the boy took some water from the river into his mouth and drank it. The water was cool and refreshing.

When he tried to sing this time, he sang properly, and the river divided and made a path for him!

He crossed over and found his sisters waiting for him on the other side. They all helped to fetch and carry water from the well and set out happily for home.

On their way back they did not find the river again.

Back home the parents were very happy because their son was now able to speak. A great feast was held, and the family celebrated this special day.

THE PRINCESS AND THE PEARL

This story was written for a six-year old girl with selective mutism – talking at home but not at school. My idea to use butterflies as one of the helping metaphors came from looking at some of the girl's drawings – there were butterflies in all of them.

I wrote this story to be given to the girl soon after her sixth birthday, without realising she had chosen as a birthday gift a felt crown with a pearl sewn on to the front. Sometimes this synchronicity happens with stories! She wore the crown to school on her birthday, and the teacher was so surprised, as she was planning to tell the story to the class the following week.

The teacher reported that slowly, slowly, there were small changes observed in the girl's behaviour. In the teacher's words: 'the story helped her to be more confident to allow her voice to be heard by me at school – in the classroom and playground – and for me to see her singing and speaking to her friends'.

A copy was also given to the parents to read at home. They reported that they were very happy with such a story gift for their family.

There was once a princess who lived in a shiny white castle high up on the rocky cliffs by the sea. This princess was known far and wide for her beautiful crown of pearls that she wore from the moment she woke up in the morning to the moment she went to sleep at night.

She wore her pearl crown while playing hide and seek with the butterflies in the castle garden; she wore her pearl crown while swinging high and low on the castle swing; she wore her pearl crown while skipping through the grass near the cliffs by the sea.

Every night before the princess went to sleep, she would take off her crown and polish the milky white pearls. Then she would put the crown to rest in its soft velvet case until the morning.

One day, while the princess was skipping through the grass near the cliffs by the sea, she tripped on a rock in the path and fell forward. The crown of pearls slipped off her head and rolled along the path. It rolled all the way to the cliff edge. Fortunately, there it stopped on a rocky outcrop, just before the cliffs dropped down to the beach below.

The princess crept carefully forward and picked up the crown. While she was dusting off the dirt and grass she noticed that one large pearl from the front of the crown was missing. She looked around – it wasn't amongst the dirt and rocks at the top of the cliffs. She walked back along the grassy path – it wasn't anywhere on the path or in the grass. She crept back to the top of the cliffs and looked over the edge. Far down below, she could see a round white pearl lying on the sandy beach, gleaming in the sunlight.

While she was watching, a large wave washed up the beach. When it washed back down, the pearl was gone. The wave had taken it back to its sea home.

The princess didn't know what to do. The sea was so big, and she was so small. How was she going to find her missing pearl? It seemed an impossible task.

She returned to the castle and put her crown back into its soft velvet case. Without all its pearls the crown seemed to have lost its beauty. The princess did not want to wear it again.

From that day onwards, life at the castle was changed. The princess didn't want to play in the gardens; she didn't want to swing on the swing; she didn't want to skip through the grass.

The butterflies were the first to notice the change. They had looked forward every day to when the princess would come out and play hide-and-seek with them. Now all she seemed to do was sit inside and stare out of the castle window.

The butterflies whispered their concern to the wind-who-knew-all-the-secrets. The wind-who-knew-all-the-secrets had been blowing around the cliff tops on the day of the princess's fall. The wind-who-knew-all-the-secrets had seen the pearl roll out of the crown and over the cliffs. The wind-who-knew-all-the-secrets had seen the wave wash up on the beach and take the round white pearl back to its sea home.

And now, the wind-who-knew-all-the-secrets told the whole story to the butterflies.

Straight away the butterflies knew what needed to be done. With a flitter and a flutter they rose together like a coloured cloud. They flew out of the castle garden, over the cliffs and down to the sea. They flew to where the waves washed backwards and forwards up and down the beach. The butterflies whispered the story of the missing pearl to the waves. Then with a flitter and a flutter they rose together like a coloured cloud and headed over the cliffs, and soon were safely back in their garden.

Meanwhile, the waves carried the whisper through the water, all the way out to where the dolphins dived and played. When the dolphins heard the story of the missing pearl, they set to work. They dived down and around, looking here and looking there, swimming in and out of the rocky reefs and searching along the sandy seabed.

For many days they searched for the pearl. Then finally one of the dolphins leapt joyfully up into the air, then swam towards the beach. In its mouth was a gleaming white pearl.

The wind-who-knew-all-the-secrets just happened to be blowing by at this moment. It saw a wave take the pearl from the dolphin and wash it high up on the sand. And there the pearl sat, gleaming in the sunlight.

Quickly the wind-who-knew-all-the-secrets blew back towards the castle. The princess was sitting inside, looking out of the castle window. The wind-who-knew-all-the-secrets did all it could to get the attention of the princess. It rattled the window latch, it blew against the glass, it shook the tree branches and it swirled up the fresh dirt in the garden beds. But the princess didn't seem to take any notice.

Then the wind-who-knew-all-the-secrets had an idea. It found a small hole in the castle door and squeezed through. Once inside the castle it blew softly around the princess and began to sing a most beautiful song. It sang about the help of the butterflies. It sang about the help of the waves. It sang about the help of the dolphins. And finally it sang about the shining white pearl lying on the sandy beach.

The princess listened to the beautiful song of the wind-who-knew-all-the-secrets. She stood up, opened the castle door and walked outside. Once she was in the garden, she was surrounded by her friends the butterflies. With a flitter and a flutter, the butterflies rose together like a coloured cloud. The princess followed the coloured cloud across the grass at the top of the cliffs, then slowly down the rocky cliff path, all the way to the beach. Once she was on the sand, she found her white pearl, gleaming in the sunlight.

What a happy day this was for everyone – for the wind-who-knew-all-the-secrets, for the butterflies, for the waves, for the dolphins, and most of all, for the princess. The crown was repaired at once, and was soon back again in full beauty on the princess's head.

And as far as I know, the princess is wearing it still, from the moment she wakes up in the morning to the moment she goes to sleep at night. She wears her pearl crown while playing hide-and-seek with the butterflies in the castle garden; she wears her pearl crown while swinging high and low on the castle swing; and she wears her pearl crown while skipping through the grass near the cliffs by the sea.

A Fisher of Words

A story to encourage patience and perseverance in children with speech apraxia and speech delays who often struggle to say many sounds and words. The 'fishing in the hole in the ice' idea came from my son Jamie. I wrote the story for his six-year old son who loves everything about water, especially waterfalls. When he couldn't get his parents to understand a word he was trying to say, I encouraged them to refer to the image in the story in a subtle way, saying 'keep on fishing' or 'dig the hole wider and deeper'.

The same story about a fisherman or fisherwoman could be used with adults who are struggling with the loss of words they used to once know. My husband and I now use the fishing metaphor to help exercise our thinking – we had grown accustomed to relying on each other for 'words' we couldn't think of by ourselves. In response to 'Can you remember the name of...', the answer is now 'Keep on fishing'!

Once upon a time in *Word Land* there were many ways to find words to make sentences. There were sometimes enough words to make a story. There were sometimes even enough words to make many stories!

In *Word Land* there was a forest of words, and in the forest every tree was covered in words like leaves. There was also a beach of words, and hiding under every rock on the sand you could find a word.

But best of all, in the middle of *Word Land* was a lake of words. Living inside this lake were many many words, like little fishes swimming everywhere – in fact, every word in the world lived in this lake. Every day new words tumbled into the waters of the lake from the waterfall at one end. They would merrily splash into the water and join all the other *fishie* words swimming around.

Living in a little house by the waterfall, on the edge of the lake, was a fisher-boy. The fisher-boy loved to go fishing every day to see how many words he could catch.

Sometimes he could only catch enough words to make a sentence. Sometimes he could catch enough words to make a story. Sometimes he could catch enough words to make many stories.

But when the weather turned very cold in the land of words, the lake froze over. The fisher-boy had to work hard to chip and dig to make a little hole in the ice so he could still go fishing. Dressed in his very warm jacket he would sit on a stool by the hole in the ice to fish. But it wasn't so easy to catch words this way.

Sometimes a word would fall off his hook and he would have to try again.

Sometimes if the word was too big, he couldn't even pull it back through the ice hole.

So, the fisher-boy had to chip and dig and chip and dig to make the hole bigger. And as he worked, he often sang his fishing song:

Fishing, fishing, all the day...
Fishing for words... what will they say?
Making sentences and stories too,
Word fishing is what I love to do!

Because the fisher-boy loved to make sentences and loved to make stories, in the cold weather he just had to work a little bit harder to catch the words through the hole in the ice.

He had to chip and dig and chip and dig to make the hole bigger... he had to work really hard! And as he worked, he often sang his fishing song:

Fishing, fishing, all the day...
Fishing for words... what will they say?
Making sentences and stories too,
Word fishing is what I love to do!

And catch those words he did!

And do you know that this fisher-boy grew up to become one of the most well-loved storytellers in all the land, because he caught so many words to make so many sentences and so many stories.

CRAFT ACTIVITY
Put many simple words on cards with metal buttons attached – use a stick with a small magnet tied to the end of a short piece of string (with the other end tied to one end of the stick).

Put all the cards into a bucket and 'go fishing'. Different games can be played depending on the age of the child – many words can be used to create a story.

A variation of this is to put letters on cards and then 'go fishing' – the letters that are 'caught' can then be used to create many different words or combinations of words.

     STORIES TO LIGHT THE NIGHT

BRIGHT LIGHT

This story was written for an eight-year old girl in England with a degenerative eye disease – it was a gift to help her, in some small way, find courage for the years ahead with her weakened condition. There is an emphasis in the story on the use of other senses to guide one's way.

The girl's auntie helped give input for the story construction (her niece loved foxes).

On a personal note, this story has helped me accept the weakened state of my own eyes as I grow older. It has encouraged me to find opportunities to use my other senses and rest my sense of sight. Sometimes, if my local beach is quite deserted, I walk along the sand with my eyes closed, relying on my sense of touch and hearing to find a way forward. Sometimes I sit in the garden with my eyes closed, enjoying the accentuated sounds of the birds and insects, and the feeling of the breeze on my skin. Or at night-time, the moonlight that I can see even with my eye lids half closed. At the end of these experiences, my eyes always feel rested and more ready to work again!

There was once a little fox who was born into the world with eyes as bright as shooting stars. Her parents fell immediately in love with her bright eyes and named her 'Bright Light'. This lively little fox lived with her family at the edge of a big forest. She spent her nights playing hide-and-seek with the forest elves, and her days creating new games with her brothers and sisters.

As the years went by, Bright Light's eyes started to dim. The dimming of her eyes upset little Bright Light very much. She slowly stopped frolicking with her elfin friends, and didn't make up any new games to play with her brothers and sisters.

One evening, Bright Light was sitting under a tree, singing a sad song to herself.

I wish, I wish, I wish so much that my eyes were as they used to be.

I wish, I wish, I wish so much that I could find new eyes to see.

I wish I wish I wish so much, my heart is really hurting,

I wish I wish I wish so much that my heart is nearly bursting.

The little fox's sad song was heard by the Spirit of the Forest, who magically appeared out of her leafy home and stood listening to the little fox's woes. Bright Light didn't notice the spirit lady at first, her eyes were so clouded with tears. But then she heard a voice and looked up.

'Dear Bright Light', said the Spirit of the Forest, 'I will tell you of a journey you can make to find what you are seeking. Only you can go on this journey, it is yours to take alone. You will need some tools that you already have – they are called your senses. And I have a small gift to help you find the way.'

The Spirit of the Forest reached down deep into the roots of her tree home and plucked out a smooth crystal which glowed with the wisdom of all the trees. Using a length of vine, she threaded it into a necklace, then handed it to Bright Light to wear around her neck.

Then the Spirit of the Forest pointed to a gap in the trees that Bright Light had never noticed before. 'If you follow this path, it will lead you to a clearing with a deep and wide pool. Here you will find what you are seeking.' With these words, the Spirit of the Forest disappeared as magically as she had arrived, leaving Bright Light with her new gift.

Now the little fox had never journeyed deep into the forest before. She had been told of scary things in there, and did not want to go near them. Just at this moment, Mother Moon shone down through the trees and bathed her in silver moonbeams. Mother Moon whispered to her: 'I can also help you on this journey. When I am shining full and bright, I can guide you with my light.'

Strengthened by the gift from the Spirit of the Forest and the light of Mother Moon, Bright Light took a deep breath. She checked her crystal was still around her neck and slowly set out along the path. Strange noises and smells surrounded the little fox, but she knew she must go forward.

Further and further into the forest she went, scrambling over rocks and twisted tree roots. Then she heard the rumbling and clapping of thunder, drawing nearer and nearer, louder and louder. 'Oh no!', thought Bright Light, 'I must find cover quickly – a storm will be here in no time at all!'

The little fox fumbled her way off the path into a deep, dark den. Cautiously, she crawled down into the hole and wrapped her bushy tail around her to keep her warm. At least in this earthen den a fox could be safe – even if she couldn't see anything. Her tummy was fluttering with fear, but she held her crystal necklace tight, and waited out the storm. After some time, she could hear that the thunder and wind had moved on, and she could smell and hear that the rain had stopped. Her sense of touch then guided her back to the path. Oh, how glad she was to have these senses!

Once out of the dark den, Bright Light noticed some moonbeams shining down through the trees, helping her to find her way forwards. She was now starting

    STORIES TO LIGHT THE NIGHT

to relax a little. The rain had smoothed the ground underfoot, and the Moon was shining brighter. She even hummed a little tune.

But as she turned another corner, the forest darkened again, and she bumped into something hard and wet. The storm must have blown a large tree across the path. There was a mountain of broken branches to climb over, but climb it she must. There was no other way.

Bright Light's senses of touch and balance came to the fore. She started the wobbly climb up the mountain of branches. They had landed in a higgledy-piggledy way, and the little fox was having to use every muscle in her body to keep herself from falling. Her sense of touch was helping her to carefully place her paws, and her balance was stopping her from falling backwards. Finally, she reached the top of the pile and sat down to catch her breath.

The moonlight was much brighter up here. Bright Light was so thankful. 'Thank you, Mother Moon, I am so grateful for your silver light.' Mother Moon smiled, glowed a little brighter, and whispered back. 'Have strength, little Bright Light, you are one smart fox. In all my millennia of being the Moon, you are one of the brightest and bravest little foxes I have ever seen.'

With the help of Mother Moon, Bright Light made her way safely down the tree mountain. She then kept following the path as it twisted and turned, leading deeper and deeper into the forest. It seemed to go on for ever.

As she walked and walked, she found herself deep in thought. She was thinking of her brothers and sisters playing so happily and carefree back at their den. Why was she the one who had to take this journey? Why couldn't she be back at home playing happily, without a care in the world?

The thoughts welled up inside her. Before long, Bright Light found herself singing her sad song:

I wish, I wish, I wish so much that my eyes were as they used to be.
I wish, I wish, I wish so much that I could find new eyes to see.
I wish I wish I wish so much, my heart is really hurting,
I wish I wish I wish so much that my heart is nearly bursting.

The tears pooled in her eyes, spilling over her cheeks and on to the crystal necklace. Feeling her tears, the crystal necklace started glowing brighter and growing warmer. The love and warmth from the crystal slowly spread through her body. As the crystal glowed, the little fox heard the Spirit of the Forest whispering to her: 'Bright Light, it's alright to cry those tears of sorrow. We have all cried them at different times in our lives. We are all on our own journey, each one so different from the other. We all must choose our own path, climb our own mountains, turn our own corners, and find ourselves. There are no highs without the lows, no ups without the downs, no light without the dark.'

Emboldened by this wisdom, Bright Light continued along the path. The crystal still felt warm around her neck as she went on her way. The forest seemed darker now than ever before, and she heard noises that were spooky and frightening... but she did not stop to listen. As fast as she could go, scrambling and sprinting around corners, she raced along the path, until suddenly she burst through into a clearing.

Once inside the clearing, the frightening noises all stopped. In fact, the little fox could hear nothing at all. The wind wasn't rustling the trees, and all the creatures were silent.

Bright Light stood still, enjoying such a peaceful place. Then she noticed a pool in the middle of the clearing, a pool that was deep and wide. Mother Moon was shining so brightly that the water in the pool was sparkling.

Drawn by the sparkles, Bright Light crept closer and closer to the pool. She reached the edge and leant down to look into the water. There, gazing back at her, were her own fox eyes.

Bright Light had never seen her own eyes before. They were beautiful, so beautiful.

Healing with Words – Poems From 'Our Kids'

By Benjamin Aukram, Austin Clark-Smith and Katie Hepton

Dr Hilton Koppe is a General Practitioner – a family physician based in the NSW Northern Rivers region on Australia's east coast.

He has developed creative writing programmes that bridge the gap between cold science and the lived human experience. His workshops have helped patients coming to terms with medical issues, and medical professionals struggling to re-find the human at their centre.

In recent years, the workshops have been adapted for use with people living with chronic and serious illness. With young patients, he emphasizes that writing should be fun. He encourages them to describe their illness with a list of single words, then write a short poem from this. Here are some examples from three young patients from a workshop with 'Our Kids' at Lismore Base Hospital, Northern NSW, Australia.

Seven-year old Benjamin Aukram has Spina Bifida. He wears splints on his legs that he calls 'Ben's boots'. Here is his poem:

It sometimes hurts

It makes me sad

It is always there

It will never go away

It won't stop me running

It won't stop me walking

It makes me strong

And it will never stop me doing anything.

Eleven-year old Austin Clark-Smith has congenital adrenal hyperplasia (CAH). Here is his poem:

> *I take my tablets day and night*
> *I sometimes feel a little different*
> *I wish it would leave me*
> *I know it makes me me*
> *I don't let it control me*
> *Because if I did, I wouldn't be me.*

Fifteen-year old Katie Hepton has a muscle disorder, and has used an electric wheelchair since she was four. Here is her poem:

> *We met 18 months after birth – he scared my parents with his growl,*
> *His grip held me like super glue – no letting go.*
> *Feeling trapped, he held me back,*
> *There was no guilt or shame – he took them – I never saw them again.*
> *Leaving me to fight for myself,*
> *Feeling trapped, he held me back,*
> *It's been 14 years now – no regret, no pain,*
> *I treat every day as if it's the last,*
> *Feeling trapped, he held me back,*
> *I have a disease, there is no cure,*
> *I have a disease, I still have hope.*

THE FROG AND THE PAIL OF CREAM

A Russian tale, retold by the author, to encourage strength and determination in fighting illness and adversity. Suitable for children and families.

There was once a frog that jumped into a pail of cream. He swam round and round, kicking and splashing, trying to find a way out. Every so often he stopped to rest. He wondered if he would ever find a way out of his predicament.

Then he started to sing as he swam. He found the singing made him stronger.

I'm a little frog, and if I stay strong,
I'll find a way out before too long!

The frog refused to give up.

He swam and swam, and sang and sang, until, without even realising it, his little feet had churned the cream into butter.

Finally, he was able to climb up on the butter and hop out – just before the milkmaid came back for her pail!

Healing Bones

By Didi Ananda Devapriya, President of the Neohumanist Education Association and AMURTEL, Romania

This story was written for the Syrian refugee children in the 'Pathways to Education' programme, whose families had fled to Lebanon because of the increasing dangers of the civil war. Football was one of the children's favourite activities in the programme, and soon, even the girls felt comfortable joining the game. The football metaphor used in this story thus reflected their passion for the game. The metaphor of an injury that suddenly disrupts life, and causes the child to fall behind his peers, was designed to reflect the situation of Syrian refugee children in the programme, whose lives had suddenly been disrupted by the war. When entering the Lebanese school system, the refugee children find themselves at a disadvantage compared to other peers, having missed months or even years of school. This can lead to them becoming targets for bullying, and they must work extra to catch up with their peers again, as Omar has had to work hard to recover his weakened muscles after the cast comes off.

This story can also be used with a child who has become temporarily immobile because of a broken ankle or leg.

Omar loved to play football! Every summer afternoon he met with friends from his neighbourhood in the field near to the village school. Nasar, Samer and Maya were his best friends, and they were always together on the same team. The four friends were the fastest runners in the neighbourhood, and when playing football it seemed as if they were connected to each other with an invisible thread. Omar could just feel their positions on the field, and knew exactly where to pass the ball.

One day when they were playing, and Samer had passed the ball to Omar, just as his foot extended to kick, Nwor and Maria reached the ball at the same time. There was a scuffle as their feet entangled and the jumbled knot of kids fell to the ground. As Omar fell underneath the pile of kids, he could feel a cracking as his right ankle gave way and twisted under him. He screamed from the sharp pain and started crying, curled up on the ground. He could not move his foot. The other children all stopped playing and gathered around him, scared. Everyone was shouting at once.

Someone ran to get the grown-ups and they soon brought him to the emergency room. His ankle was broken, and the doctor set his leg in a plaster cast.

During the first days, his ankle was very swollen and painful. Luckily, the pain soon faded, and Omar started to walk around his house with the help of crutches. Now, he missed his friends. It wasn't easy, but he was determined to visit his friends, so he hobbled carefully across the field strewn with stones to where all of the neighbourhood children gathered every day to play. He sat on a rock, warm from baking in the sun's rays all day, and leaned his crutches against them. His friends were happy to see him – and Samer came to give him a big hug. But there was a group of kids who whispered between themselves, looking in his direction and snickering. Omar couldn't hear what they were saying, but still he felt his face get hot and red. He looked away from them and focused intently on watching his friends Samer and Maya play, cheering for them.

It took almost eight weeks for his bones to heal. The cast was itchy and hot, and he couldn't wait to get it off. Time seemed to crawl by so slowly and it was boring to just sit at home when everyone else was outside playing and having fun.

At last it was time to go to the doctor and have the cast removed. The doctor used an electric saw that made the cast buzz and tickle against his skin, and then he used some scissors to snip it open. His leg felt cool and light, but he noticed that it seemed thinner than his other leg. Indeed, when he stood up to walk, the healed leg felt weak and he had to move carefully.

The doctor taught him some exercises to strengthen the muscles and get his leg to return to normal. Although the exercises were much easier than all the warm-ups Omar had been doing every day to practise for football, they felt so much harder than he expected. But Omar was determined to be able to run fast and play football again, so he kept practising and practising. Day by day, the muscles grew stronger.

Summer vacation had ended, and instead of spending long days outside playing football Omar had been practising and practising getting stronger again. Omar and all the children in the neighbourhood returned to school. After school the children gathered to play football in the field. Finally, Omar was able to join his friends, and though he couldn't yet run fast, and he was a little scared of getting hurt again, he was happy to be together with his friends. Samer and Maya had missed playing together with Omar too.

At last, the team was complete again!

THE BLACK STONE

By Andreja Krenek and Erika Katačić Kožić, storyteller, Zagreb

This story was written to help a 17-year old girl, Kristina, accept the use of a wheelchair (something she was strongly opposed to). The teenager had been diagnosed with muscular dystrophy. The typed-out story, along with an amethyst ring, was given to the girl by her mother one evening – and the next morning, the girl told her mother that she could make peace with being in the wheelchair.

Six years later, when I was back working in Zagreb, Kristina arranged to meet me to share her news of her achievements as an advocate for disability services. She was currently studying at a university in Croatia and has fought (with great success) for wheelchair access – ramps and an elevator have now been installed!

Before going to the next world, Grandmother passed a certain black stone on to her grand-daughter, saying the stone should never be separated from her hold, for it is the keeper of a great secret.

The girl took the stone. She carried it with her wherever she went. With time the stone seemed heavier and heavier... and the girl began adjusting her activities accordingly. She could not go ice-skating any more because the stone would pull her down and she would fall. Getting up would be difficult. She could not roller-skate either. Or run.... Riding her bicycle also became impossible. The girl could not go swimming by herself, for the stone would pull her to the bottom.... The steps that she climbed daily on her way to school were becoming an ever-more difficult obstacle to overcome. Almost unnoticeably, she was adjusting her normal daily routines and seemingly small activities according to the burden of her stone. The girl combed her hair differently, brushed her teeth differently, and ate differently.... She slowed her step, yet she did not give up. The girl carried the stone's weight with dignity, every single day, as her grandmother had requested.

One day, while walking slowly and with great difficulty, the girl tripped and fell. She had fallen before, but this time as she fell, the stone slipped from her hold and cracked open as it landed on the ground, revealing its brilliant purple from within, its inner colour and shine. Illuminated by the light of her stone, the girl continued her journey through life.

    STORIES TO LIGHT THE NIGHT

Copy of the letter from Kristina, who was helped by the story:

Dear Susan,

Thanks to your knowledge and assistance in writing therapeutic stories, and the workshop that Erika and my mum attended, they wrote
a beautiful story that gave me strength to go on and to lift my head
high – no matter how difficult it can be at times, to get up each day
and continue with a smile.

Each of us has some sort of stone to carry in our lives, and it is up to us
to find the beauty in our stone so we can carry it more easily and be at
peace with our destiny.

The story is special and very dear to me; it has certain elements with
which I feel a special connection.

Thank you for sharing your gift. You are a great teacher, and your workshop students write more than just stories, their stories have that special
touch not found in many stories.

Kristina Ivatović

Little Shell and the Dancing Pearls

By Saška Klemenčič, M.Sc., University Bachelor of Pedagogy and M.Sc. of Andragogy, NLP – Master Praktik and NLP coach, trainer for self-management, Slovenia

This is a story about growth through suffering many years of grief and loss. The story journey and metaphors could be of help in many difficult situations and for many different ages. Saška attended my Therapeutic Story Seminar in Llubljana, and later emailed me to say that she found the idea to use the pearl and the shell from a story exercise at the seminar with random words/symbols (see Table of Story Words for Random Story-Writing Exercise, p. 175).

In Saska's words: 'I wrote this story for myself. I cannot better describe my challenge as I did through this story. The red spot represents at least three things: my artificial eye – I lost my eye when I was three years old; my skin disease Atopic Dermatitis – which appears from time to time mostly on my face and on my hands; and my feelings of guilt, anger, shame and pain, because I trusted people who were not trustworthy. I was manipulated by them, which cost me a lot of money. Some people have told me that sometimes it is as if I was invisible... because I was.... I didn't want to open myself and risk not being accepted... and sometimes when I was giving a lecture, I was not consistent... some people said so... they looked at my spot instead of my pearl....

Now I have an answer in this story.'

Soon after she was born, a big red spot appeared on the inside and outside of Little Shell. Sometimes it grew bigger, sometimes it was smaller, but it always persisted. It was growing so noticeable that it could soon be seen by all around it, and questions were being asked about it by the other shells and sea creatures.

Because it was unusual for a shell to have such a big red spot, it was very uncomfortable for Little Shell to talk about it. Soon she figured out that the best way was for her to stay closed and somehow invisible. This way she wouldn't have to answer all the questions. Small shells have small pearls which are not as interesting as her red spot.

Therefore, Little Shell became used to staying closed. When she tried to open a little bit, she was immediately assailed with sharp stones. These small stones hurt her, and the pain bothered her for a long time. So she preferred to stay closed.

The more she grew, the more she noticed how beautiful other shells became when they opened and showed their pearls. But Little Shell stayed closed.

Sometimes she secretly admired the others. If she didn't have such a red spot, she could proudly reveal herself like they did.

One day, when there was a large gathering of all the shells, she opened a little bit in a tiny dark corner. She just wanted to see the reaction. But no one noticed her. It was like she was invisible. But still, little stones came inside her and reminded her of her pain.

She just told to herself what she couldn't tell the others. And she shaped and sharpened her little pearl, using the tiny stones. And slowly her pearl grew bigger.

One day Little Shell felt that her pearl was so big that it was painful to keep her shell closed. She felt it was time to open herself up and show the world her pearl, no matter what anyone would say. But she was scared. She was afraid of the sharp stones. Some of her wounds were still not healed. However, inside her pearl she knew there was something precious she would like to show the world.

She began to open herself from time to time. Sometimes she just peaked out a little bit of her shell. However, because the pearl was now so big, every time Little Shell opened, some of the small stones fell out and she felt much more comfortable. But because she was blinded by the sunlight shining down through the water, she would close herself down again.

Eventually there came a time when Little Shell would just open wide. She was trying to open herself wide enough so that no one would notice her spot. But it was unusual, what she was doing. The other shells and all the sea creatures started to stare at her. Beside her beautiful pearl they also saw her red spot. They didn't know where to look. Should they watch the pearl, or should they watch the spot. The more she was trying to hide the spot, the more they were looking at it. In the end it was not only the spot which was red, but all of Little Shell turned red.

One moonlit night when an ocean wave rolled her close to the beach, she heard a cry for help. She was looking around when she noticed two shells stuck between rocks. They couldn't come out. There was a tiny hole between the rocks, but they couldn't see it because they couldn't open wide enough.

The wave whispered to Little Shell that she should help them. She felt sorry for them, and without even thinking of her red spot she just opened wide. In that moment the bright moon lit up her pearl and she began to shine her pearly light across the water. Now the two shells could see the way out of the darkness. They were able to follow her pearly light. As soon as they swam from the narrow hole in the rocks back to the wide sea, they started to do a happy dance.

Meanwhile the Little Shell stared at her reflection in the water, and for the first time she could really see her pearl and her red spot. She realised that the spot was not so ugly as she thought. The red colour of the spot made the colour of the pearl even more special and unique. The pearl was so big now that it almost completely overshadowed the red spot. And what everyone could see was the beautiful pearl and only the small piece of red colour. The red spot was still there, but nobody paid attention to it. Also, the Little Shell felt at peace with it. For the first time in her life she could be open and feel good. Finally, everything seemed right.

Once back in the sea, the rescued shells opened themselves and showed their pearls toward Little Shell who had saved them. And the moonlight lit up their pearls as well. Now three pearls were shining brightly. And their light was so strong that the red spot became even paler. All the little wounds from the sharp stones began to heal.

The mighty light attracted all the other shells. One by one they opened, and their pearls started to shine brightly. The moon was watching them with a big smile on her moon face – she embraced them with her Light. The shells filled their pearls with that Light. When they were full of Light, they just threw away their casing. Now they were free to dance. All the pearls held each other's hands and danced happily.

From far away it appeared as if they were shining like a beautiful pearl necklace.

 STORIES TO LIGHT THE NIGHT

Random Story-Writing Exercise

This approach to making a story can encourage your imagination to flutter and fly, as it can help to bypass logical thinking. Randomly pick two cards (see the card-making instructions in the table below) and use these to craft a story. This can be done as a fun exercise (even a party game!). Sometimes when you feel blocked, or subjectivity is getting in the way, this exercise can help you break through.

Almost every story has a beginning (introduces the problem), a middle (wrangles with the problem) and an end (problem resolved). This is a simplistic explanation, but it can be helpful for beginning writers.

I am not suggesting this as the only way to craft a story – but you may be surprised how it can help your imaginative thinking.

The previous story, 'Little Shell and the Dancing Pearls', has been created this way. The writer was 'stuck' in her subjective connection to her situation, and the random approach helped to free her from this. She picked out two cards – 'shell' and 'pearl'.

Table of Story Words for Random Story-Writing Exercise

Make small cards with one word on each card – I have used gold card for my set. Spread all the cards upside down on a tray or table (so the words cannot be seen). Choose two cards and create a short story – add extra characters to your story if needed, but be careful not to clutter the story journey. There are empty squares for you to add your own ideas to make more cards. There could be thousands of cards, but I suggest you keep them to an 'easy to manage' number.

TREE	BELL	DOOR	PRINCE	HORSE	TEAPOT	ROPE	FLOWER
SPADE	FEATHER	CAT	MOON	POT	BEE	CAVE	CHAIR
BEAR	PATH	KEY	WAND	STICK	GRAND FATHER	NECKLACE	GRAND MOTHER
STONE	GOLD	HUT	FARMER	HAT	RING	GLOVES	DOLPHIN
CRYSTAL	BAMBOO	SHOE	BOY	SILVER	SHELL	PEARL	MIRROR
GIRL	BRIDGE	BUTTERFLY	TURTLE	RABBIT	DRUM	STAR	CASTLE
COAT	PRINCESS	BIRD	RIVER	FROG	ELEPHANT	KING	MOUNTAIN
FISH	TABLE	FOX	BOAT	LION	DANCER	QUEEN	CLOCK
BEACH	GARDEN	FIREFLY	ANT	NEST	KANGAROO	SUN	WALL
TIGER	PEACOCK	SNAKE	SCISSORS	APPLE			

7   LOSS OF PLACE

In this chapter you will find stories for children, families and communities who have lost their homes in bushfires, floods and other environmental disasters; stories for those who have had to move out of their home for various reasons; and stories for those who have had to leave their home country and settle elsewhere.

To help you find your way, I have summarized the background to each story as follows:

THE BAMBOO FAMILY – written to tell to a class of young children (4–6 years of age) after a typhoon had damaged many homes and farms (p. 178).

THE ANTS AND THE STORM – a story used with kindergarten children after an earthquake had damaged their school (p. 180).

THE RABBITS AND THE BUSH FIRE – a story for a four-year old boy whose home had been destroyed by fire (p. 182).

PRINCE CARP – a story about a warrior doll published after the 2011 tsunami in Japan (p. 184).

THE KALACHUCHI DOLL – a resilience tale for children (4–8 years of age) after loss of toys and furniture and property through natural disaster (p. 186).

THE MEMORY BLANKET – a resilience story about knitting for all ages of family and community (p. 188).

THE SONG OF LIFE AND THE SONG OF WORK – a story for all ages of family and community who have to rebuild their homes after natural disasters (p. 190).

THE FLOWERED KIMONO – a story for older children, teenagers and adults written to give hope, and to help build resilience after loss through natural disaster (p. 192).

THE MIGRATORY BIRD – a story written for refugee children to offer hope to those who had to leave their homes and travel long distances to find a new place to live (p. 195).

Two Stories for Syrian Refugee Children:
UPROOTED (p. 198) and **THE NEST BUILDERS** (p. 200) – written for refugee

families to help give optimism and hope for the future.

LINDELWE'S SONG – a story about the healing power of singing, written to honour the struggle and resilience of the peoples of South Africa during the oppression of Apartheid (p. 202).

THE LAVENDER NEST – written to give strength to an older couple facing the prospect of having to move from their dream home to a small apartment (p. 205).

THE BAMBOO FAMILY

By Aimee C. Chua, psychiatrist, Ilolio City, Philippines

This story was written to tell to a class of young children after Typhoon Yolanda struck the Philippines. Many homes were damaged, and the typhoon's widespread devastation severely affected the country's agriculture and fisheries sector.

The story was shared as a puppet show – only minimal materials were needed, and movement and song were incorporated for the children to imitate. It was told in the local dialect, so the story has local words for the kinds of rain and winds and waves.

The teacher reported that the story seemed to help reduce the children's anxiety – the children empathized with Tu, laughed, and even imitated the character in their own play.

In a little clearing near the sea grew a bamboo family with shoots and old stems living together mightily, merrily, swaying gently, eek, eek, eek in the breezes. Through sun and storm the bamboo family grew together, living happily with the small birds that built their nests among its leaves and spines, the mice that lived in a hole near its roots, the ants and bugs and little animals that sought shelter in its shade.

Tu was a young shoot in the bamboo family, bright green with some leaves and spines but quite thin. Very thin, in fact, so that his mother, Ella, named him Tu, for tukog, a coconut palm leaf midrib. Tu was often ribbed and bullied by cousins all around, jostled and elbowed when the breezes allowed. This made Tu quite sad, but Ella told Tu to just be patient and bear it. She told him that one day, with rain and sun and earth nurturing him, he too would grow tall, strong and stout like all the others.

One day, the bamboo family woke up feeling a different wind, something quite familiar because many winds visit the land where the bamboo family lived, but also something quite different. This wind made the clouds swirl high up in the sky and whipped the leaves of the plants and trees. It upset the female cousins of Tu because this particular wind made them look topsy-turvy – giving them unexpected trims and make-overs. It frightened the bugs and the little animals so that they all ran away and hid, Tu knew not where.

Whistling and whining, the wind blew and blew and blew. The waves in the sea grew from mounds into hills, and then into mountains. Then the wind brought rain, at first a drizzle, then a shower, then a deluge of water. Water from the rains and also water from the sea whose mountains wandered lost into shore.

Tu was fascinated at first, but then he became frightened and huddled close to his mother. Ella sung him a lullaby to soothe him... *ili, ili, tulog anay, ari diri imo nanay...* and he finally drifted off to sleep.... crook, crook, crook.

Many hours later Tu woke up, sleepily opening his eyes. He felt astonished as he beheld the sight in front of him. Then shock crept into his leaves and stem, as he saw some of his cousins bent and broken, uncles swept out to sea, aunts left a few feet short, and his own leaves all trimmed except for two.

Tu cried quietly, afraid of further upsetting his mother, Ella, who appeared all anxious and aquiver. But Ella felt her little shoot distressed; and so she hummed and swayed... *hmmm...* to calm herself so that Tu would cease to be afraid.

Hmmm... Tu swayed and imitated Ella. They saw the blessings in the new landscape – those uncles that were swept away would be made into houses by the people nearby, the cousins would be more flexible now, the aunts would get new leaves... what other blessings do you see?

THE ANTS AND THE STORM

In May 2008 an earthquake measuring 7.8 on the Richter scale hit Chengdu in the heart of Sichuan Province, China. A school in Chengdu suffered major structural damage, and while thankfully no adult or child in the school community was hurt by the earthquake, the school was closed for many weeks, and many families of the school lived in tents in the school ground till repairs could be made to their homes.

The kindergarten children were safely extracted from their school building, but watched the walls collapsing and experienced the ground shaking. In a storytelling training in Chengdu, I encouraged the teachers to work on the following story to help the young children understand and cope with the traumatic event. The school has a large pond in the centre of its grounds, and one of the favourite walks for the young children was exploring for insects and birds around the edge of this pond. The teachers used these ideas for their story. They felt that telling it as a simple puppet show, over and over again, helped reduce the children's anxiety about the earthquake events.

There was once a large family of ants that lived in many little grass houses near a pond. Around the pond were beautiful willow trees. The ant children played in and out of the fallen willow leaves, and the willow trees shaded the little houses. It was a good place for the ants to live.

One day, however, a big storm came across the valley and blew in the doors and windows of the grass houses. The wind was so strong that even the ground was shaking, and all the ant houses toppled down and fell into cracks in the ground.

Fortunately, the mother ants had known of the coming of this big storm. Just in time they led all their children out of their houses and down to the pond. The helping willow trees dropped many leaf boats on to the water, just near the edge of the pond. One by one all the ant families were able to cross on to the leaf boats and stay afloat on the water. The mother ants sang their children to sleep with a soothing lullaby, and they stayed safely on the leaf boats all through the night.

When they woke up the next morning the wind and rain had gone, the ground had stopped shaking and the sun was shining. The leaf boats floated back to the bank and the ants climbed back on to the ground. The mother ants then set to work busily building new houses in the grass.

Soon all was as before. The ant children played in and out of the fallen willow leaves, and the willow trees shaded the new little houses. It was a good place for the ants to live.

The Rabbits and the Bush Fire

This is a story to help sooth anxious behaviour.

BACK STORY: This story was written many years ago for a four-year old boy. One day at pre-school, a normally very settled little boy arrived like a whirlwind. Matthew proceeded to knock things over and tip things upside-down, and playtime was extremely challenging for all concerned.

His mother, while putting her son's bag into his locker, explained that the previous evening a fire in the home had burnt half their house down. Matthew and his family had escaped to the garden and watched all the bedrooms burn to the ground. His mother had tried to explain to her son that the house was covered by insurance and they would be able to rebuild soon, but of course Matthew had been deeply affected by the whole experience. That morning at school Matthews behaviour was like the flames of a fire!

Finally, it was lunchtime followed by our daily rest, and Matthew fell fast asleep, totally exhausted. While the children were resting an idea for a story came to me, a story that I thought might help Matthew understand, in a more imaginative way, the traumatic event of the previous evening.

Rabbits were Matthew's favourite animals, so I chose a rabbit family for the main characters in the story. My message, through the use of metaphor, was twofold: the rabbit children were safe, and slowly their environment was returned to normal.

This story showed the powerful effect of using an imaginative versus a rational explanation for a young child.

I waited until Matthew had woken up, and then gathered the whole group of children for a story time on the veranda, just before the arrival of the parents. Even though there was no time to 'polish' the story, it was loved by the whole group and for the next two weeks they asked to hear it again – Matthew was especially keen to hear it over and over again.

The story had a remarkable effect on Matthew. When his mother arrived to pick him up on this first day of the story, he ran to meet her at the gate and patted her on the arm and said, 'Don't worry Mummy, everything's going to be alright!'. She looked at me and said, 'What have you done, Susan?'. I suggested that she call me later that night when her children were asleep and I would tell her a story. Which I did!

There was once a mother rabbit who lived in a hole in the ground in the middle of a green grassy field. This mother had many babies, and every day the baby rabbits would enjoy playing, running and jumping in and out the long grass around the edge of their home.

One day, Mother Rabbit had to go away on a short journey. She left her babies sleeping, safe and snug in their rabbit hole, and set out across the field and along the dusty track. While she was away a bushfire started up in a nearby gully, and was given an extra push by the hot summer wind and swept across the green grassy fields.

Later that day when Mother Rabbit was travelling back home, she saw to her horror that a fire had travelled before her. The green grassy field was now blackened stubble, and the ground was too hot for Mother Rabbit to walk on. 'Were her babies still safely asleep in their home?', she wondered?

Mother Rabbit had to wait till the cool of the evening before the ground was ready to step across. In the light of the twinkling stars, she made her way carefully to the edge of her rabbit hole and peered down.

What a relief to find that her babies were still sound asleep, safe and snug in their home. Mother Rabbit was so happy. She joined her babies down in the rabbit hole and they all slept till the next morning.

Every day the little rabbits watched their green grassy playground slowly grow back. It started first with little green shoots peeping out of the blackened ground. Taller and taller the little shoots grew, until the field was full of tall green grass once again. And once again, as before, the baby rabbits would enjoy playing, running and jumping in and out the long grass around the edge of their home.

Prince Carp

This story was written for a Japanese collection of stories entitled *Stories to Grow the Hearts of Children*. It was published after the 2011 tsunami. Children and adults alike can be comforted and strengthened by the metaphorical message within this simple tale about a broken doll that is rescued from the mud and makes a new friend. An obstacle is overcome, a difficult task achieved, a character transformed.

Prince Carp was a warrior doll that used to live in a little child's bedroom. Prince Carp used to be the most admired toy of all the toys in the bedroom. He was strong and handsome, and he wore a warrior dress that was made with little pieces of metal that looked like shining fish scales.

But now things were different. When the great wave came and flooded the land, Prince Carp was washed out of the bedroom window, swirled around in a black river, then left lying in a great muddy pile of bricks and rocks and wood. One leg was ripped off, and both arms and most of his body were cracked in many places. And the warrior dress, made from shining metal scales like the carp fish, broke into a hundred pieces and was washed away.

Prince Carp did not feel like a Warrior Prince any more. For many days he lay squashed in the muddy pile, his head and one leg poking out from the mess of bricks and rocks and wood. Prince Carp thought his wonderful life had come to a terrible end.

Then one day a little boy came walking by. The little boy saw the doll sticking out of the messy pile and excitedly climbed up to pull it out of the mud. He carried it back home and washed it clean. Then, with his father's help he glued up the cracks in the arms and body.

The little boy's mother found some scraps of leather, and with needle and thread she stitched together a patchwork warrior dress, and a leather cap.

Prince Carp was not so happy with his cracked ugly body, and he was definitely not happy with his patchwork leather dress and cap. And he felt so ashamed to only have one leg – who ever heard of a one-legged warrior doll?

But the little boy didn't seem to notice that his new doll had only one leg. He didn't mind about the cracks in the arms and body. He didn't mind about the warrior dress stitched up from patches of leather.

This little boy had lost all his toys when the great wave came. This little boy was so excited to have a new toy to play with again.

When *Kodomo no hi* (Japanese Boys Festival) came around, the little boy took his new doll to the festival. He found a coloured feather in his garden, stitched it on to the doll's leather cap, and called his doll 'Prince Feather Cap'.

The warrior doll was happy to hear his new name. Over time, the name was shortened to 'Prince Cap', which sounded almost the same as the doll's original name.

Slowly Prince Cap grew used to his cracked body and patchwork leather dress. Slowly Prince Cap grew used to having only one leg.

Slowly Prince Cap grew to love his new owner, and for many years they lived happily together.

THE KALACHUCHI DOLL

This story was written for the children of the Philippines, adapted from the previous 'Prince Carp' story (p. 184). It was used by psychologists in evacuation centres after Typhoon Yolanda, together with the gift of donated second-hand dolls and stuffed toy animals. 'Kalachuchi' means 'frangipani flower'.

The story could be changed to suit other traumatic events (e.g. when property has been destroyed by a bushfire).

Kalachuchi was a princess doll that used to live in a little child's bedroom. Kalachuchi was the most adored toy of all the toys in the bedroom. She was so beautiful it seemed the sun shone out of her face, and her yellow and white dress radiated warmth and joy.

But now things were different. When the great storm came and flooded the land, Kalachuchi was washed out of the bedroom window, swirled around in a fast river, then left lying in a great muddy pile of tin and rocks and wood. One arm was ripped out of its socket, both legs were cracked in many places, and the Kalachuchi dress was now in shreds.

Kalachuchi did not feel like a princess doll any more. For many days she lay squashed in the muddy pile, her face and one arm peeking out a little from the mess of bricks and rocks and wood. Kalachuchi thought her wonderful life had come to a miserable end.

Then one day a little girl came walking by. The little girl saw the doll sticking out of the messy pile and excitedly climbed up to pull it out of the mud. She carried it back home and washed it clean. Then, with her father's help she glued up the cracks in the legs.

The little girl's mother found some scraps of cloth, and with needle and thread she stitched together a patchwork dress.

Kalachuchi was not so happy with her cracked ugly legs, and she was definitely not happy with her patchwork dress. And she felt so ashamed to only have one arm

 STORIES TO LIGHT THE NIGHT

– who ever heard of a one-arm doll?

But the little girl didn't seem to notice that her new doll had only one arm. She didn't mind about the cracks in the legs. She didn't mind about the dress stitched up from patches and rags.

This little girl had lost all her dolls when the great storm came. This little girl was so excited to have a new doll to play with again. When the Panagbenga Festival came around, the little girl took her new doll to the festival. She picked some Kalachuchi flowers to make a flower crown for the doll's head, and called her 'Kalachuchi'. Kalachuchi was delighted to hear that her new owner was calling her by her real name!

Slowly Kalachuchi grew used to her cracked legs and patchwork dress. Slowly Kalachuchi grew used to having only one arm. Slowly Kalachuchi grew to love her new owner, and for many years they lived happily together.

The Memory Blanket

By Tjenka Murray

This story was written for a class knitting project (7–8-year old children) at a school on the south coast of New South Wales, Australia. Tjenka wrote it because, in her words: 'I wanted to tell them a story about knitting that was reassuring and created an image of the craft project. I wanted the purpose of the blanket to be positive.'

Sad memories are included along with happy memories, including the recent bushfires that affected the school and wider community. The fires caused devastating loss of forests and animals and homes.

As the blanket stays with the class in the classroom for many years, it holds the memories of the class, and it can be added to each year.

An adjusted story, and a similar kind of memory blanket, could be made in family and community situations, with all ages of knitters.

In a land far away, there were two children, Saffron and Indigo. They lived in a small town, in a house on the hill.

The people of this town had a wonderful tradition; every year they would make a memory blanket during the long winter. People would sit by their fire, remembering the year and knit the squares for the new blanket. And as they knitted, they would knit in memories of the year; things not to forget, things that were special, things that were sad and things that were happy, things that were lost and things that were found... many kinds of stories of families and friends and animals and places.

When autumn came, the word went around; from mother to son, from brother to sister, and father to daughter, it was time to begin. This year two children, Indigo and Saffron, were going to learn to knit so that they could make a square for the memory blanket too.

Out came the wool and out came the knitting needles; some wool was new, and some was saved, and colours were swapped and wound and shared around.

Everyone found needles the right size; and cast on the stiches and began to knit.

And so Indigo and Saffron learnt to knit. At first, they tangled and then they dropped, then they twisted, then they stopped, and then they got it just right. They counted the stitches again and again, and soon to their delight they had finished a whole square.

As they sat knitting and talking, they knitted in their memories, and their words became patterns and their thoughts became colours, and were woven into the threads and knots, bright and strong.

Indigo knitted in the blue of the sky and the green of the hills, and Saffron knitted in the sunshine in yellow and gold. And they both made extra squares, knitting the bright red of the summer fires and the burnt colours of the forest.

They knitted and knitted. Some days the memories were sad and long, and sometimes the memories were small and funny, and they knitted them in, all the same.

Sometime near the beginning of spring, the best knitters in the town gathered up everyone's squares and began to sew them together. Stitching and sewing, they sewed this one with that, one memory next to another, one colour just right beside the other.

Indigo loved seeing the patches stitched together. She helped by laying some out, and Saffron knitted just one more square.

And so, as the first blossoms of spring marked the end of winter, the Glorious Blanket was finished. Everyone celebrated the new blanket, and the new knitters too, as there were always children like Saffron and Indigo learning to knit, and there were always people to teach them.

And so, the memory blanket's journey began, and its memories lived on in many places.

First it went to live on a cosy chair to warm and comfort those who sat there, and then ... well I wonder whom the blanket is sharing its memories with now?

Craft Activity
Here is a simple pattern from Tjenka for first-time knitters to knit squares for a blanket: You will need 6mm needles and 16 ply/bulky wool. Cast on 20 stitches, knit as many rows as needed to make a square. When there are enough squares to make a blanket the size of your choice, you can choose to either sew or crochet them together. It is also a good idea to crochet an edging to finish it off.

The Song of Life and the Song of Work

A story to help restore the song of life and the song of work. It is about birds having to rebuild nests after an environmental disaster that destroyed their trees and homes. I wrote it for a Japanese publication of resilience tales following the 2011 tsunami, and based it on the true life story of a village where only one pine tree remained. It was adapted for use by teachers and parents following the weeks of devastating fires in Australia – the storm and giant waves were changed to 'fire and smoke images' and the trees were changed to eucalyptus.

There were once two little sun birds that lived in a nest in a pine tree by the sea. One was a mother bird and one was a father bird. The little sun birds were nest builders.

Every day they kept themselves busy gathering sticks and twigs and weaving them together to make their nest warm and safe. They loved to sing as they worked. All day long they sang their nest-building song.

Sometimes a strong wind came in from the sea and blew bits of their nest all the way to the ground. Then the little sun birds had to work hard and long to repair the damage. As they worked they sang their nest-building song. Sometimes a storm cloud came down from the mountains and the heavy rain washed bits of their nest all the way to the ground. Then the little sun birds had to work hard and long to repair the damage. As they worked they sang their nest-building song. They were continually gathering, weaving and singing; gathering, weaving and singing; gathering, weaving and singing.

The little sun birds were happy with their nest-building life. And of course their nest building had an important purpose! Every spring, the warm and safe nest was the home for tiny little eggs. Every spring, tiny little sun birds hatched from the tiny little eggs. Every spring, tiny little sun birds were fed and cared for by the mother and father bird.

Then, when the little sun birds were big enough they flew off to other trees to begin their new life as nest builders, all the while singing their nest-building song.

Life went on, and after many years there were many little sun birds living contentedly in many nests in many trees by the sea.

But one day everything changed in the life of the little nest-building birds. Far out from the coast, a storm began swirling and twirling around like an angry beast, sending raging winds and giant waves towards the shore. The waves flooded the land and many trees were washed away. The wind blew so strongly that the nests left in the remaining trees were completely blown away.

Some of the little sun birds managed to fly up high in the sky to escape the flooding water. They circled and circled around until they were too tired to keep on flying. Then they flew back down to find somewhere to rest, landing in the branches of the pine tree that had stood strong through the storm. They huddled together, shivering with cold. Many of their family had gone, their homes had gone, and their song had gone.

But little birds cannot rest for long. Little birds need to fly. Little birds need to build nests. Their song had gone but the work needed to go on.

Soon the little sun birds began to fly far and wide to gather sticks and twigs. The song had gone but the work needed to go on. They worked through the autumn, they worked through the winter, they worked through the spring – gathering and weaving, gathering and weaving, gathering and weaving.

Slowly but surely many new bird nests began to fill the branches of the pine tree that stood strong. The little sun birds worked hard and long. The song had gone but the work needed to go on.

By the middle of spring, the nests were ready to be the home for tiny little eggs. The nests were safe and warm, and many tiny little sun birds hatched from many tiny little eggs. The new little sun birds were cared for by the mother birds in their warm and safe nests; and miracle of miracles, they began to sing a new song.

When the new little sun birds were big enough, they flew off to other branches of the pine tree to begin their life as nest builders. And as the new little sun birds worked, they sang a new nest-building song. And so life went on. The new little birds worked all day long, and as they worked they sang their song.

And around the strong tree, slowly, slowly, very slow, some new little pine trees began to grow. Hopefully it would not be too long before these new little trees would be strong – strong enough for many more little sun birds to build their nests while singing their nest-building song.

The Flowered Kimono

A story suitable for older children, teenagers and adults. It was written to give hope and to help strengthen resilience after the Tsunami ravaged the coast of Japan in 2011. It is included in the Japanese publication by Tokyo Shoseki of a collection of stories entitled *Stories to Grow Children's Hearts.*

It can also be used as a story for hope in times of 'tsunami waves' of grief. A colleague found great comfort in this story during a difficult divorce process. It had relevance in our challenging Covid19 time when adults were asking for resilience tales to give some hope, to offer a tiny light at the end of the tunnel. It can be read or told using a woman or a man as the tailor/seamstress.

Once upon a time there was a tailor who made the most magnificent silk kimonos in all the land. His shop was in the middle of a garden in a small village by the sea. The villagers used to say that he stitched the garden, the hills, the ocean and the sky into his fabrics, the embroidered patterns were so beautiful. People came from all over the land to buy his silken wares.

The tailor lived alone, working every day on his designs, and doing very well from his sales. But there was one kimono he would never sell. It was pale green, like the rolling hills that stretched down to the sea, and it was embroidered with every kind of flower that grew in the land. No one could persuade the tailor to part with this treasure. He hung it in his shop window in a strong frame behind the glass, for all to see but for none to buy.

For many years, life continued as normal, with the tailor working every day on new designs and new kimonos. But one day an unimaginable tragedy came to the tailor's village. Without any warning, far out from the coast the ocean reared up high like a great beast, sending a giant wave towards the shore. The great wave covered the whole village, turning all the houses and shops, and everything in them, upside down and inside out. The villagers, together with their children and their animals, were swirled around in the black mud. Some were sucked back out to sea. Some survived and some did not.

The tailor was visiting the city on this day. When he returned, all he could see was black mud and mess – he hardly knew if this was even his village, so broken and mixed up everything appeared. Then he recognized a tree from his garden, the only tree in the village that had stood strong throughout. He frantically began digging in the mud around the tree, looking for his flowered kimono. Day after day he dug, week after week he dug. He found bricks and wood, and built himself a small room to sleep in. Day after day he dug, week after week he dug, desperately looking for his precious kimono.

Eventually, in a sodden pile of mud and broken glass, wrapped round some roots of his tree, the tailor found his silken beauty, battered and beaten, ripped and torn. He laid it out on an old board that he was now using for a table. The embroidered flowers, once so vibrant and alive, could hardly be seen – the kimono was black with mud. The tailor wept and wept, bending his head in sorrow over the muddy silk.

Then something unexpected happened. The tailor's tears dropped on to the kimono and everywhere they landed a little spot of green silk began to shine through the black mud. Quickly he fetched some soap and water and began to gently rub and scrub, and after much work the kimono was clean again. But the battering of the wave had caused the threads of the embroidery to hang limp and lifeless, and there was so much mending to be done.

The tailor continued digging, looking for his spools of embroidery thread. After many more days of digging and searching he found the box of threads that he was looking for, but they too, like the kimono, were black with mud. By now the tailor was exhausted, and the thought of trying to clean all the threads was too much for him to bear. He wept and wept, ready to give up this task.

The tailor's song of sorrow was carried by the wind all the way up the valley and into the hills. Still he wept, and his song of sorrow was carried by the wind all the way over the hills and up into the mountains. Still he wept, and his song of sorrow was carried by the wind all the way into the mountains and up to the sky above.

High in the sky, hiding in the clouds the sky spirits heard the tailor's song of sorrow, and decided to come down to earth to help him. They flew down to the box of spools and pulled on the ends of each coloured thread, carrying them together up into the clouds. High into the sky the muddy threads were stretched out, like a black band from earth to heaven.

Then the sky spirits called on the cleansing rain... pitter patter, pitter patter, pitter patter. The tailor was woken out of his sorrow by the sound of the raindrops... –pitter patter,pitter patter, pitter patter. When he looked up into the sky he saw a shining rainbow of coloured threads, washed clean by the rain, stretching from heaven down to earth.

With great joy, the tailor reached up to take hold of the rainbow. He carefully began winding each colour back on to its spool, until his box was once again full of shining threads. Now he could begin the task of mending his precious kimono and embroidering new flowers into the silken green fabric.

For a year the tailor worked on this task, every day working a new petal on to a new flower. Eventually the flowered kimono was repaired and hanging once again in the window of his new little shop, in the middle of the garden in the small village by the sea.

Now the tailor was ready once again to create beautiful clothing for the people in his land – stitching patterns of the garden, the hills, the ocean and the sky into his silken kimonos.

THE MIGRATORY BIRD

By Dr Alys Mendus

This story was developed from a storytelling workshop that Alys led with a Community in Athens working for Die Freunde with the Syrian refugee children on Lesbos. She told it twice to a group of unaccompanied minors on Lesbos, 11–18 years of age.

INTRODUCTION FROM ALYS

The thinking behind this story was to give hope to those who must leave their homes and travel long distances to find a new place to live. The intention of the story was also to nourish the idea of friendship and care from those they would meet in their new home. The bird in this story only travels in one direction, mirroring the journey of many refugees. It also includes different climates, a journey over the sea (which was particularly poignant for those on Lesbos who had come from Turkey on blow-up boats) and then, with guidance from a friend, finding food, shelter and hope in a new land. It was told as a puppet show to make the lack of common language less of an issue, using simple wool-felt bird puppets and coloured cloths. At the end of the story I asked everyone to cup their hands together before the bird went around the group, giving everyone some sunflower seeds to eat.

Several members of the Die Freunde team have stayed in contact with some of the teenagers from Lesbos as they have travelled to Europe and settled in Germany and Scandinavia. Many have shared how helpful the storytelling, eurythmy, art therapy and friendship that they experienced on Lesbos were for them at such a desperate time.

Setting the scene: It is a wet afternoon and there is a clatter of chairs as the group settle in a circle around me. Syrian boys and young men housed in makeshift porta-cabins on the island of Lesbos, waiting to be escorted to Athens. They are the unaccompanied minors: the young people sent alone or with siblings to make the journey overland to Europe to gain asylum for their family. And I am at this moment the storyteller. I speak slowly as my story is being translated into Arabic....

(A yellow cloth is on the floor, a hand-made felt bird perches on the cloth.)

This is a story about a bird.

The weather was getting cooler and the bird knew it would soon be time to head to warmer climes. So it said 'goodbye' to its friends and family, and had something to eat. Then it set off on its journey, flying up high above the golden plains, soon leaving them far behind and flying over the open sea.

(I pulled back the yellow cloth to reveal blue cloth underneath.)

Up and over.

Round and down.

It wasn't long before a storm picked up which blew the bird sideways.

(I made blowing noises, and the bird visibly moved sideways.)

The bird flew out of the wind, and then the rains came.

(At this point I wafted a blue silk over the bird puppet.)

The bird flies out of the rainstorm and is now tired and hungry and a long way from home.

Despondently, the bird flies on. At the same time, a little bird is flying along and sees the larger bird and says,

'Hello Bird! Where are you going? Why are you looking so sad?'

The bird replies, 'I am tired and hungry and looking for somewhere warm to live....' 'Follow me', said the little bird.

And it did.

Up and over.

Round and down.

(I pulled away the blue cloth to reveal a green cloth below.)

Soon the green land was in view, with bushes and flowers and buzzing bees.

The birds landed.

They looked around, found some delicious food and somewhere to make a new nest.

They lived happily ever after.

NOTE FROM ALYS REGARDING THE LAST LINE

The story could easily end after the second-last line when the birds are safe and have a new home. However, at the time we really felt that we needed to give the boys some hope. In the two weeks we were there, two tried to commit suicide. They were so distraught to have got all the way to Europe then find themselves incarcerated.

CRAFT ACTIVITY

Make a bird. See Patterns and Templates, p. 282.

Two Stories for Syrian Refugee Children by Didi Ananda Devapriya, President of the Neohumanist Education Association and AMURTEL Romania

General Introduction from Didi

Both these stories, 'Uprooted' and 'The Nest Builders', were designed for Syrian refugee children whose families had fled to Lebanon because of the increasing dangers of the civil war. On their arrival in Lebanon, the families were forced to live in very crowded, uncomfortable, unhygienic conditions. Many of these families were middle-class people who owned businesses, land etc. – so finding themselves now so poor and in squalid conditions was a particularly rude shock. Some children had witnessed unspeakable horrors during bombings and military strikes. All had experienced the fears and stresses of being uprooted from their homes and finding themselves and the adults that they depend upon in very vulnerable, insecure situations.

I was invited to Lebanon to help train staff (some of whom were refugees and mothers themselves) for AMURT Lebanon's 'Pathways to Education' project that helped these children to prepare for the transition towards integration into the public school system. A healing, trauma-sensitive environment was created. Many refugee children had been out of school or never attended kindergarten or school due to the disruptions of the war and the instability and poverty of refugee life. The project allowed children to regain their childhood and access the normalizing routines and structures of a creative educational setting. I emphasized therapeutic storytelling as an important element in helping the children to integrate their experiences and begin to heal.

The metaphors were designed to give optimism and hope, and show that, with support (as that which the Pathways Programme was striving to offer), the children will be able to regain some sense of normalcy. Indeed, part of the healing effect of the stories was on those who would be providing the programme for the children, as it helped them to gain perspective on their role in supporting the children.

Uprooted

By Didi Ananda Devapriya, President of the Neohumanist Education Association
and AMURTEL, Romania

Introduction by Didi
This nature metaphor story, the transplanting of the tomato seedling, symbolizes being transplanted not only into a new country but also into the new education system. When I shared this story with the women I was training, their faces illuminated with smiles and their eyes brightened. It seemed to help them to get a perspective on their new role and new life.

A tiny tomato seed was planted in the warm, dark earth inside of a safe green house. Soon, a tiny green shoot had sprouted through the earth and began reaching up towards the sunlight. It grew, and grew.... And then one day, a shovel came, and roughly dug into the earth next to her, and in one sudden lurching movement the tomato seedling was dizzily free of its familiar bed of earth. A small chunk of earth clung to her tiny hair like roots. Several of the roots stung as they had been severed when the seedling had been torn from the ground.

The seedling was crowded into a tray with many other little plants. They could barely breathe. And then a motor hummed, and suddenly the earth was moving underneath them and rumbling and jostling. They fell over on to one another, and some of their fragile leaves snapped off.

A long time passed, and the little seedlings just waited, huddled together. Most mornings they received a brief shower of water from above. But a long time passed without water... they were so thirsty. The little plants couldn't keep growing towards the sun. They began to wilt.

Some of the leaves were turning yellow. They cried out for water – they wanted to grow again.

At last their cries were heard. A concerned voice said, 'Oh – these plants need to get into the ground!!! Who left them here?'

The little seedling again found herself moving through the air, and then she was settled into a carefully prepared hole, already soaked with water. The half-covered roots were then snugly covered up with earth. The little seedling was happy – but so exhausted that she just slumped over on to the earth. She didn't even have the strength to stand up straight – especially with the rays of sun beating down as the sun rose high into the sky.

There were other tomato plants nearby – strong and tall. They seemed to be laughing at the sadly wilted newcomers. Already they had yellow flowers brightly decorating their branches that would turn into red tomatoes in a few more weeks.

That night when the hot sun set behind the stony mountains, a cool moon rose in the sky and gently shone its healing light on the little tomato seedling. The moon told the seedling – 'You are safe now and can let your roots stretch into the ground again. I will send morning dew for you to drink and grow strong, and soon you will catch up with the other plants, and you too will have beautiful yellow flowers and lovely juicy tomatoes!'

The next morning it wasn't easy, and the little seedling had to struggle, but already she was standing up a bit straighter. The farmer came and planted a strong pole next to her and gently tied bits of string to her stem to support her to grow nice and tall. Though she was smaller than the others and had to work hard to grow, day by day the little plant was climbing higher and higher thanks to the pole. The farmer took extra care to give her steady showers of rain and a little bit of extra fertile black manure so she could catch up. Soon the tomato plant was doing what tomato plants do – stretching her leaves up to the sun and growing, growing, growing.

Before long, yellow buds unfurled on its branches. In a few more weeks, when the flowers had dried up, they left behind small, round, green knobs that began to swell every day. The green tomatoes warmed in the summer sunshine, and began blushing into red. The little tomato seedling had grown into a tall, strong tomato plant just like the other plants, and offered its juicy, sweet, red tomatoes to the farmer.

THE NEST BUILDERS

By Didi Ananda Devapriya, President of the Neohumanist Education Association and AMURTEL, Romania

INTRODUCTION BY DIDI
The metaphors used in the following story reflected the natural setting of the ancient cypress forests of the Syrian refugees' homeland. When I first told this story to the group of women that I was training to be the teachers of a Child Friendly Space, several were themselves Syrian refugees. When I was telling how the little bird family reached the city and were crowded into a dirty, narrow crack in the wall, there was an excited gasp and twittering in Arabic. One of them translated, 'It is just like our story!'. They were now all leaning forward in excited anticipation to see what would happen next. It seemed very empowering for them to have this recognition.

When I was next in Lebanon, I was happy to find out that this story had been actively used in the curriculum.

Once there was a beautiful forest, thick with ancient cedar trees whose twisting branches spread out wide, creating dense pools of cool shade on the rocky, dry earth below. There were many, many golden bellied birds living in the trees. Two birds had been busily gathering twigs from the abundant forest to build their nests and start a new family. The mother bird laid five tiny blue eggs and soon, five baby birds were born. The family was very happy, and every day just before the sunrise they sang the traditional song of the forest birds to welcome the new day and greet the rising sun.

The morning sun has risen, all the birds are singing,
Let's sing together as one and greet the newborn sun,
Sing together as one and greet the newborn sun.

Then the mother and father birds would fly off into the forest to gather cedar berries for the little ones and twigs for their nest.

One night, a crackling sound woke up the birds. The air was thick with smoke, and flames were everywhere. All the birds in the forest were flying away, and the family joined them. It was hard for the baby birds to keep up, and in the smoky air it was difficult to see. The mother and father frequently stopped to rest on a branch but only for a few minutes, because the flames were still everywhere and it wasn't safe. Finally they left the forest and entered a strange new land. There were no trees and it was night-time. The bird family were very tired from their difficult journey to escape the forest fire.

Big drops of rain started to fall from the sky. The birds could not find a tree, but they found a building with a crack in the wall just big enough for all seven to enter. It was a very small space and they had to squeeze to get inside. It was uncomfortable and dirty, but they were safe and grateful to be together.

The next morning, just before the sunrise, the bird family woke up, and as they did every morning, they went outside to sing and greet the rising sun.

The morning sun has risen, all the birds are singing,
Let's sing together as one and greet the newborn sun,
Sing together as one and greet the newborn sun.

The angels in the sky smiled, and the sun was pleased by the beautiful song of the birds, sending golden rays which dried the rain from their feathers, warming them up after the cold night. In the forest, thousands of birds sang together in chorus to greet the sun, but here, in the city, there were very few voices joining in. Still the bird family sang bravely together. They sang to the beginning of a new day. Their beautiful song woke up the little children sleeping inside the houses of the city. They ran outside to listen to the beautiful birdsong. Then they ran back inside to find some bits of bread to share with the birds so that they would stay and keep singing.

The mother and father bird then flew off to gather berries and twigs for their nest. It wasn't as easy to find twigs in the city as it had been in their lovely forest. But they kept gathering scraps and bits of twigs wherever they could find them. Soon they had enough to build another nest. It was on top of the roof of the house of some of the children they had befriended. It wasn't the same as their nest in the forest, and they missed the shady leaves and beautiful scent of cedar trees. But their new nest was clean and safe, and they were happy to be altogether. Every morning they sang their song to the sun, and the city was filled with the joyful singing of birds.

Lindelwe's Song

This is a story that I wrote many years ago about the healing power of singing. I wanted to honour the struggle and resilience of the peoples of South Africa during the oppression of Apartheid. I presented it as a gift to the women who were attending my training courses in Cape Town. Its metaphors, journey and resolution were inspired by the following comment made to me by a Xhosa friend, Nomangesi Mzamo, whose husband was incarcerated on Robben Island along with Nelson Mandela.

'Without our singing we would never have found our way through the thorns of apartheid.'

The story has since found its way into many Educare Centres and schools in the Cape Town Townships. Another Xhosa friend, Nombulelo Majesi, once described it as a healing fairy tale for the new South Africa.

For many years after this, whenever I would visit Africa I was asked for it again and again by the children and adults I met and worked with – some of the children gave me the nickname 'the pumpkin lady'. In Kenya, a group of teachers turned it into a story that was played out with the children in dance and song. In Australia it was performed at a national conference as a puppet show.

The story has had global relevance in our challenging Covid-19 time when adults were asking for resilience tales to strengthen and give hope.

The song simply means 'a golden pumpkin is sitting in the middle of a field' – you can sing it in your own language and make up your own tune.

Once upon a time, in the middle of a field next to a village, a tiny pumpkin seed started to grow. It slowly spread out its green tendrils and leaves, and very soon a pumpkin appeared in the middle of the pumpkin patch. It grew and grew and grew, until it was the biggest and most beautiful golden pumpkin that the villagers had ever seen.

But this was no ordinary pumpkin, and this was no ordinary field. Because as the pumpkin was growing, around the pumpkin patch was growing a circle hedge of thorn bushes. These bushes were thick with thorns – thorns as long as your finger and as sharp as a needle. The bushes were so close together that by the time the

STORIES TO LIGHT THE NIGHT

pumpkin was ripe and ready to be picked, no-one could get through the hedge to reach it.

The villagers had a meeting to decide what could be done. At the meeting, an old grandfather said: 'I have a sharp axe – I will try to chop down the hedge of thorns.'

The grandfather took his sharp axe and started to chop through the hedge, but every time he chopped through a branch, another one grew quickly in its place, and by the end of the day he had given up. This was no ordinary pumpkin, and this was no ordinary field.

Then one of the mothers of the village said: 'I have a strong spade – I will try to dig under the hedge of thorns.'

The mother took her spade and started to dig down, but the roots of the thorn bushes were so strong and close together that by the end of the day she too had given up. This was no ordinary pumpkin, and this was no ordinary field.

Then one of the young boys of the village said: 'I am such a good tree climber – I will try to climb over the hedge of thorns.'

The boy started to climb up the branches, but the thorns were as long and sharp as needles and they tore his clothes and pricked his skin. By the end of the day he too had given up. This was no ordinary pumpkin, and this was no ordinary field.

Then strolling into the village came Lindelwe, a young girl known to have the most beautiful voice in all the land. When she heard the problem, she walked past the villagers, sat down on a rock next to the hedge of thorns, and started to sing:

Ithanga elikulu, Ithanga elikulu; lishleli ebobeni, lishleli ebobeni.

Lindelwe's singing was so beautiful that all the animals in the surrounding fields came hopping and running to be closer to her to listen.

Ithanga elikulu, Ithanga elikulu; lishleli ebobeni, lishleli ebobeni.

Lindelwe's singing was so beautiful that the birds in the sky flew down to sit in the trees to listen.

Ithanga elikulu, Ithanga elikulu; lishleli ebobeni, lishleli ebobeni.

Lindelwe's singing was so beautiful that the worms and caterpillars crawled out of the ground to sit at her feet to listen.

Ithanga elikulu, Ithanga elikulu; lishleli ebobeni, lishleli ebobeni.

Lindelwe's singing was so beautiful that even the clouds in the sky came down low to listen.

Ithanga elikulu, Ithanga elikulu; lishleli ebobeni, lishleli ebobeni.

One little cloud came so low that it was hovering right in front of her. Lindelwe stopped singing and smiled at the watching villagers. Then she stepped into the middle of the little cloud. The cloud lifted her up, up, up and over the hedge of thorns and right down into the pumpkin patch.

Lindelwe was now able to pick the beautiful golden pumpkin. She stepped back into the cloud and it lifted her up and over the hedge of thorns and carried her all the way to the village.

The villagers then chopped and cooked the pumpkin for an enormous feast that evening.

Together they celebrated how Lindelwe, with her beautiful singing, was able to find a way over the magic hedge of thorns to pick the most wonderful, most golden pumpkin in the land.

The Lavender Nest

By Anja Jarh, teacher, Slovenia

This story was written at a seminar I ran in Ljubljana in Spring 2018. Anja's inspiration was her mother who had been fighting cancer since she was 27 years old. She was never happy where she used to live, and she and Anja's father, after many years of searching, had built themselves a beautiful home with a magnificent view over the green landscape below, stretching all the way to the Alps. But they didn't live happily here for very long. They soon found out that their house was to be pulled down due to the new highway that was going to be built there, and they would have to relocate. This was devastating news, and the mother's health again started to deteriorate.

Anja chose the stork as the main character of this story for various reasons. The stork is known to 'bring babies' – her mother keeps saying that her grandson (Anja's son) is her best medicine. There is a stork family living in the village where the parents live.

Her mother is also devoted to gardening and making everything look neat and orderly around and in the house. She carefully chooses the spot for every plant and flower. There are many shrubs of lavender around the house.

Anja writes: 'The first reaction, after reading the story, was mostly silence, but the only comment of my parents was that "they are not this stork and they will do everything in their power for the house to stay where it is now". They do not read the story often, but I wove them a small lavender nest with a clay house inside, and this is sitting on their table in the dining room. Their visitors ask them about it, and they proudly tell them the stork story which usually moves and fascinates the guests. There are people among them who might lose their own house if the new highway is built there.

This story, first of all, was therapeutic for me, as I was emotionally involved in the events revolving around it. But I also noticed a change in my mother, who has somehow accepted the possibility that she might have to move again. My parents are now searching for a new place, and they aren't so sad any more.'

On the highest chimney, high up above all the roofs, a stork was building a nest and enjoying the beautiful view over the sunlit landscape from her home. The nest was very special – different from the others and admirable. The stork placed each twig carefully on a very specific place of the nest. Everyone who saw it was thrilled about this stork and her work. How skilfully she was building the home for her family!

But on a stormy night the strong wind uncovered all the roofs of the village houses and destroyed all the chimneys. The sight of the village in the morning was really devastating. Each and every nest was destroyed. The storks cried from worry, but then gathered in a flock and flew up into the empty sky. They didn't know where the wind was going to take them. They flew and flew, looking at parts of the landscape they had never noticed before, even though they had flown past them many times in the past. The wind took them far and about the landscape.

They flew here and there. Eventually they landed one evening on the edge of a forest on an old farm. They intended to spend the night there, and a mighty tree gave them shelter. When they woke up in the morning, they enjoyed the magnificent view over the green landscape. The sun glittered in a clear river that flowed merrily among the blossoming meadows, and the birds joyfully trilled their most beautiful songs. At this sight, the storks looked at each other. They knew right away that they would be able to build their nests here even more beautiful than those they had before.

This time the nests were made even stronger and with loving care. The stork that had built her home on the highest chimney now wove her new nest out of lavender twigs, which made it special. With its smell the lavender attracted admiring attention and the stork was thus even prouder of the nest she built for her loved ones.

CRAFT ACTIVITY
Thoughts from Anja: I wrote the story by hand on a piece of paper and drew some lavender in bloom next to it. Out of thick hemp thread I crocheted (interlaced the thread into) a small nest and stuck a few twigs of dried lavender into it. Into the nest I put a small clay house with the words 'flowers grow after rain' written on it.

8 ENVIRONMENTAL GRIEF AND LOSS

There are eight stories in this chapter covering different environmental themes – all can be used with children, teenagers and adults as a springboard for family and school discussions, and community projects.

Six of the stories have journeys that begin with greed and/or lack of caring, and end on hopeful tones of sharing and caring:

THE TREE OF LIGHT (p. 208).
THE PEACOCK'S FEATHER (p. 217).
THE SHADOW GIANT (p. 222).
THE LIGHT OF LIFE (p. 225).
GRANDMOTHER AND THE DONKEY (p. 229).
THE MULBERRY TREE (p. 232).

The other two stories, **MESSAGES IN THE SAND** (p. 214) and **THE SWAN'S SONG** (p. 227), explore the drastic situation of ocean pollution and loss of species, and end with just a hint of a possibility, in the hope that the message will be heard and acted upon.

THE TREE OF LIGHT

This rhyming story has metamorphosed from the original text version, 'Garden of Light', published in my first book, *Healing Stories for Challenging Behaviour*. Over the years many versions of the original story have had global reach – it has been made into a puppet show by the musical Department of the University of Manila, using waist-high puppets. It has been turned into a musical play by V- Excel Educational Trust, performed by high-school students in India.

More recently, an updated version has been used by an environment movement in Europe called BROZ, an NGO active in nature conservation in Slovakia and Austria (https://broz.sk/), beautifully illustrated by a Slovakian artist called Simoonka for conservation brochures and conservation park billboards.

The main difference in this version is that King-Didn't-Care doesn't die, but, with the help of the Nature-Weaver and many little children, transforms into King Care.

I think it is one of the most important stories I have written.

There was once a beautiful garden that stretched far and wide,
From the valleys to the plains, from the hills to the seaside.
In this beautiful garden lived every bird, every butterfly, every bee,
In this beautiful garden grew every flower, every plant, every tree.
In this beautiful garden all the children loved to play,
And they were healthy and happy playing all day.

In the middle of the garden, spreading branches oh so old,
Was a great and wondrous tree with leaves of shining gold.
Deep amongst its roots lived a Nature-Weaver sprite
Who cared for the garden and the golden Tree of Light.

The Nature-Weaver wove her nature threads each day,
In and out the garden and around the children's play.
In and out the roots and around the shining tree,
In and out the flowers and the children dancing free.

As long as the Nature-Weaver wove her loving spell,
Across the wide land, all was happy and well.
The tree shone its golden light every day,
And the children had somewhere beautiful to play.

One day, it happened, a new King took over the land.
This new King thought he was so very GRAND!
He didn't care about flowers and plants and trees.
He didn't care about birds and butterflies and bees.
He didn't care if the children had beauty in their play,
Or if they were healthy and happy every day.

His name was King-Didn't-Care – although he did care about himself!
And for himself he wanted treasures, wealth, and much more wealth.
King-Didn't-Care only knew one thing that gave him delight –
Gold, silver and jewels, sparkling and bright.
He ordered his servants to dig deep mining ditches,
And build a grand castle to store all his riches.

Slowly, slowly, the garden was chopped down,
To dig more treasures for the King's crown.
After a long time of digging for riches galore,
The beautiful garden was........ NO MORE!

There were no more flowers and plants and trees.
There were no more birds and butterflies and bees.
There was nowhere beautiful for the children to play,
To keep them happy and healthy every day.

Without the garden and without the children's play,
The Nature-Weaver couldn't weave her dance each day.
The once-golden tree turned a very dullish grey,
And the children puzzled how things had turned this way.

The garden was forgotten as the many years passed by.
The children played on bare ground under a sorry sky.
King-Didn't-Care didn't care that the garden was gone.
He spent time in his castle all the day long.
Counting treasures is what gave him delight –
Gold, silver and jewels – sparkling and bright!

But one day, the King looked out and was shocked to see
In the far distance, the dying grey tree.
'What an ugly sight',
he said, with a fright,
'This dull grey tree I must try to hide –
It makes me feel *uncomfortable* inside'.

The servants set to work building a wall so high,
Around the ugly tree, under the sombre sky.
The wall had no windows, the wall had no door.
The King was pleased – he couldn't see the tree any more!

No one could get inside – no one could get through,
And the Nature-Weaver didn't know what next to do.
She sat amongst the tree roots, alone in her room,
And remembered the garden that once used to bloom.

On the night after the wall was complete,
King-Didn't-Care struggled to settle into sleep.
Next morning in his mirror he saw that he was grey,
The grey of the clouds on a dark stormy day.

   STORIES TO LIGHT THE NIGHT

At the sight of the King the servants were appalled,
Many doctors in the land were urgently called.
They tried many herbs and potions and pills,
They had never seen anyone quite so ill.
King-Didn't-Care seemed to be fading away,
Growing greyer and paler by the day.

At this time... one may ponder why,
A crack appeared in the stone wall so high.
This crack was very small, hardly noticed at all,
But playing close by was a child... also very small.

The child seemed to know exactly what to do,
He went up to the crack and squeezed right through.
On the other side he saw the tree that was dying,
And amongst the tree roots he heard a soft sighing.

When the Nature-Weaver saw him, her smile was so bright,
It lit up the tree roots with golden light.
'Come closer', she whispered, 'dear child, be bold,
I have a story that longs to be told.'

The Nature-Weaver told of the flowers and trees,
She told of the birds and butterflies and bees.
She told of the dance she would weave each day,
In and out the garden and the children's play.
She told of the tree that shone golden bright,
She told of the children so happy in its light.

The little child's eyes, in wonder, grew wide.
'We must bring back the beautiful garden', he cried.
'We must bring back the life to the great grey tree
So it can light up our land and shine on you and me.'

'There is surely a way', the Nature-Weaver sighed,
'But I am too old, and I am too tired.
This task is too great for me by myself,
I will need many children to give their strong help.
Go back through the wall, gather all that you can find –
I hope you've come in time; I do hope you've come in time!'

The boy squeezed out through the crack in the wall,
And called for the children, one and all.
Girls and boys together followed him back
To the high wall, then squeezed through the crack.
The Nature-Weaver welcomed them all with glee
As they gathered around the dying grey tree.

The Nature-Weaver picked up a box from her shelf,
'These are my treasures, I collected them myself.
They are from the garden before it was chopped down,
Thousands of seeds – white, red, black and brown.'
The children peered into the box, so excited!
The Nature-Weaver saw their bright eyes, so delighted.
She taught them how to plant all the different seeds,
And how to tend to each seed's special needs.

Each day they came back through the crack in the wall
And helped with the new garden, one and all.
Soon new plants began to grow with their care,
And bees and butterflies danced in the air.

When the grasses were tall and the plants were in bloom,
The Nature-Weaver could now dance out from her room.
Once again, she could weave her loving spell each day
In and out the garden and around the children's play.
In and out the roots and around the special tree,
In and out the flowers and the children laughing free.

As the Nature-Weaver danced, the tree shone sparkling bright,
It flooded the new garden with warm and golden light.
Its roots grew deep and strong and spread under the wall,
Cracking the stones and causing the wall to....... FALL!

The Tree of Light shone its gold across the land.
Its sparkle reached the windows of the castle so grand.
The King arose and bathed in the light,
And rejoiced in this gift of gold so bright.

He danced out of the castle, he danced to the tree,
He joined hands with the children, happy and free.
The garden nursed him back to good health –
At last he knew the *real* meaning of wealth.

Today the Nature-Weaver weaves her magic spell,
And once more, as before, all is happy and well.
The wondrous tree shines its golden light each day,
And the children have somewhere beautiful to play.
'King Care' is the new name given to the King,
And of his good deeds the children love to sing.

They sing of the garden that stretches far and wide,
From the valleys to the plains, from the hills to the seaside.
They sing of the birds, the butterflies, the bees,
They sing of the flowers, the plants, and the trees.
They sing of the dance of the Nature-Weaver Sprite
And they sing of the wonder of the golden Tree of Light.

Messages in the Sand

An environmental story dedicated to
the saving of our oceans.

For a long time, a strange monster had been growing in the waters of the ocean. However, because it was hidden below the water, the people who lived on the land didn't know about its size and hideous potential.

The monster had grown so large it now had more than a thousand arms... and at the end of each arm were more than a thousand hands with many (too many to count) fingers... creepy, crawly, slippery, slimy fingers.

The monster didn't have a face, and it didn't have a nose or eyes or ears – but at the end of each finger was a mouth... it is difficult to imagine just how many thousands of mouths! And every mouth was hungry – hungry for anything and everything – from rubbishy bits of plastic, to scraps of metal, to dirty oil and chemical concoctions. How the monster loved chemical concoctions of any kind!

The monster had grown so large that its more than a thousand arms had entirely surrounded the land. They were now reaching into ports and harbours, and up rivers and streams. In fact, there was hardly a watery realm that didn't have a part of this creature living within it.

And with every year this hideous 'thing' continued to grow. But the people carried on with their everyday lives, unaware of this creature taking over their beloved waters.

Eventually there came a time when the monster had grown so big that it could no longer hide its horrible form below the water. Slowly, very slowly, parts of its revolting shape began to poke out. Creepy, crawly, slippery, slimy fingers began to reach up and out and everywhere.

People were shocked at what they were seeing. Could this be real? Why hadn't they noticed it before?

 STORIES TO LIGHT THE NIGHT

They gathered in huddles along the shore. They gathered in huddles around the ports. They gathered in huddles up and down the rivers. 'Something must be done', they said, and they looked to the *Leader* for help. 'Kill the monster', they cried, begging the *Leader* to do something about it.

The *Leader* called in the *experts*. After much considering and consulting, an outcome was reached – the Monster must be captured, and if it couldn't be captured it must be killed. The people of the land were happy with this decision... anything to help the ocean and waterways return to their safe and peaceful state.

The *Leader* called on the *Navy*, and the people watched proudly as the *Navy* sent out boats with nets and ropes. But this was an impossible task. How do you net a monster with more than a thousand arms? How do you tie up a monster with more than a million fingers?

Meanwhile the monster had a wonderful feed of the nets and ropes.

Then the Navy sent out boats with guns, many guns. What a shock to discover that every time the guns fired bullets, no matter what size, the monster seemed to swallow them like snacks. The boats returned to stock up on different weapons – knives, spears and harpoons. But to the monster this was a feast, and it seemed that this creature had an insatiable appetite.

The people of the land were in shock.... The *Leader* couldn't do anything to solve this terrible situation. What kind of a 'thing' was this that could make a meal of all kinds of weapons?

Meanwhile, in a cave in a very deep part of the sea, Great-Grandmother Turtle woke from her dreaming and straight into a nightmare. The water above was filled with slimy darkness. The sunshine that usually stretched down to touch her with its golden rays was completely blocked out.

Great-Grandmother Turtle knew she had to do something. She had lived way back in the time before the monster had existed, and for years had been witness to its horrible growth. And now that the sunlight had gone, not another moment could be lost.

She sent out a message to all her children and grandchildren and great-grandchildren. Her message travelled across the ocean and into the ports and up and down the waterways. It was whispered by the swaying seaweed, it was passed from small fish to large fish, it was carried by the ocean currents.

Her message reached thousands of turtles, young and old, small and large. After listening to her wise words, they set out on the task – each one swimming towards different beaches at the edges of the land, around the harbours and along the rivers.

In the message the turtles were taught six human words by Great-Grandmother and a special way to deliver them to the people on the land.

In the quiet of the night, and at the lowest point of the tide, every turtle, young and old, large and small, swam to shore. On every sandy beach and every sandy river flat, each turtle set to work. With their strong flippers pushing them forwards and backwards, illuminated by the soft and silvery moon, they slowly but surely wrote these words in the sand:

LOVE THE OCEAN

The next morning, as the sun rose across the land its golden light shone on the letters with hope and promise. The families who lived close to the beaches and the rivers came down to walk and play on the sand. They saw the writing and they were filled with wonder. The children skipped around and jumped up and down the lines and curves. They lay down and felt the warm shapes on their skin. They decorated each letter with shells and pebbles. They put their ears to the sand and heard the wisdom.

Then the tide came in and washed the message away.

The next night the turtles once again came up on the sandy beaches and sandy river flats and set to work. With their strong flippers pushing them forwards and backwards, illuminated by the soft and silvery moon, they slowly but surely wrote new words in the sand:

STARVE THE MONSTER

Once again, the next morning the message was seen by those who came down to walk and play. They saw the writing and they were filled with wonder. The children skipped around and jumped up and down the lines and curves. They lay down and felt the warm shapes on the skin. They decorated each letter with shells and pebbles. They put their ears to the sand and heard the wisdom.

Then the tide came in and washed the message away.

THE PEACOCK'S FEATHER

This environmental story was inspired by a recent visit to Rajasthan, India. I was privileged to have a peacock cross my path while on a walk through a sunlit forest. Its beauty took my breath away!

The story addresses the theme of 'loss from taking too much' – the unsustainability of not allowing time for regrowth and regeneration. The gardener in the story has been given the name Rusa, in honour of a wise female Vaidya (Hindi for 'doctor') who lived in the eighth century, in a time where female doctors were almost non-existent. The word 'Maharaja' in Hindi means 'Super King'; the title 'Rajkumar Prithvi' means 'Prince of the Earth'.

The final crafting of this story, including the addition of the Hindi lullaby, was a special collaboration with Ameen Haque, the founder of 'Story-wallahs', a group of storytellers in India who work with teachers, parents and counsellors, and who also specialize in telling stories to children – 'wallah' means folk or people.

For those interested in finding similar stories in existing folk literature on the consequences of greed, I suggest you look up 'Reaching for the Moon' (a Nigerian folktale); 'The Golden Goose' (The Jataka version, not the Grimm's version); and 'The Glass Cupboard' by Terry Jones.

There once lived a Peacock who was known far and wide for being the most precious and magnificent Peacock in the land. In fact, it was said that the jewelled colours in his beautiful tail feathers held the secrets of the rainbow itself.

The Peacock lived in the garden of the Maharaja's palace. He was well looked after, and fed many kinds of delicious food. Every night he was led inside to sleep in the corner of the Maharaja's room. His bed was in a large wicker cage lined with silken velvet cushions.

The Maharaja was very proud of his magnificent Peacock and liked to show off his beauty. Whenever there was a special occasion the Maharaja would use tail feathers from the Peacock for his costume, and more feathers for the decorations at the festivities. When an important visitor came to his palace the Maharaja would give some of the jewelled feathers as a gift. One year the Maharaja demanded many feathers from the Peacock's tail to adorn the back of his new golden throne.

His advisers warned him against using so many of the Peacock's feathers. But the Maharaja would laugh and say, 'Don't you know that Peacocks can always grow more feathers?'.

Rajkumar Prithvi, the Maharaja's son and heir, who had known and loved the Peacock as a friend since he was a young boy, pleaded with his father to stop taking so many of the feathers. But the Maharaja would scoff and say, 'Don't you know that Peacocks can always grow more feathers?'.

For many years, the Peacock continued to please his master. The Maharaja would demand more and more of the rainbow-coloured feathers, and for many years the Peacock would grow new feathers to replace them.

However, the day came when there were no more feathers left in the Peacock's tail and the Peacock was too exhausted to grow any more. When this was known by the Maharaja, he quickly grew angry. So, the Peacock stayed in his softly cushioned cage and refused to come out.

Many weeks passed and still the Peacock had not come out of his cage, nor had he grown any new feathers. The Maharaja became more and more angry and impatient. One day he picked up the wicker cage and carried it outside his bedroom to the top of the Palace wall. 'If you can't give me beautiful feathers you are of no use any more', he shouted. Then he flung the cage, with the Peacock inside, right off the top of the wall and walked back to his room.

This cruel act was seen by Rusa, one of the palace gardeners. She was watering some pots of flowers close to the edge of the wall. Rusa had always been very fond of the Peacock, and was shocked to see him treated in this way.

That night under cover of darkness, Rusa crept out of the palace gates and followed a path that wound beside the high wall. Moving slowly forward she used her hands to guide her way. Eventually she felt the top of the wicker cage. Then she heard a faint whimpering noise, and was relieved to know that the Peacock was still alive. The silken velvet cushions must have protected him in the fall.

Whispering words of comfort, Rusa carefully reached into the cage, lifted out the trembling Peacock and wrapped him in the long folds of her sari. Carrying him against her chest, she slowly retraced her steps along the path by the wall and back through the Palace gate.

Rusa's little hut was in the far corner of the Palace gardens, and it took quite some time for her to make her way there, unseen by the Palace guards. When she was safely inside and her door was bolted, she lay the Peacock on her bed and covered him with a soft rajaee to keep him warm. Then she lit a fire and placed a pot of water on a hook over the fireplace.

 STORIES TO LIGHT THE NIGHT

Now it was time for Rusa to use her healing skills. She set to work, chopping different herbs, leaves and roots to put in the pot to simmer. While the plant broth was cooking, she took a jar of healing ointment over to her bed. She uncovered the Peacock and began to gently massage the ointment into his cuts and bruises, all the while singing to him:

Tham ja re Tham ja, thodi der so ja, Bahut door jaana hai, thoda sa tham ja,
Pause my friend, pause, rest for a while, You have to go really far, rest for a while
Ye raat dhalegi, savera hi hoga,
Savere talak mere raja tu so ja.
This night shall pass, and a new dawn will break,
So, my friend, rest till the sun rises again.

Very soon the soup was ready and Rusa managed to feed the Peacock a few spoonsful of the healing broth. Then she lay down on the bed next to him, cradling him in her arms, and very soon they were both fast asleep.

The next morning, after feeding the Peacock more spoons of soup and tending to his wounds, Rusa left him sleeping in her bed and set out to do her day's work. She bolted the door behind her and joined the other gardeners. They were talking in hushed tones.... 'Did you hear the Maharaja threw his beloved Peacock off the wall! Did you know that the cage was found this morning and it was empty! Perhaps the Peacock was taken by a wild animal? See how upset the Rajkumar Prithvi is, moping around the garden, missing his friend so much.'

With an inner smile Rusa kept on with her gardening. She knew that the Peacock's life depended on her not telling anyone her secret, even though she longed to share it. She felt a special affection for Rajkumar Prithvi, and knew how relieved he would be if he knew the truth, but she could not take any chances. The Peacock's safety and well-being had to come first.

Every evening, once she was safely back inside her hut Rusa fed the Peacock more of her healing broth, and after a few days he was also nibbling on some finely chopped pieces of fruit and vegetables. She continued with her treatments, and slowly, slowly, the cuts and bruises healed.

Within a month, the Peacock had fully regained his strength and Rusa began to see signs of new tail feathers growing. She was so happy. But she was also concerned. She knew the time had come for her to move the Peacock out of her hut. She had to shift him before the feathers grew any longer or she would not be able to hide him in her sari as she had done before.

The next night, when the moon was half a circle in the sky, Rusa wrapped the

Peacock in the folds of her sari and held him firmly against her chest. She unbolted her door and slowly made her way across the Palace gardens and out the palace gate, safely avoiding the guards on duty. With the silver moon lighting the way, she followed the road away from the Palace, across the river and into the forest.

Once in the forest Rusa followed a little path until she could hardly see her way forward. She stopped near a tree with wide branches and a friendly shape. With a gentle kiss goodbye, she lifted the Peacock up to roost on one of the branches. Then, with tears in her eyes, she hurried back home.

Time passed. There was not a day when Rusa didn't wonder about the Peacock. She knew she had done the right thing to return him to the forest, so she just had to trust that all was well with him in his natural home.

By now the Maharaja was growing too old to rule, and he had requested for his son, Rajkumar Prithvi, to take his place. Grand festivities were planned for the coronation.

Rajkumar Prithvi wanted to give his father a special gift on the day of his crowning. After much thought, he had decided to build him a cool and shady garden to enjoy in his older years. As many new plants were needed for this, he called Rusa and some of the other gardeners to join him on an expedition to the forest. They loaded small carts with gardening tools and empty pots, then hitched them to donkeys. Off they set, out through the Palace gates, across the river and into the forest. Rajkumar Prithvi slowly rode in front, stopping his horse every so often to point out plants and little trees for the gardeners to dig up and put in the pots.

Once the carts were full, they stopped by a stream for the donkeys to have a rest and a drink. Rajkumar Prithvi, being a very kind young man, happily shared his princely feast with the gardeners. They sat together in a clearing near to the stream, under a tree that had wide branches and a friendly shape.

Rusa finished her meal quickly, then stood up and looked around. She sensed the Peacock may be close by, and she wanted to warn him to stay hidden.

Suddenly, to the surprise of everyone looking on, a most unusual sight happened. A magnificent Peacock came strutting out of the forest and up to Rusa. He slowly walked around her, nudging his head against the skirts of her sari. Rusa was so happy to see him she forgot her fears. She bent down and gently rubbed her hands over his body in a warm and joyous greeting.

After a few minutes the Peacock stepped out into a place on the grass where the sunlight was shining in golden rays down through the forest canopy. He turned full circle, fanning his tail to reveal a most beautiful display of rainbow jewelled feathers. Then, in a flash of colour, he disappeared into the thick forest.

Rajkumar Prithvi had been watching all this – the loving connection between

Rusa and the Peacock, and the Peacock's fan of coloured feathers sparkling in the sunlight. It was the most beautiful sight he had ever seen, and he was sure that this was the Peacock that used to live in his Palace. How happy he was to know that his childhood friend was not only still alive but looking stronger and more beautiful than ever before.

In this instant Rajkumar Prithvi realised how special it was that the Peacock was now back in his natural home. He walked across to Rusa and embraced her with love and gratitude.

'I make this promise, to you and all who live in my kingdom, that after my coronation, I will declare this forest as a protected place. It is my heartfelt wish that the Peacock can live here with no fear of harm.'

Rusa beamed an inner and outer smile. Then she looked down and saw, lying on the grass, a beautiful tail feather.

She picked it up and handed it to Rajkumar Prithvi.

'The Peacock has left you a coronation gift', she said: 'May it guide you to rule wisely and fairly for the rest of your days.'

THE SHADOW GIANT

An Environmental Fairy Tale written to address greed and power.

'GREED IS MY GAME AND POWER IS MY NAME'

Once upon a time, in the not-so-distant past, there lived a Giant. This giant was the strongest, largest and most destructive creature ever to have lived on the earth.

The mysterious thing was that no-one had ever seen this giant, but many had experienced its dark shadow as it travelled around the world, leaving destruction behind it wherever it went. The people called it the Shadow Giant.

The Shadow Giant was continually busy, day and night, night and day, moving backwards and forwards, stamping its dark presence on the earth, in the ocean and in the air... deep black cracks in the ground, engulfing waves of black water and mud on the coastlines, burnt and blackened forests in the valleys and the mountains, and swirling masses of polluting fog everywhere.

No-one knew where the Shadow Giant came from and where it lived. And no-one knew when and where it would next use its dark force.

Nothing was safe from this Giant – not the peoples of the world, nor the animals of the land, nor the creatures of the sea. All were vulnerable to its power. Even the birds, who usually could fly fast enough to escape its path of destruction, were slowly being affected by the swirling black fog that was spreading through the air.

The Queen of the Heavens, who lived high up in her Silver Castle above the clouds, was hearing news of these terrible events from her feathered messengers, the birds. She was growing more and more concerned about this Shadow Giant and the evil work it was doing on the earth below. She decided to call a meeting, and sent out an invitation to all the birds around the world.

On the day of the meeting, the Queen of the Heavens was seated on her silver throne, resplendent in her flowing rainbow gown. All around her were gathered many birds – birds from every part of the world, birds of all colours and shapes and sizes, birds of the land and birds of the sea, birds of the day and birds of the night.

Patiently and intently the Queen of the Heavens listened to each and every bird – between them they had seen every kind of destruction caused by this Shadow Giant. When all the stories had been told, the Queen spoke to the gathering:

> There must be a way to overcome this dark force that is taking over the earth. Every enemy has a weakness! Fly back to where you have come from and try to find where this Shadow Giant lives – then you can observe what the weakness of this creature could be. Report back to me as soon as you can.... I don't think we have much time!

The birds flew back to their homes around the world and kept a vigilant watch on the Giant's path of destruction, trying as much as they could to track down where it lived. Days passed, weeks passed, months passed.

When it was almost a year since the birds had been sent on their quest, an old owl finally found the answer the Queen was looking for. He had flown into a deep mountain cave, searching for something to eat, following a rock tunnel which led into an expansive cavern.

Inside this cavern was a huge, dark, mumbling, rumbling figure. It was of no definite shape – in fact its shape seemed to change size and form with every sound it made. Sometimes it filled most of the cavern like a giant squid with many writhing tentacles; other times it turned into a monstrous, bear-like figure and stamped angrily around the room.

The owl hid in a far corner of the cavern and watched and listened, as owls can do very well. After a while he began to make some sense of the mumblings and rumblings, as they seemed to be chanted over and over again.

> *All for me and me for all, devouring all things big and small,*
> *Greed is my game and Power is my name.*

Finally, the hideous dark creature curled itself into a large ball and fell asleep. The owl quickly and quietly flew out of the deep cave. Then he began the long journey across the sky, all the way to the castle of the Queen of the Heavens. As he flew higher and higher, he kept chanting the awful mumbling rumblings so he would not forget them.

> *All for me and me for all, devouring all things big and small,*
> *Greed is my game and Power is my name.*

When the Queen of the Heavens heard the story of the Owl's experience, she had no doubt that the Owl had found the home of the Shadow Giant. And when she heard the mumbling rumbling chant, she immediately recognized the Giant's weakness:

The Shadow Giant only cares for itself – it only wants power for itself!

Then the Queen of the Heavens called for her feathered helpers. 'Fly out around the world and sing this message to the people. If they work together and care for each other, then they can slowly but surely overcome this dark shadow that is affecting the earth.'

Strength in caring, strength in togetherness can overcome the giant's selfishness.

The birds flew out to all parts of the world, birds of all colours and shapes and sizes, birds of the land and birds of the sea, birds of the day and birds of the night. And as they flew, they sang the message from the Queen of the Heavens for all on the earth to hear.

And to this day, the birds are still singing their song. Sometimes they even drop feather messages which flutter softly to the ground. When the people find these beautiful feathers lying on the ground... in the garden, on the street, in the forest and on the beach... they know that this message has been sent directly to them. They pick up the feathers, they wonder at their form and beauty, and they remember the message that has been sent to them by the Queen of the Heavens.

Strength in caring, strength in togetherness!

And slowly but surely, the wisdom of the *Song of the Birds* is helping the people of the world to overcome the dark power of the Shadow Giant.

THE LIGHT OF LIFE

This story was written for a Japanese collection of resilience tales entitled *Stories to Grow the Hearts of Children*, published after the 2011 tsunami. It aimed to address both the shame and the selfishness that can happen after environmental disasters (to some of those not affected by misfortune).

There was once a town that was nestled around a cove by the sea. In this town were many homes, and in every home there was a shining lantern. The shining lantern in each home shone on the family that lived there, and the lantern light helped everyone grow wise and strong. Golden like the sun, it sparkled by day. Like the twinkling stars, it sparkled by night. For many years, the lantern lights sparkled in every home, and all was well in the town.

But one day a giant monster came in from the sea, dragging behind it a very dark bag. This monster hated anything that sparkled or shone. It hated anything with shining lights. Its plan was to capture all the lanterns and take them away in its dark bag. The monster worked quickly and ruthlessly as it swept across the town. It reached into the homes, stole the sparkling lanterns, and put them in its bag. Then, carrying a very full, very heavy bag, the monster retreated to the sea.

The town was left in darkness and sorrow. At first it seemed that the monster had taken every lantern from every home. Without the lantern lights, how could life possibly go on?

But slowly, some tiny lights began to twinkle in a few houses scattered around the dark cove. Fortunately, in its haste the monster had missed these homes and each of their lanterns.

A meeting was held in the town square. The folk who still lived in homes with lanterns gathered together. They agreed that they, as the fortunate ones, must find a way to spread their lights across the rest of the town and share them with everyone. They wanted to help the others who were living in darkness and sorrow. They knew that their lights could help find a way forward.

The fortunate ones travelled up and down the dark streets, taking their lanterns with them to show the way for others. Then they returned to their homes and opened wide their windows and doors so that the lantern lights could shine out across the town.

But there were some fortunate ones who didn't come to this meeting. Instead they drew their curtains and tightly closed their doors, and kept their lantern lights hidden. They were heavy with shame – why was their home not touched by this terrible monster that had done such damage elsewhere across their town; why was their home still lucky to have its lantern light while others were in darkness? They kept their windows and doors closed, stayed inside their homes with their families, and refused to come out.

Days passed, weeks passed, months passed. While some folk were busy finding ways to share their lights, some were still hiding inside their homes, hiding their lights.

Autumn winds began to blow, and after this a long winter gripped the land in its icy fingers. Then came the hope of spring!

Birds sang, bees buzzed, butterflies fluttered, new flowers opened. The warm sun shone down on the homes with closed windows and doors.

The children in the closed-up homes felt the warmth of the spring sun calling them, and they couldn't accept being inside one more day. They flung open the curtains and burst open the doors, and they tumbled out into the streets to play.

From this day forward, thanks to the children the lantern lights in the closed-up homes now shone out of all the windows and doors. They shone across the town and up and down the dark streets. They merged with the other lanterns until the town was flooded with light again, as it was once before.

For many years after this, the shining lantern lights continued to help everyone grow wise and strong.

Golden like the sun, they sparkled by day.

Like the twinkling stars, they sparkled by night.

The Swan's Song

An environmental story written to accompany an art exhibition with the theme of 'loss of habitat' by Lynn Taylor entitled INDIGO BREW, Melbourne, 2019 – https://www.studio-taylor.com.au/

The Spirit of the Swans looked upon her wide brown land. She was worried... very worried.

For thousands of years she had watched over her family down in the world below. She had felt proud of their beautiful black wings that could fly them from coast to coast, and their strong necks that held their heads high above all others around them. Here was a bird so loyal and so loving... with so much to teach to all in the world.

For generation upon generation, her swan family had survived through many ups and downs... fire and flood, wartime and peace, the cold and the heat....

But never had there been a crisis like this – a crisis that did not seem to have a solution.

For swans to have babies they need nests. To build their nests they need fresh grasses and reeds. And for fresh grasses and reeds to grow and thrive, they need clean waterways... lakes, harbours, rivers, swamps and wetlands.

But fresh grasses and reeds, once a normal gift of nature, were becoming harder and harder to source. Rivers were drying up, swamps sitting stagnant, lakes polluted, harbours and inlets piled high with oily slicks and plasticky bits.

The Spirit of the Swans was desperate to find a way for change. She let out her loud and long bugle-like sound, followed by a range of softer crooning notes – a desperate song to all in the land below to heed her clarion call.

But no-one seemed to take notice.

So the Spirit of the Swans called on the Four Winds... the Wind of the North, the Wind of the South, the Wind of the East, the Wind of the West... to take her song across the land.

The Four Winds carried the song through the night and through the day, over the mountains, across the plains, along the valleys, into the forests, and along the rocky coastlines.

The children in the land heard the music carried by the winds – children living on farms, children living in cottages by the sea, children living in cabins in the mountains, children living in homes and high-rise apartments in the cities – all children everywhere.

They heard the music and looked up. And the song entered their hearts.

GRANDMOTHER AND THE DONKEY

A story written to address the growing loss of 'clean' environments and to encourage children to have litter awareness. It was turned into a puppet show, then toured through kindergartens in the Cape Town Townships. The effect was immediate – as the puppeteers were packing up the show, the children would be running up to them with handfuls of litter. I believe the story has a universal environmental message and could be used with all ages. The Xhosa song was written by one of the puppeteers, Maria Msebenzi.

NOTE: the song could be rewritten in any language.

Once upon a time, in the southern lands of Africa there lived an old grandmother. Her children and grandchildren had moved into the town, and she was left by herself on her farm in the country. But grandmother never felt lonely because her favourite child was *nature* itself, and there was always so much to do to take care of *nature*.

Grandmother especially liked to see her *nature child* wearing a beautiful dress, a flower dress, and so she spent most of her time tending a garden and growing beautiful flowers. Her best friend was a little brown donkey who worked all day pulling a cart to carry buckets of water for the flower garden. Then on Saturdays he would carry Grandmother on his strong back, pulling a cartload of flowers behind him, setting off for the market at the edge of town. Grandmother would dress him up with a special hat ringed with flowers and a brightly coloured cloth on his back.

At the end of the day, when all the flowers had been sold Grandmother would use the money to buy food for herself and oats for the little brown donkey. They always had enough to eat, and for a long time they were very happy together. The donkey loved Grandmother, and Grandmother loved the donkey. As they worked in the flower garden, she would often sing to him this song:

Oh, a donkey is a wonderful thing; a wonderful thing is a donkey.

Imbongolo yinto entle kahle; into ekahle yimbongolo.

However, as the years went by, Grandmother was growing older, and there came a time when she was too old to work in her flower garden and too old to live out in the country by herself. So one day she packed all her belongings into the donkey cart, put the flower hat on the donkey's head and the brightly coloured cloth on his back, and together they set off to town to find a new house, a town house, to live in.

Now Grandmother had not been into town for a very long time, and as she travelled up and down the streets on the way to her new house, she was shocked and saddened to find what an untidy place it had become. There was mess and garbage piled up everywhere. Instead of gardens of flowers there were gardens of mess and garbage.

'What are the people doing to *nature's child?*', cried Grandmother. 'How can they dress her in such an ugly dress?' And she sat down amongst the tins and bottles and plastic bags outside her new house, and started to cry. While she was crying, the little brown donkey came close, bent down and whispered a secret in her ear. Slowly Grandmother's tears stopped, and a smile crept across her wrinkled face. 'Of course, little brown donkey, what a wonderful idea', she said, and then she started to sing:

> *Oh, a donkey is a wonderful thing; a wonderful thing is a donkey.*
> *Imbongolo yinto entle kahle; into ekahle yimbongolo.*

While she was singing, she unpacked all her belongings into her new house. After a cup of tea for herself and some water and oats for the donkey, she set off down the street with the donkey and an empty cart. As she walked, she started to pick up the garbage and load it on to the cart. And as she worked, she sang:

> *My nature's child is ugly and grey,*
> *She needs a change of dress today.*
> *Let's pick up the garbage and clean up the mess,*
> *Then plant seeds to grow a flower dress.*

It wasn't long before the children in the street heard Grandmother's happy singing. They came out from their houses and started to help. By the end of the first day with the children working hard, all the garbage in the first street had been picked up. It was loaded on to the donkey cart and taken to the garbage tip. Then Grandmother dipped her hand into a bag of flower seeds that she had brought from her country garden. She gave seeds to all the children to take back home and plant in front of their houses.

The next day, with more children helping the second street was cleaned up.

The next day, the third street was tidied. In this way, with the children working with Grandmother and the little brown donkey, every street in the town was soon cleared of all the mess. And with the flower seeds planted in front of all the houses, soon *nature's child* had a new town dress, a beautiful flower dress.

Now Grandmother was able to enjoy the beauty of the flowers in the town. Meanwhile the little brown donkey was kept busy carrying water up and down the streets for all the gardens, and collecting new garbage every day.

From that day to this, if anyone in the town had any garbage to throw out, they would put it in their bins and wait until the donkey cart came by to load it for the tip. Each day the children would pick flowers from their garden and weave a fresh flower ring for the donkey's hat.

If you ever visit this town you will hear the people singing praises to the little brown donkey – the little brown donkey who helped Grandmother give their town a beautiful new dress, a flower dress:

Oh, a donkey is a wonderful thing; a wonderful thing is a donkey.
Imbongolo yinto entle kahle; into ekahle yimbongolo.

THE MULBERRY TREE

By Jenni Cargill-Strong

This is a story of how a child overcomes her grief at the loss of her favourite tree. It is based on the real-life experience of the teller. An audio version is on Jenni's album 'The Story Tree and Other Nature Tales', available as a digital download at www.storytree.com.au

Before Lucy was born, her dad planted a mulberry tree. As she grew, it grew. By the time Lucy was big enough to climb into it, the tree was strong enough to take her weight.

The mulberry tree grew on the wild side of the garden, in any direction it felt like growing – even over the fence. Its roots thrust deeper into the earth and its branches arched gracefully towards the sky.

Lucy had a special branch in the mulberry tree. It was strong, straight and worn silky smooth by her hands, feet and bottom. Lucy would imagine that the mulberry tree was one of many in a great jungle of trees. It was a steamy jungle, full of wild things – and Lucy was one of them. She would climb up into her special branch and hide behind the green, heart-shaped leaves. She'd sit so still, so still, that the humans wouldn't even know she was there.

In the winter the mulberry tree was naked, but elegantly so. Tiny green leaf-buds and little green, hairy fruits would form on the branches. Then the leaves would slowly unfurl.

As winter turned to spring, the berries changed colour: from green to white, to pink, to red and finally to a sweet, juicy, luscious purple.

In the Summer, Lucy and her family would picnic in the shade of the mulberry tree.

In Autumn, Lucy's dad gave the mulberry tree a light pruning. When he appeared with his pruning saw, Lucy would say, 'Don't cut my special branch, Dad, will you?'.

    STORIES TO LIGHT THE NIGHT

Dad would smile, ruffle her hair.

'No, possum, I would never cut your special branch.'

Over the fence from Lucy's place was an empty yard. There the grass grew tall and the weeds swayed in the wind. When Lucy was four, Ed and Mavis Andrews bought the empty plot of land, and Lucy watched as the grass and weeds were mown flat, the timber skeleton was built, and the golden bricks were laid.

The Andrews moved in. They were friendly neighbours, but unlike Lucy's family they were neat, tidy and very particular. Ed Andrews did not enjoy messy, purple mulberry splodges landing on his flower beds.

'Alex, you should cut that tree down. It makes a terrible mess', said Ed.

Dad scratched his head and offered to cut back all the branches that hung over the fence. Lucy watched nervously. After that the mulberry tree wasn't quite as elegant, but Lucy still had her special branch and enough leaves to hide behind.

Every Summer holiday, Lucy and her family went camping at the beach for five whole weeks. One year they came home to discover that Lucy's beautiful mulberry tree wasn't beautiful any more. All the branches and leaves were gone and all that was left was a stump.

Lucy ran straight to her room and wept. She wept rivers and lakes. She wanted to run to Ed and shout, 'Mr Ed Andrews! How could you kill my special tree with my special branch? It wasn't hurting your stupid flowers!'

But Lucy didn't say anything.

Dad had strong words with Mr Andrews about it. Lucy refused to go out into the back yard. Conversations over the fence didn't happen any more.

One day there was a knock at the door and mum called, 'Lucy, someone is here to see you'. Mr Andrews was standing at the door, awkwardly holding a new little mulberry tree.

'Here you go Lucy.'

Lucy's face got hot, tears stung her eyes and her tongue wouldn't work.

'Thanks, Ed', said mum.

Mr Andrews rushed back home.

Lucy and her dad started talking about where they could plant the new mulberry tree. They searched all around the garden, front and back, but there wasn't a spot that felt right.

The next day Lucy and her dad were out walking when a little Willy Wagtail flew down to the path in front of them. Lucy pulled her dad to a stop.

They watched as the bird waggled its tail, chirped, and hopped off a little in front of them. Lucy giggled softly. They carefully followed the bird and soon it led them, one hop and skip at a time, into the new community garden.

'Oh', said dad. 'I forgot there was a community garden starting down here. Wow. It looks great.'

There was a big circle in the middle, as if it was waiting for something.

'Oh dad. Do you think we could plant our mulberry tree here?'

'Maybe. We'll ask.'

Dad found the right people to ask and they loved the idea. The following Saturday, dad and Lucy planted the tree.

They carried the tree in a wheelbarrow with a shovel, a trowel, and some rich compost. They dug a nice deep hole, gently put the compost in the hole, planted the tree and watered it.

Slowly, the mulberry tree grew. Its roots thrust gradually deeper into the earth, and its branches arched gracefully towards the sky.

Lucy was so happy with the new tree that she made up a little song:

Oh mulberry tree, oh mulberry tree
You sway with me
Oh mulberry tree, oh mulberry tree
Your fruit's so sweet
Purple are my hands,
Purple are my feet.

One autumn, it rained for weeks. Lucy's garage had a few feet of water in it. Kids put on wet suits and played in the flooded parks on their boogie boards.

The mulberry tree in the middle of the community garden sprang to life. The next spring it bore its first crop of mulberries. After a while, it was strong enough to hold not just Lucy, but kids from all around the neighbourhood. In mulberry season, after school, they'd sit in the branches, feasting like chattering monkeys.

You can probably guess the colour of their lips, hands and feet!

9   OTHER KINDS OF LOSS – TRUST, CO-OPERATION, CONTROL, BALANCE, RESPECT

There are many other kinds of loss that don't fall into the previous chapter categories, yet it felt important to include them in this collection – stories for the loss of trust, loss of control, loss of co-operation, loss of balance and the loss of respect.

THE LAKE AND THE SKY –a story to rebuild trust in life and the world, written for children aged 3–12 (p. 236).

THE LITTLE FISH – written for a six-year old boy to help build acceptance of the present and trust in the future, and to support the boy to cope with everyday changes (p. 238).

THE RAINBOW GNOMES AND THE CAVE OF SECRETS – written to address a lack of trust between children in a class of 4–6-year olds (p. 240).

THE RAINBOW STONE – a story to help a group of eight-year old children recover trust in the wonder and beauty of the world (p. 243).

THE BEEKEEPER AND THE HONEY CUP – written to help a five-year old boy find a way to control his anger in a more socially acceptable and fun-like way (p. 247).

THE BRUSH AND THE PAN – a rhyming story to help encourage discussion when there has been a loss of co-operation between friends or family or community groups (p. 249).

THE CIRCLE FRIENDS – written for an eight-year old girl who had controlling friends (p. 252).

THE SPACE BETWEEN THE MOON AND THE STARS – a story that restored harmony and balance in the life of a professional woman who had developed Post-Traumatic Stress Disorder (PTSD) caused by vicarious and accumulative trauma (p. 254).

KING SUN AND QUEEN MOON – a story to encourage respect and caring between boys and girls, and men and women (for all ages) (p. 256).

THE LAKE AND THE SKY

By Mayumi Murphy

A story to rebuild trust in life and the world. Mayumi works with children between the ages of 3 and 12 in a town that had recently suffered terrible bushfires. She wrote this therapeutic story both in English and in Japanese to use in her Japanese classes.

The response from an eleven-year old student was: 'I liked the story a lot. I feel things look a little brighter now.' A nine-year old student said, 'I love the story. I'd like to be the pink robin or the wind' (meaning that she could help people who were going through difficult times).

A parent who has two young boys (aged 7 and 10) commented, 'The story is beautiful: it describes so perfectly how it feels to go through an experience like we had with our sons. The days of the fires were at times so very dark, but now the sun shines more often, even though the clouds will always appear at times!'

There once was a lake in the middle of a forest.

The lake was always looking at the sky. She liked watching the clouds, imagining different animals moving through the blue sky. She also enjoyed the breathtaking show of colours at sunrise and sunset. Gazing at the moon and the stars at night left her feeling so peaceful.

But one day the sky became covered by a dark, heavy cloud. The whole world went grey and gloomy. It rained day after day after day. The lake thought, 'It feels like I'll never see the blue sky again. Everything is dark and grey. No more colour or light in my world, not even the twinkling of a star.'

As the dark rainy days continued, she felt more and more sad. She was fearful of getting stuck in a colourless world, and was feeling quite hopeless without the light.

A pink robin that lived in the forest saw the dark coloured lake from the sky, and saw her sadness. He flew up high in the sky and called the wind. The bird asked the wind to blow the dark heavy clouds away for the lake. So the wind gathered its power and, little by little, blew away the heavy clouds.

The sunlight started to come through the clouds. As the sky became blue, the colour returned to the lake. When the lake saw the blue sky again, she said to the sky, 'I thought I'd never see you again. I missed you so much.'

The sky said, 'I missed you, too. But I knew you were there, even when I couldn't see you. I knew the cloud would move away one day. Nothing stays the same in this world.'

When night-time came, the lake said to the moon and the stars, 'I'm so happy to see you. I thought I'd never see you again.'

One of the stars said to the lake, 'We are always twinkling. We are always here – shining night and day. We are always here, just like the pebbles at the bottom of the lake.'

From that day on, the lake felt so much better knowing that the blue sky and the stars were always there, even when she couldn't see them.

THE LITTLE FISH

By Jill Tina Taplin

This story was written for a six-year old boy who, in Jill's words, 'struggled with the strangeness and difference of everyday life. He was a child who did not seem to have good control of his body, his running style was awkward, and he could easily be described as clumsy. He seemed to be very sensitive to touch, and would react quite strongly, for example with a push, to what seemed like a normal touch to others.'

The story's intention was to help build acceptance of the present and trust in the future, and to support the boy to cope with the changes that happen in daily life.

Jill told the story to the whole group in the kindergarten for a few days, and then gave it to the boy's parents to use at home, which reportedly they did. After some time, the boy seemed to manage more comfortably socially and in staying with the mood of the group. In Jill's words 'he was more able to swim with the flow'. Jill hopes that her story supported this evident progress.

Once upon a time, high up between the two biggest mountains in the world, there was a sheltered valley. In the valley was a deep, deep lake. It was very peaceful and quiet there. The huge mountains kept the stormy winds away, and only gentle breezes ruffled the waters of the lake. In the lake there lived a little fish. He swam through the quiet waters and nibbled the waterweed, and he was happy. His life was very peaceful.

One day a large bird flew across the lake. His sharp eye spotted the little fish swimming along under the water. All at once the bird folded his great wings and dived straight down through the water to the little fish. He caught the little fish before he could even guess what was happening, and carried him away across the mountains.

The bird carried the fish far away to another lake, and into that new lake he dropped the little fish. This lake was quite different to his old home. The water was not fresh and pure and clear. It was muddy and dirty. This new lake was beside a great city, and the people living in the city threw all their rubbish into the lake. It made the little fish feel most uncomfortable, and he swam around and around, looking for some cleaner water. He was swimming near to the shore of the lake when he suddenly saw a strange shadow coming towards him through the murky water. In a moment he was caught, and lifted out of the water in a net. The poor fish was carried twisting and gasping in the net for a while, and then tipped out into a small tank.

The water in the tank was not dirty like the lake water, but it tasted stale and old to the little fish. The tank was very small, and he could hardly swim in it. There was no waterweed to nibble, only a little dry dust on the surface of the water, which did not taste good. The little fish was very unhappy and wished he were back in his mountain lake. Outside the tank there were lots of people. They came and peered at him and talked loudly to one another. The little fish was afraid of the staring faces and the loud voices.

Then one day things changed again for the little fish. He was taken from his tank and put into a great rushing roaring river. Now he was swept along by the water. In the lake he had been able to swim wherever he wanted to, but now he had to go where the flow of the river took him and he could not stop to nibble the waterweed. He was knocked about by the churning water and his head ached with the roar of it, but he was swept on and on.

At long last the little fish was swept out into the sea. Here, he was no longer buffeted about as he had been by the river water, but was soon lulled to sleep by the rhythm of the waves.

When he awoke he began to explore his new home. It was huge, so huge that he could not find any boundaries to it. He could swim wherever he wanted to. The water was strange to him; it was salty, but it was clean and good to live in. He could find seaweed to nibble, and then he found that there were other little fishes, just like himself. He enjoyed swimming about with them. They told how they had found their way down rivers to the sea, and he told them his strange story.

As time passed, he became a big fish who could swim strongly through the oceans. When he had been taken from his mountain lake by the bird, he had been afraid. He had not liked the dirty lake or the little tank where he had to eat dust and the people stared at him. He had been afraid when the great river had swept him along, but now he was not afraid or unhappy any more. He had found his true home in the mighty oceans.

The Rainbow Gnomes and the Cave of Secrets

By Élodie Guidou, kindergarten teacher

This story was written to address a lack of trust between children in a class of 4–6-year olds.

Élodie writes: Last year some older children started to whisper secrets to each other. At some point it brought a very unpleasant atmosphere in our little kindergarten family. Some children started to feel rejected and some suspicions were arising. Many children were very upset, and I could sense a growing loss of trust in the group: the children telling secrets were losing their sense of 'being inclusive' (which we work hard on in Kindy). The children being excluded were losing their sense of belonging. I felt I had to tell a story that could bring everyone back together again, and that would help them to share what they had in mind.

A friend told me that in her family day-care she was saying, 'No secrets, only surprises'. It was winter time, and in our culture, gnomes are very much part of winter stories, as they are traditionally busy digging out some crystals.

And so, the story was born.

I told it with puppets using gnomes wearing the rainbow colours, and with a crystal stitched on their hat. Each gnome also had a crystal matching with their colour (as told in the story). It really helped to bring the magic at story time.

After sharing it for a week, most of the children stopped telling secrets, and if some told secrets, one child would say, 'No secrets, only surprises'!

The unhealthy tendency was slowly washed away, and our atmosphere of sharing was back.

Once there were seven brother gnomes who lived deep down in the earth, in a light-filled cave. All day long they would hammer and hack to find some hidden crystals.

They loved each other dearly and always sang jolly songs. The cave was full of music and joy.

In this particular cave, the crystals were always very light and transparent, always the same. So all day long, the seven brothers would work hard and find crystals. Then the stones would spread their light on the sleeping seeds and trees outside their hidden cave.

One day, Red Gnome, who was always working very hard and was often very grumpy, found a red crystal. It was so special that he decided he wouldn't share this crystal with his brothers, and instead he hid it.

The same day, Orange Gnome, who was also working very hard but was more patient than red gnome, found an orange crystal. He found it very special, and also hid it.

The day after, the same happened to Yellow Gnome: he found a yellow crystal, and he was so full of joy, that he hid it. Green Gnome, who is quite slow but likes pretty things, found a green crystal, and loved it so much that he hid it.

Blue Gnome and Indigo Gnome, who are often very teary, also found crystals of their own colours, and for once they didn't cry, so they hid them.

Only Violet Gnome, the youngest of all the siblings, didn't find anything, and patiently, with courage, continued to hack with his long and strong axe.

After some time, Red Gnome started to feel very heavy with his secret, so he whispered it to his brother Orange Gnome, and Orange Gnome felt relieved to share the same secret.

And strangely that day, the same thing happened between Yellow and Green Gnome, and between Blue and Indigo Gnome. They told their secrets to one of their brothers, but not to all of them.

After this they all became very suspicious of each other, and started to watch what their brothers were doing, hoping that their precious secret wouldn't be revealed.

More and more secrets started to fill the room, and more and more whispers were bouncing from one wall to another.... The cave was full of secrets, and the gnomes had lost their happy songs and tempers.

Only Violet Gnome remained happy. But he could see that his brothers were not, and it sometimes left him feeling sad too. Especially because he didn't know what was going on. He so wanted to help them.

One day he found a crystal, very special, because it was of his own colour. And it was quite small. It gave him a very good idea to cheer up his dear brothers. He stood in front of them and said with a big smile (hiding his crystal): 'My dear brothers, I have a surprise for you.'

And with happiness, he showed them the shining crystal.

All the gnomes opened wide their eyes and mouths, and felt very embarrassed inside....

Red Gnome grumbled: 'Well I have a surprise too.'

And he showed his red crystal. Orange Gnome did the same, and all the brothers followed, feeling relieved that there were no more secrets, only surprises.

But then, something very astonishing happened. As their crystals sat next to each other, they started to shine more and more intensively, until their light passed through the rocks and shone on the trees and plants out of the cave.

The gnomes ran out to have a look, and they saw the most magnificent rainbow they had ever seen in their life. What a surprise!

From that day, they never kept any secrets from each other any more, they only shared surprises.

Story Games

To extend the story Élodie hid some crystals in the sandpit, and the children were very excited digging them out. She reported that it helped to bring a sense of belonging as they had to work together to find the treasures.

She also played a little game where the children had to sit in a circle with their eyes closed. One child tip-toed behind them all, leaving a sack full of crystals behind a child's back. Then this child had a turn to do the same. Here is a song that could be used:

'Heigh ho, trip and trap, Hey di ho carries treasures in his sack.
And if you're very quiet, and do not make a sound,
You might just find some treasures to be found.'

THE RAINBOW STONE

By Becky Whitcombe, early childhood educator

By Becky Whitcombe, early childhood educator

INTRODUCTION BY BECKY

This story was written to help a group of eight-year old children recover trust in the wonder and beauty of the world – before hearing this they were having difficulty getting rid of disturbing scary images that they saw from the internet. Given the influence of images and their tremendous sticking power, the children found it impossible to fall asleep at night. There was screaming, tears and fear of being alone.

The journey of the little girl gives hope and reassurance that these pictures can fade away and that we ourselves have the power to release them. The reflection image was inspired by the English folk tale 'The Brownies'. The only prop was a piece of blue silk at the storyteller's feet, with the rainbow stone waiting to be revealed by the small wave.

After the presentation of the story there was a collective sigh – as if they had all been caressed by the words and its magical ending. Each child was handed a pebble with a rainbow on it to help their own dreams come alive. It was received with such reverence and awe.

Following the story, the children were each given the chance to pick a few cards in the colours of the rainbow. They were each instructed to write their favourite dreams on each card. Some chose dream land of the puppies, fairies, candy, football, chocolate and of course butterflies and rainbows! Many stuck these cards to a mini poster and drew pictures next to them.

After a week or so I had a few parents tell me that their child had their dream poster up near their bed, and before nodding off chose their dream to pop in their head. Many were sleeping with the rainbow stones as well, trying to make it warm in order to give it power. Their negative images had eased with time, and the children felt supported by the story on hearing it each night before bedtime. Within a month the few children who suffered the most from these scary images were able to settle themselves nicely before slumber, and felt safe to enter their chosen dream land.

There once lived a lovely little girl. About your age [pointing to listener]. She was a delightful happy girl who loved to go on adventures.

Every day she would set off into the woods behind her house. She would skip around the meadows, she would skip around the trees, she would sing to the flowers, the birds and the bees.

Mother Nature was her whole world, and she was ever so happy and safe there.

She collected pine cones to make huge volcanos, she would make little sailing boats using strong bark with twigs and leaves, and she would love to look at the huge majestic tree trunks and all their markings. She would see animals in there, swirly patterns and sometimes faces that she knew. Most of the time she saw grandma's face!

She was so happy in the woods – exploring, frolicking and playing.

One day as she walked home from school, she met a young boy from her neighbourhood. He asked, 'Did you hear about the bird? Outside our school gates?'

The little girl said, 'No, no I didn't.

The boy then told her that a group of kids found it dead with all its feathers off: it had no face, and some of its insides were all squashed! Oh, it was so cool!', he said.

'That poor little bird', she thought.

She told the boy to stop talking and that she needed to go home straight away.

So she did. She ran all the way home. When she arrived, she felt much better being away from the boy and his bird story. Her mum saw that she looked sad, and gave her a warm hug and made her some hot chocolate.

The afternoon carried on as always. She played with her dolls, read some books, had her tea, then a bath and yawned her way to bed.

After her mother and father kissed her goodnight and turned off the light she was ready to fall pleasantly asleep. But she didn't!

As soon as she closed her eyes there was the bird. With no feathers, no face, all squashed.... She screamed! She cried! She even tried to shake her head... 'Leave me, leave me', the little girl pleaded... but it would not leave her.

Oh her mother tried to soothe her with song, and her father tried to calm her with cuddles, but nothing really worked.

She ended up crying herself to sleep that night.

Unfortunately, it was like this for many days. And the little girl grew exhausted....

One afternoon she went into the woods to cheer herself up, but all she saw was the dead bird.

She saw it in the running stream, in the pine cones and in the tree trunks.... She felt so sad that she could not see anything else.

She fell into a slump next to a tree and cried and cried.

While she sat and cried, she asked, 'Why can't I simply see rainbows and butterflies?'.

'Hoot hoot', said a wise owl from above.

'Your crying has woken me; I cannot simply let you be... why do you shed so many tears?'

STORIES TO LIGHT THE NIGHT

The little girl began to tell him the whole story of the boy, the bird and the way it was found, and that it was all she could see everywhere she looked. And she was so tired, as she had not slept for days.

'Ah', said the wise owl... 'that is easy to tame, it is merely a wish to say in your name. Did you know your heart has more power than your head?

'What do you mean?', said the little girl.

'There is only one person who can release this, you see, only one person who can set it free. Head down to the magical lake, I say, this is where your troubles fade away. As the moon sits way up high, look in the still water and say goodbye.'

The little girl looked puzzled; 'Who do I say goodbye to?'.

The wise owl continued, 'You just need to say this rhyme... 'Zooma zooma zee, zoom zoom zee, I wish I wish I wish to see, Who is the person to set this all free, Who is this person, could it be...?' The little girl asked, 'That's it? That's all I say?'

'Indeed, indeed; now be on your way', said the owl.

So the little girl set off through the woods towards the lake.

She waited till the moon rose high and then stood to look in the still water.

And then she said, ' Zooma zooma zee, zoom zoom zee, I wish I wish I wish to see, Who is the person to set this free, Who is this person, could it be...?'.

She looked around for this person to appear... she saw no one. She was alone. Just her, the moon and the lake. In the distance she heard 'Hoot hoot'.

She took a deep breath and rubbed her eyes, looked in the lake and tried once more.

'Zooma zooma zee, zoom zoom zee, I wish I wish I wish to see, Who is the person to set this all free, Who is this person, could it be...me!!!!! Me? Me? I am the one with the power to set it free?'

And at that moment the lake made a little wave that brought up a small stone to her feet.

She picked it up and turned it over, and there were rainbow marble colours. And just then a butterfly fluttered by.

She smiled broadly and took the stone and laughed all the way home.

She hugged both her parents ever so tightly and said, 'I cannot wait to go to sleep tonight!'. She started to do a little dance as she sang: 'I am the person to set this free, I am the person; It is me! I am the person to set this free, I am the person; It is me!' That very night she settled down into her bed, holding that stone so tightly... wishing oh wishing with all her might.

As the stone started to feel warm the butterflies came. They fluttered around her head, tickled her skin then flew off. She felt so happy and calm, and fell deep into a dreaming sleep.

The precious stone lived under her pillow by day and was held in her hand at night. The stone grew warm in her hand and helped her dream. One night she was running through a field full of sunflowers, another night there was a rainbow, another night more fluttering butterflies.

And in the daytime the little girl returned so joyfully back to the woods to play with the pine cones, sail boats in the stream and see patterns in the trees. And once again, as before, she found herself singing to all the flowers, birds and bees.

She was so happy that once again her eyes could see all the beauty around her.

CRAFT ACTIVITIES
Paint rainbows on smooth pebbles or stones.
Make 'dream cards' as described in the story.

THE BEEKEEPER AND THE HONEY CUP

A story to help a young child find a way to control his anger in a more socially acceptable and fun-like way. It was presented to a five-year old boy on his birthday, together with a hand-made doll with a jacket with bee-buttons down the front, which helped as a constant reminder of the story.

There was once a beekeeper who lived in the middle of a large flower garden. At the edge of the garden were many beehives. In the hives were many bees... not just hundreds of bees... thousands of bees.

The beekeeper kept thousands of bees for one main reason. He loved to eat lots and lots of honey. Not just a teaspoon of honey. Not just a dessert spoon of honey. A great big tablespoon of honey at any one time!

His favourite jacket had bee-buttons to remind him of how much he loved his bees and loved his honey.

Every day the beekeeper would collect the honey from the hive in a little wooden honey cup. But sometimes there was not enough to fill his wooden cup. Sometimes the bees could not find enough flowers to collect enough pollen to make the honey. Sometimes the days were rainy, and the garden was wet. This made it very difficult for the bees to do their work.

When there was not enough honey to fill his cup, the beekeeper would get angry. Not just a little bit angry. Very angry! And when the beekeeper was very angry, he would scream and shout and throw things about. He would shake his fists in the air and complain bitterly that life was unfair.

However, all this angry behaviour did nothing to help the bees make honey. In fact, when they heard the angry sounds they would fly away from the screaming and shouting, and not come back to the flower garden till things were quiet again.

Life went on this way for a long time – sometimes there was honey, and all was well. But sometimes there was no honey, and the beekeeper would scream and shout and throw things about. He would shake his fists in the air and complain bitterly that life was unfair.

One day the beekeeper grew so angry and made such a loud noise that the whole garden seemed to shake with his anger. Even the wind up in the sky swirled wildly around because of such a noise. And as the wind swirled and blew, the clouds grew dark. And as the clouds grew dark, the Thunder Man was woken up from his important sleep.

'WHAT'S ALL THIS SCREAMING AND SHOUTING AND THROWING THINGS ABOUTING?', roared the Thunder Man down to the little beekeeper.

'DON'T YOU REALISE YOU HAVE WOKEN UP THE THUNDER MAN? DO YOU HAVE TO MAKE SUCH A NOISE?'

The beekeeper was quite disturbed when he heard the Thunder Man's roaring. He called up to him in his very small voice and tried to explain the problem.

'HO HO HO', said the Thunder Man, 'SUCH A FUSS ABOUT SUCH A SMALL THING. WHY DON'T YOU JUST DO THE ANGRY DANCE WHEN YOU ARE FEELING UPSET? THIS WAY, THE BEES WILL STAY IN YOUR GARDEN AND I WILL BE ABLE TO HAVE MY SLEEP.'

The beekeeper had never heard about such a thing as an angry dance. He asked the Thunder Man to tell him more. So, the Thunder Man explained to the beekeeper how to do the ANGRY DANCE.

SAY HUFF AND BRUFF, AND STAMP THE GROUND,
KNOCK BOTH KNEES AND TURN AROUND.
DO THIS WHEN THINGS DON'T GO YOUR WAY (3 times),
AND LIFE WILL GET BETTER EVERY DAY.

The beekeeper thanked the Thunder Man, and the Thunder Man went back to his cloud home to continue sleeping.

From this time onwards, whenever there was not enough honey to fill the bee-keeper's wooden cup, he would do the ANGRY DANCE three times, like this:

HUFF AND BRUFF, STAMP THE GROUND,
KNOCK BOTH KNEES AND TURN AROUND.
HUFF AND BRUFF, STAMP THE GROUND,
KNOCK BOTH KNEES AND TURN AROUND.
HUFF AND BRUFF, STAMP THE GROUND,
KNOCK BOTH KNEES AND TURN AROUND.

All the bees were much happier now that the beekeeper didn't scream and shout and throw things about.

Life settled down in the garden of flowers. And do you know what? Because the beekeeper was less angry, the bees seemed happier. And the beekeeper's cup was more often filled with honey than not.

     STORIES TO LIGHT THE NIGHT

THE BRUSH AND THE PAN

A story poem to help encourage discussion when there has been a loss of co-operation between friends or family or community groups. The rhyme and humour lend it for use for all ages.

The brush and the pan were the best of friends,
They thought their friendship would never end.
They worked together day and night,
Cleaning up all the dust in sight,
Sweeping up all the fluff so light,
Keeping their home so tidy and bright.

Then, without warning, one unusual day,
Things went horribly, terribly astray.
The brush announced (out of the blue):
'It is much more important – the work that I do'.
'No, No', cried the pan, 'that is not true,
I am so much more important than you.'

They jostled backward and forward this way,
And no work was done the entire day.
The jostle turned to a quarrel, the quarrel to a fight,
The fight to a fierce argument that carried into the night.

The argument tore them both apart,
The argument broke their brush-and-pan hearts.
The pan hid in the corner – to be used no more,
The brush stayed out of sight, behind the door.
Their home grew quiet – hardly a sound was heard
Except the noise of the wind and a lonely night bird.

The days and the weeks and the months passed by,
While the dust and the fluff kept piling up high.
The wind blew around the brush-and-pan home,
And the night bird kept singing a song of its own.

After a very, very long time had passed by,
The dust and fluff had piled up so high,
The brush and pan were now buried from view,
And they didn't have a clue as to what next to do!

That evening, the night bird sang a new kind of song,
Calling the wind to come and blow wild and strong.
The wind blew and blew as hard as it could,
Squeezing into the house – through a crack in the wood.

Once the wind was inside, it blew over the floor,
It blew open the windows and open the door.
It blew dust and fluff outside in a swirl,
Then went on its way with a whirl and a twirl.

Now only the song of the bird filled the night,
It reached out to the friends to help with their plight.
The pan came out from its corner, to hide no more,
The brush appeared from its spot behind the door.
The friends joined in the song,
Wondering what had gone wrong....
Then they hugged each other and set to work,

   STORIES TO LIGHT THE NIGHT

Cleaning up patches of fluff and dirt.

Now the brush and the pan are the best of friends,
They know their friendship will never end.
They work (and sing) together by day and by night,
Cleaning up all the dust in sight,
Sweeping up all the fluff so light,
Keeping their home so tidy and bright.

The Circle Friends

In the land of shapes, amongst the squares and the triangles and the pentagons (to name but a few), lived three circle friends. One was red, one was blue, and one was yellow.

The circle friends loved doing everything together.

The circle friends loved going everywhere together.

Every day they could be seen out and about, playing and having fun – rolling along the ground, spinning fast and bouncing up and down. So many movements that they could do!

Their bright colours brought such joy to all who lived there.

However, something was happening that seemed to go unnoticed for a long time. The blue circle and the red circle were taking turns as the leaders in the play, and the yellow circle was more and more following everything her friends wanted to do. She hardly took a turn at being a leader, and as much as possible she would hide between her two friends. Sometimes, as they all rolled along the ground, or spun fast, or bounced up and down, the yellow circle could hardly be seen at all.

Then one day, this was noticed! It was noticed in the Royal Shapes Castle itself – by the regalest in the land of shapes – *The Queen of All Shapes*.

Every day *The Queen of All Shapes* would visit her Grand Mirror Room to check on all the shapes that lived in her Queendom. In this Grand Mirror Room was a mirror for every kind of shape – a square mirror, a triangle mirror, a pentagonal mirror and many more – including, of course, a circle mirror.

Now as you may already have imagined, these were not ordinary mirrors. Every one of the mirrors was magical. When *The Queen of All Shapes* looked into them, instead of seeing her regal self she could see what all her shape subjects were doing across the land.

And for quite some time, when she looked into the circle mirror each day, *The Queen of All Shapes* had been noticing something not quite right. She could see that the yellow circle shape was more and more hiding between her friends and not showing her beautiful, round, shining yellow self.

Finally, *The Queen of All Shapes* decided to offer some queenly help. She lifted her regal hand, lent in towards the mirror and blew a kiss to the yellow circle that was rolling along between the circle friends. The kiss turned into a little wind that whooshed and swirled and whirled around the mirror.

Back in the real shape-world, in real shape-time, the yellow circle suddenly experienced a bit of a whoosh, a bit of a swirl, a bit of a whirl. She saw a new winding path she had never noticed before, and a friendly wind was helping to blow her towards it. It felt good to flow with this little wind, so she decided to follow the new path.

This led her to a different part of shape land that she had not known about. It was so exciting – well, a little bit scary, but mostly exciting! So many new things to explore, so many new shapes to meet! Hexagons and octagons and nonagons and dodecagons and hexa-decagons. Rectangles and ovals and stars. Trapezoids and parallelograms.

The yellow circle couldn't wait to tell her friends. Next time she met them rolling along, she led the way to her new discoveries, and together they enjoyed exploring and playing.

Meanwhile, in the Royal Shape Castle *The Queen of All Shapes* continued her daily visits to the Grand Mirror Room. When she looked into the circle mirror, she was happy to see the yellow circle having fun, rolling along, spinning fast and bouncing up and down, shining her yellow light across the land. *The Queen of All Shapes* would smile to herself and continue working. Then, at the end of the day, after taking off her velvet gown and golden circle crown, she would relax with a cup of tea in the Royal Shape Gardens.

THE SPACE BETWEEN THE MOON AND THE STARS

By Beate Steller, M.A.P.S., M.A.Ed., B.S.W. (Hon.) R.N.

I thank Susan's therapeutic story training for encouraging me to write my own story that enabled a profound healing shift in my life that had become out of balance.

I wrote this just over seven months after I was diagnosed with Post-Traumatic Stress Disorder (PTSD) caused by vicarious and accumulative trauma. As a professional and simply as a human being I have supported people through trauma, loss and grief for many years. I had been feeling dizzy and exhausted for a while, and did not recognize these signs as a symptom in myself. Then one day I heard a story that triggered me and I was brought to a sudden stop. I lost the physical connection with my legs and had to seek medical help. This is when I was diagnosed by a very insightful young medico, reassuring me that with help I could re-wire my brain, strengthen my personal boundaries and refocus my life/work balance. The PTSD had the potential to be transformed into Post-Traumatic Growth. It meant undergoing life-changing psychological shifts in thinking and relating to the world, which would contribute to a personal process of change that is deeply meaningful. I was very committed to do this inner work, and had support along the way. However, it was the process of writing a therapeutic story for myself that totally and un-expectedly released a huge shift in my thinking and relating to the world. It has been a profound breakthrough. The resolution of my therapeutic story literally restored harmony and balance in my life.

A long time ago there lived a young woman who was known for being so helpful to all the life and people around her. Wherever Helpy went, she would carry other people's burdens and problems. Whenever she left a place, people commented on how much lighter they felt.

However, Helpy's legs had become tired and heavy. They had been carrying many stories and burdens of other people's lives. Sometimes she could not even feel her own limbs any more, and she started to wobble while trying to stand upright. And often she was dizzy.

Helpy was popular and always had people around her. One day, her friend said to her, 'Have you seen the amazing Moon and Stars lately? There is so much Space out there in the Universe. If you want to see them you must wait till it is very dark. I can stand on one leg and reach out and feel balanced in so much Space.'

Helpy's heart sang with joy when her friend was talking about the Space between the Moon and the Stars, and had not felt that lightness in her heart for a long time. She also noticed her friend was steadily balanced on one leg as she told Helpy her story.

That night Helpy waited till everyone was asleep and it was very dark. She left her house and crept to the clearing at the edge of the bushland, then opened her eyes wide and looked up to the night sky. There were no Moon or Stars sparkling up in the Space. Her heart was not singing. Her head dropped and she noticed a heavy weight around her shoulder. Had the Moon and the Stars fallen on her shoulders too?

As Helpy was standing in the clearing she heard the night owl hooting in a tree near her, calling her close, offering some owl-wisdom. 'The only way you can see them is to go back to the dark spot in the clearing, close your eyes and go deep inside yourself and deep into the silence of the night. This will help you find the Space.' The owl then said, 'You might have to do this a number of times before you can see the Moon and the Stars and the Space between them'.

The next day, the young woman waited till it was very dark and crept out to the clearing again. She did not look up, but instead closed her eyes and went deep into the inner silence, the inner Space. She kept her eyes shut for a long time. Then after it had become completely silent inside her, she slowly opened her eyes.

However, Helpy's heart did not sing. She felt lost and frightened. She still had the feeling of the weight of the Moon and Stars on her shoulders. Then she remembered what the wise owl had said to her: 'You might have to do this a number of times.' So Helpy crept back to her home and returned the next night, and the next night and the next night.

After doing this many times, one evening as she opened her eyes she saw that the Moon and the Stars were way up high in the Universe. They were sparkling and there was lots of Space between them. She had never seen anything like this before. She didn't feel lost any more.

Her heart was singing with a soft voice. She stayed with that tender melody and she felt balanced. The heaviness that had been sitting on her shoulders had disappeared. As she looked down, she noticed that she had shifted the weight of her legs and she was balancing on one leg, just like her friend had told her she would.

Everything that belonged in the Cosmos – the Moon and the Stars – had returned back to the Space. She had forgotten that this is where they had always belonged.

Now she remembered, and her heart was singing.

KING SUN AND QUEEN MOON

This story was written to encourage respect and caring between boys and girls, and men and women. It is based on ideas arising from a group workshop in Chennai and was included in a collection of community stories for use by different groups of storytellers in India.

King Sun and Queen Moon ruled the kingdom of the sky. It should have been a happy reign, but King Sun was always arguing that he was far more important than Queen Moon. After all, he shone round and full and bright all through the day, and the people in the land below were awake and alert when he was high above them.

Queen Moon was sometimes round and full, but often she was hardly there... just a thin sliver in the sky.... And most people in the land below were asleep when she was reigning in the sky above them.

The argument had gone on for so long that Queen Moon had accepted King Sun's importance, and often she saw herself more as a servant to the King, and not as the Queen herself.

This story was written to encourage respect and caring between boys and girls, and men and women. It is based on ideas arising from a group workshop in Chennai and was included in a collection of community stories for use by different groups of storytellers in India.

Life was destined to continue like this for ever if it was not for a little weaver bird that roamed the sky, both day and night. This bird decided it had had enough of King Sun's arguing and wanted to find the true answer to this question.

In its quest for truth, the little weaver bird visited the Old Star Owl, known across the heavens as the wisest of the wise. The little bird presented the question: 'Is King Sun more important than Queen Moon?'

The Star Owl opened its large eyes and looked out across the sky. It pondered for a while, then said to the little weaver bird,

The next morning the weaver bird flew up and gathered golden threads of light from the rays of King Sun.

The next night the weaver bird flew up and gathered silver threads of light from the beams of Queen Moon.

Then the little bird set to work, weaving in and out, in and out, creating a sparkling crown of silver and gold. When it was finished the little bird placed the woven crown high in the arch of the sky.

The next morning, as King Sun began his climb up into the daytime sky, the sparkle of the crown caught his eye. He reached out and placed it on his head and it fitted so perfectly that he wore it with joy.

That night, Queen Moon found the crown on her journey, high in the arch of the sky. The sparkles caught her eye, and she reached out and placed it on her head. It fitted so exquisitely that she wore it with joy.

From that day to this, King Sun and Queen Moon always wore the woven crown on their journey across the sky. When Queen Moon was round and full the crown fitted perfectly. But even if Queen Moon was just a thin sliver in the sky, by some special magic the crown still fitted beautifully.

And from that day forward, King Sun never argued that he was more important than his Queen. They both continued to wear the sparkling woven crown, day and night, and peace reigned in the sky kingdom.

10   CYCLES OF LIFE AND CHANGE

This chapter includes stories that share a 'bigger picture' of the cycles of life – the metamorphosis of a caterpillar to a butterfly; the cycle of the seasons; the cycle of water and the journey of a snowflake. Some traditional stories from different parts of the world bring their wisdom here.

Here is a summary of each theme:

APPLE LEAF – a composting story for pre-school and kindergarten children about the cycles of life and death in nature (p. 259).

THE BUTTERFLY – a tale of death, life and transformation – for all ages (p. 262).

LITTLE STAR'S JOURNEY – a story for a young child of the cycle of life, using images and ideas from Mexican culture (p. 264).

THE SPARKLING RIVER – a flood story of a river that goes through a cycle of destruction and recovery – for children aged five years and upwards (p. 266).

THE LEGEND OF CHUAB – part of the creation myth from the islands of Palau – a cycle-of-life story for older children, families, schools and communities (p. 268).

FLY EAGLE FLY – a folk tale from Ghana with a 'resurrection theme' – for older children, families, schools and communities (p. 270).

STREAM, DESERT, WIND – a Sufi parable about change and transformation – for older children, families, schools and communities (p. 271).

THE CREATOR WOMAN AND THE DOG – a Native American story with the theme of 'how trouble becomes transformation' – for older children, families, schools and communities (p. 273).

SNOWFLAKE IS FALLING... a story-poem to encourage discussion with older children and families about transformation and metamorphosis, and individual 'patterns' or destinies in life (p. 275).

Apple Leaf

By Toni Wright–Turner

A story for pre-school and kindergarten-aged children about the cycles of life and death which are around us all the time, in nature and in our lives.

The Apple Gum is an Australian native and is not deciduous, so the whole tree doesn't change and drop leaves all in one season. This story is about one leaf on the tree, and this is very typical of gum trees – dropping leaves all the time.

Once upon a time there was an Apple Gum Tree on the edge of the garden. The garden was full of flowers and herbs, vegetables and shrubs. The plants in the garden chatted happily as the winds blew, the raindrops pattered, and great Father Sun shone. They knew the rain fairies and the sun fairies, and they were friends with the elves who tended them daily. The children who came to work in the garden were gentle and kind to all the plants. It was indeed a happy garden.

There was one small glossy leaf on the Apple Gum Tree which stood proudly overlooking the garden. Apple Leaf was friends with everyone. His world was perfect, and Apple Leaf wanted it to always stay the same.

Then one day, something changed. Apple Leaf woke one fine summer morning not feeling his usual glossy green self. Father Sun shone and the sun fairies came down to visit, but they didn't notice Apple Leaf today. They busied themselves with the new baby leaves and the new flowers in the garden below. Apple Leaf was fading more and more. Gone was his beautiful soft green glow. Day by day he was becoming more brittle. Apple Leaf cried, for he wanted to be the most beautiful leaf for ever.

When the gusty autumn breezes came to the garden, Apple Leaf could not hold on to his tree any more. Down he fluttered to the earth below. At first, he was frightened, for he had never been to the earth before. But soon he made friends with the grasses nearby, the beetles who tunnelled under him and the ants who scurried over him. Every day he saw Father Sun, felt the breezes blow across him and the soft raindrops patter on his now brown coat.

Then his old friend from the garden, Daisy Petals, came fluttering down beside him, her beautiful flower finished. The two friends were pleased to meet again. After that, day by day they were joined by others... leaves and grasses, petals and twigs, all like themselves, withered and brown, fallen from plants in the garden. Sometimes the autumn winds would twirl them into a dance, but mostly they lay, watching and waiting, wondering what would become of them. The sun fairies came to visit the garden less now, and the days grew cooler.

One day Apple Leaf heard the children coming. They were talking and laughing, carrying rakes and forks, one pushing a wheelbarrow. They stopped near Apple Leaf and his friends, and one child, seeing Apple Leaf, picked him up joyfully.

'Look, look, this one is just right! And look at all these!'

Soon, Daisy Petals and all the others were raked into a pile and put in the wheelbarrow with Apple Leaf.

Bump, bump, bump went the wheelbarrow as the children took turns pushing it along. They were excited about their load, and talking about the compost they were about to make.

'What is this compost they talk of?', wondered Apple Leaf, 'and where are we going?' He didn't want to leave the garden that had always been his home. Then Apple Leaf felt the wheelbarrow tip and he went sliding, and landed in a soft sheltered bed with all his friends tumbling in beside him. More and more leaves and twigs, grasses and fallen flowers were gathered into the bed with Apple Leaf – until it was quite full. At last the children put a blanket of Mother Earth over the bed.

Inside their new earth bed, Apple Leaf and Daisy Petal listened as the wind blew and the raindrops pattered. Sometimes the sun fairies would visit briefly and warm the earthen blanket. The friends snuggled up together, glad to be out of the winter winds, away from Jack Frost's icy fingers, safe from winter's cold. They grew sleepier and sleepier until, yawning, one by one they fell fast asleep and slept the whole winter long.

One morning Apple Leaf awoke as a little earthworm tunnelled past him.

'Wake up, sleepy heads!', said the worm. 'Springtime is here. Time for you to work.'

'Work', thought Apple Leaf, '– what work can a faded leaf do?' And he rolled over and went back to sleep. But it wasn't long before the children arrived, and he was woken again.

'Let's see if our compost is ready', they called. They lifted Mother Earth's blanket off all the friends in the bed. The sun was shining brightly. Apple Leaf looked around for Daisy Petals. She was nowhere to be seen – all around was rich moist earth.

'Daisy Petals, where are you?', he called.

'Just here, but where are you?'

　　　　　　　STORIES TO LIGHT THE NIGHT

As all the friends awoke, they found themselves transformed – gone were their brittle brown coats – all were now soft, moist and earthy. The children were pleased when they looked in, and ran off, returning with wheelbarrows and shovels, eager to dig out the new soft compost and take it to the garden.

It was springtime and they were working again after the cold winter. Where Apple Leaf was turned into the garden earth, the children planted a tiny marigold seed. She was very frightened for she had never been away from mother marigold before. So Apple Leaf wrapped his new self around the seed, sheltering and feeding her, helping her to grow.

Day by day, the little marigold grew stronger with Apple Leaf's help. First, she sent roots down into the earth, and then stretched her leaves up to the sun. At last the day came when marigold was ready to open her first flower. Deep inside the opening bud, Apple Leaf looked up and saw that he was back in his own garden, beneath his own mother, Apple Gum Tree. Apple Leaf was very happy!

THE BUTTERFLY

I rewrote this story from an anonymous source – it is a simple tale about death, life and transformation, for children aged four and upwards. This is especially beautiful when presented as a puppet show – see the activity at the end of story.

Although this story has been written to tell to children, its metaphor of transformation speaks to all ages. Drawing on the thousands of accounts of 'near-death experiences' that she has accumulated over the years from persons of all ages and circumstances, Elizabeth Kubler Ross developed the image of the butterfly's emergence from a cocoon as a symbol for the new beginning that such experiences portend for us when we die.

With tired wings an old butterfly once fluttered over a field. It made its way towards a green bush, and laid a tiny egg under a leaf and crawled away.

The egg was left in the care of Mother Earth. During the day, the sun warmed it from above; at night, the earth warmed it from below. The leaf protected it from rain, and so it was well cared for. The glow of life of the old butterfly had gone out, but in its egg lived a spark.

Already after only a few days there was a gentle movement under the delicate skin. A sunbeam played around the green leaf of the plant, calling, 'Come out, come out'. There was a pulling and stretching in the egg, the skin tore, and out came a tiny yellow caterpillar, covered with little dots and with skin as smooth as silk.

The little creature crawled towards a green leaf, which then became its garden, house and food. The edge of the leaf was especially good to eat, and the tiny caterpillar began to gnaw out little corners. After a few days almost all this leaf was gone, and the sunbeam said, 'It's time to find your way into the wide green world'.

So the caterpillar began its journey, crawling from bush to bush, from leaf to leaf. As it crawled it munched, and as it munched it grew. It crawled and munched, it munched and grew. Soon the tiny caterpillar had grown into a very large caterpillar.

By this time summer was coming to an end, and the autumn winds were blowing across the fields and through the bushes. The sunlight seemed to say, 'Find a quiet place to rest'.

The caterpillar crawled down between some rocks into a dark and quiet space. Mother Earth wrapped it in her warm arms, and the caterpillar fell into a deep sleep. While it slept through the long winter, delicate elves wove a special gown for it. With their mysterious fingers they wove the sparkle of the stars and the glow of the rainbow into the cloak.

Spring came and brought some sunny days. The warmth of the sun reached deep into the earth. While flowers were opening to the light above ground, a butterfly was waking up below the ground. The caterpillar had died, but in its place a butterfly was climbing up through a crack in the rocks, climbing up towards the light. It could hear the flower song and it could feel the warmth of the spring sunbeams.

It opened its beautiful new wings and flew up high.

Craft Activity
Tell the story as a puppet show, using your body (seated on the floor) as the 'theatre' – you need a green cloth over your lap (for the garden) and some puppets made from coloured combed fleece: the caterpillar starts off very small, with new and larger ones hiding in the folds of the cloth as he eats and grows bigger. You can also use coloured combed fleece to make the butterfly – hang it by a thin thread from a small twig so you have something to hold on to when you need to help it to fly.

Children can also be helped to make their own caterpillars and butterflies and do their own puppet shows.

LITTLE STAR'S JOURNEY

A very simple story of the Cycle of Life, using images and ideas from Mexican culture shared by illustrator Zavet Monroy (included after the story). My writing has been guided by Zavet to specifically tell or read to a young child growing up in Mexico; and on her suggestion I have left a space in the middle of the story** for personal additions/sensory adventures to be added before or during the sharing with a child – other things to see, smell, touch, taste, hear and do. For example, if the child has recently fallen off a bike, you could put this in; or if you have visited the beach and rolled down the sand dunes, you could add this; and you could engage the child in adding his/her own ideas – these may be real experiences and/or made-up ones. The story could be adapted for use in other parts of the world by changing the sights and sounds and smells and tastes that the Little Star Child may experience.

A *Little Star Child* was preparing for the long journey from his sky home to spend time in the world below.

He was looking forward to enjoying so many beautiful things. He had heard wondrous stories about what he would find down on the earth – the smell of the flowers, the taste of the fruits, the sounds of the birds, the touch of butterfly wings, and the sights of green mountains and white beaches.

To help get ready for this special adventure, *Little Star* had to first put on his very own suit of skin. Mother Moon wrapped *Little Star* warmly in a silver moonbeam hug and helped him squeeze inside the new suit – it felt soft and warm and wonderful. Father Sun circled him with a golden glow of light.

Little Star was one of many star children making the journey. Sometimes the little stars twinkled 'hello' to others they passed who were returning home. Sometimes they stopped briefly to hear their snippets or tales, then continued along their way.

Each of the star children wondered if they might spend a short time in the world, a long time or a very long time. But no matter the length of their stay, they hoped to enjoy many things – the colours of the festivals, the smell of orange blossom and cinnamon, the taste of tortilla and *elotes*,* the feel of soft grass under their feet, and the song of the thrush and little coquette and many other wonderful birds. They looked forward to the many adventures they may experience, like …**

After their adventures, when it was time to return home, *Little Star* and all the other star children knew just what to do. They would take off their skin suits and then, light as air, they would begin their journey back to the sky. They had to travel across rivers and over mountains, and find their way through hot lands and cold lands and windy lands. It was a long way!

Finally, they would reach their sky home and once again shine their bright light down into the world.

---

*Grilled Mexican Sweet Corn

MEXICAN CULTURAL THOUGHTS ON 'CYCLES OF LIFE' FROM ZAVET MONROY, ILLUSTRATOR, MEXICO CITY

For me, the subject of death is something very profound because it inevitably talks about life. Perhaps that is why death is celebrated in Mexico. My way of perceiving it, already merged and transformed with all the culture that I have received from my ancestors, is seeing death as something sacred, since it is a symbol of transformation. Without knowing what specifically happens after death, the idea of life is always present. For example, when a loved one dies, I do not know where she (or he) is going, but in me, she is reborn, through memories and the way I perceive what her life was, now giving life to a memory. That is also a rebirth. That person is being born again in my way of remembering him or her.

On the other hand, my way of perceiving my own death is taking life into account first. Life is like a small open door where you can see a little light. When I get closer, I let myself be seduced by the sensations that can only be experienced in life. I let myself be dressed in a skin to obtain the senses and with them, live life. Being aware of death, it is how I can enjoy life, because when it is time to die, I will take off my skin clothing to return to where I belong. These are the images that I would personally like to share, in story form, with my four-year old son.

For all this, it is important to celebrate death, since it is death that teaches us to live, to enjoy, to be reborn. This does not mean that when a loved one dies, we do not feel sad and it is a very dark moment, but it is part of the transformation that all beings close to that person experience.

All this I see represented in all daily experiences. For example, a pandemic like the one which, as I write, we are experiencing is the process of a death that also announces a next life. The same with night and day, sleep and wake up.

In Aztec culture the Mictlán legend talks more about what happens after death. The road to Mictlán is like a purification process. It consists of nine levels that must be overcome in order to reach the King and Queen of the Underworld, and then the Spirit can be released. At the end of this long journey to Mictlán, the deceased have to deliver to Mictlantecuhtli the tributes that have been given to him before 'waking up on the riverbank', since it would not be fair to arrive before the very Lord of Death empty-handed. This for me is about reaching my death, and giving up my skin and my senses, and being free again in a place where I don't need 'matter'.

THE SPARKLING RIVER

I wrote the following story during a time of devastating floods in Brisbane – it was used in primary schools with children aged five years and upwards.

A sparkling river goes through a cycle of destruction and recovery, while the river dwellers are helped by a different kind of sparkle.

The story has since been modified and translated into two Filipino languages – Tagalog and Visaya – to be used by teachers in the communities in Southern Philippines which suffer from floods each monsoon season.

There was once a town built on the banks of a long and winding river. The people who lived in the town loved their river – its waters sparkled in the sunshine, many boats moved up and down its lazy flow, bicycles and cars travelled along paths and roads on its banks, and children played in the parks along its way. By night, the moon and stars and the lights of the town were reflected in the river's silky stillness.

The people who lived in the town were proud of their river that sparkled by day and sparkled by night.

At certain times during the year, the rains would fall, and the sparkling river would grow brown and swollen and flow swiftly by. But when the rains stopped, the river would settle down again, and all would be as clear and sparkling as before.

However, there was a week when the rains fell so heavily that the river filled up and swelled over its banks and into the town. The muddy brown waters flowed into houses and shops and schools. Many people had to move out of their homes and sleep in large halls together, in many beds all in a row.

When the rains stopped, the sun shone once again. The brown waters slowly flowed back out of the houses and shops and schools. The brown waters slowly flowed back down the streets and into the river and out into the ocean. And as the brown waters flowed back into the river, they left a coating of mud on everything.

It took many months and much work for the mud to be cleaned up. It took many months for the river to lose its muddy brown colour and regain its sparkle.

However, during this brown, muddy time, the people of the town discovered a new kind of sparkle. It was a sparkle in the eyes of helping neighbours. It was a sparkle in the eyes of helping strangers. It was a sparkle in the offer of a helping hand that came from all over the land and from faraway lands.

This new kind of sparkle helped give the people of the river town much hope. They carried this with them through all the muddy days and muddy weeks and muddy months.

They carried this with them until once again, their river was sparkling in the sunshine.

They carried this with them until once again, the moon and stars and the lights of the town were reflected in the river's silky stillness.

THE LEGEND OF CHUAB

This cycle-of-life story is part of the creation myth from the islands of Palau in the western Pacific Ocean – its theme of the consequence of 'taking too much', to the point where all the food from the sea and the food from the land had been consumed, is very relevant today.

The story could provide a springboard for discussion with older children, families, schools and communities.

Long long ago, before the time of humans, the sea was empty. The spirits under the sea and the spirits above the sea were lonely, and they longed for company. From the darkest part they caused a volcano to erupt, and the molten rock formed a high mountain which became an island. It was here that the power of the sea, together with the power of the sky, created a giant clam, Latmikaik.

Latmikaik could not move or speak... it just continued to grow. It grew and it grew and, finally, the turbulent waters forced its giant lips open and all forms of life came flowing out ... crabs, eels, fish, crocodiles, dugongs, sharks... and many birds and butterflies flew up into the sky.

But Latmikaik had one more to birth. Once again, its lips opened, and a giant creature crawled out.

The creature's appetite was monstrous. It cared about nothing else but eating. 'More, more, more, bring me more!', was the daily cry.

Over time the creature grew into a mighty giant. It was called Chuab. As it grew, its appetite increased, and soon the villagers had to use a ladder to reach its mouth. Soon there was nothing left to eat... nothing for the giant, and nothing for the villagers. The sea was empty of fish, and the land was empty of fruits and coconuts.

When there was no food left the giant called for the villagers to bring their children. Of course, they did not want to give their children to Chuab, and so they worked out a plan. While the giant was sleeping, they piled coconut stalks and husks against its giant body, and then lit the fire.

By the time Chuab woke up the burning flames had created a wall around it and there was no escape. Seeing the fear in the people, for the first time the giant creature understood how selfish and cruel and greedy it had been.

Chuab realised it needed to die so it could give back to the people what it had taken. Slowly the giant body toppled over and broke into many pieces. Each piece where it fell became a new island – 340 islands in total. Soon the sea around each new island was teeming with fish, and on the land grew many fruits and coconuts.

And this is how Palau was created.

FLY EAGLE FLY

When I was working in South Africa many years ago, I listened to a radio interview with the Bishop of Table Bay, Cape Town. He described the following story that he told his eight-year old daughter who was dying of cancer.

The story was taken from a folk tale from Ghana with a 'resurrection theme', and the Bishop felt it had really helped the daughter and the whole family cope better with the reality of her coming death. The tale is recounted below.

There was once an eagle chic that was born in a nest of chickens. A farmer had been walking in the mountains and had found the egg lying on the ground, and had taken it home to his hen to help hatch it.

The eagle chic grew up with all the other chickens but always had a feeling it could fly high – but there was no one who could show it what to do.

The farmer's boy took it and tried to help it – first from the top of a ladder, then from the roof of the house. But these two tries were not high enough for the eagle to really feel its wings.

Then the boy and the farmer took the eagle back to the mountains where it had come from. Together they placed it on the edge of a high cliff. This time the eagle chic took off from the edge of the cliff. It felt the air beneath its wings and the sun on its feathers and soared higher and higher.

Soon the eagle was back high up in the sky where it belonged, and it flew up towards the sun.

STREAM, DESERT, WIND

This little tale is a Sufi parable – a beautiful story about change and transformation. It could be used with older children, teenagers and adults, accompanied by painting or drawing scenes from the stream's journey, or a weaving of the colours of the journey (see the activity after the story).

Like 'Fly Eagle Fly', this is another story of death and transformation. Something dies and is then reborn in a different way.

A stream was born high on a mountain. It rushed around stones, over waterfalls, across fields, and through forests and valleys. Finally, it reached a great desert and pushed its water against the sand. Then the water disappeared. The stream, that was feeling so confident with its life up to this point, could not believe what was happening. 'My water is disappearing – how can I cross this desert?'

Then the stream heard a whispering. It seemed to be coming from the sand itself – 'Ask the wind – it knows a way to cross the desert'.

'The wind can fly', thought the stream. 'All I can do is disappear into the sand. I can't cross this desert.'

'Allow the wind to carry you', the voice whispered.

'But then I will have to change. I don't want to change – I want to stay as I am.'

'If you continue to flow into the desert, you are changing – you are either going to disappear altogether or you will become a swamp.'

'But I want to stay myself', said the stream. 'How can I get to the other side and still be myself?'

'If you remember your true self, you will know this can never change', whispered the voice.

The stream then remembered a long-forgotten dream about being carried in the arms of the wind. It let go of the earth below and allowed itself to rise in a vapour.

The wind flew with it far across the desert, all the way to the mountains on the other side. Finally, it was released as soft rain high on the top of a mountain.

With this the stream was born anew. It rushed around stones, over waterfalls, across fields, and through forests and valleys. And as it rushed along, it had watery memories of its true and essential self.

CRAFT ACTIVITY
Using a cardboard guide, make a piece of weaving using lengths of wool in the colours of water, wind, sand, stones, forests and mountains.
See Patterns and Templates, p. 283.

THE CREATOR WOMAN AND THE DOG

This Native American story, referenced to the Apache and Sioux Tribes, has been told around the fire and in homes and cultural gatherings for thousands of years. With the theme of 'how trouble becomes transformation' it is possibly more relevant today than ever before; and with deep respect to its origins, a summarized version is included in this section.

It is an extraordinary tale, with the journey a constant cycle of creation and unravelling and new creation. According to cultural understanding of its meaning, this is a good thing, for if the black dog ever fails to unravel the rug and the rug is finished, the world as we know it will come to an end. Chaos has happened to the world before. And it has always recovered from its unravelling. The Creator Woman knows what will happen when she leaves her weaving to tend to the pot. The Creator Woman knows that she will have to begin her task anew when she returns.

This philosophical understanding is reflected in wall art in Berlin by Erich Fried, that says, 'He who wants the world to remain as it is doesn't want the world to remain at all'.

The story could provide a springboard for discussion with older children and families.

There is a cave, a special cave, in the side of a mountain – no one knows which mountain or which cave. It is the home of the knowledge of the wonders and workings of the world. Inside the cave lives a wise Creator Woman.

Although everyone knows the Creator Woman is there, no one has ever seen her. With an old black dog as her only company, she sits in front of a roughly made loom spending all her days weaving. She is working on a beautiful rug, using pine needles and porcupine quills and other things of beauty from the forest.

She rarely stops her work, only leaving her weaving to stir the great clay pot that hangs over a fire in the back of the cave. The fire is so old it might just be older than time itself.

The stew in the pot is also very old... and very important. It contains the roots and seeds of all the herbs and plants and grains in the world.

If the woman fails to tend the pot, the stew may burn, and the Creator Woman knows that this must not happen.

Every so often the old woman rises, looks at the black dog, and then slowly moves to the clay pot at the back of the cave.

This gives the black dog time to get up and go to where the weaving lies on the floor by the loom. The dog takes one loose thread after another in his mouth and begins to pull on them.

While the old woman continues to slowly stir the stew, the dog slowly unravels the rug to its starting point.

When the Creator Woman returns and sees the chaos that her companion has done, she sighs a big sigh. Then she sits down to begin her work all over again.

As she weaves, she sees new visions and thinks of new patterns, and her old hands begin to give them shape and form. She has now forgotten the rug she was weaving before.

Thus, down through the years the Creator Woman and the dog have continued their ritual of weaving, unravelling and reweaving, but the rug is never completed. This is a good thing, for if ever the rug is finished, the world as we know it will come to an end.

SNOWFLAKE IS FALLING...

This story-poem was inspired by the following quotation from Goethe. He wrote these thoughts in the Swiss Alps while staying near the magnificent Staubbach Falls:

> 'The soul of man is like water: it comes from heaven, it returns to heaven, and again to earth must go, ever changing.'

The poem could be used to encourage discussion with older children and families about transformation and metamorphosis, and individual 'patterns' or destinies in life. For instructions for making paper snowflakes see Patterns and Templates, p. 285.

Snowflake is falling, new life is calling,
The pattern of a star tells the secret of who you are...
Tells the secret of what you can be... only you can see!

Softly landing on mountains below,
Where will you go?
Will you rest on a green branch,
Or flutter to the ground while having fun?
Will you fall into a hole,
Or land on a rock and melt in the sun?

Will you merge with a bubbling stream,
And be part of water that helps keep things clean?
Will you tumble over a waterfall so high,
And into mist return to the sky?

Or fall to the river below....
And continue along...
Across the great land... growing wide and strong...
Rushing fast, meandering slow,
Eventually reaching the sea,
The jewelled sea of eternity...

Snowflake is falling, new life is calling,
The pattern of a star tells the secret of who you are...
Tells the secret of what you can be... only you can see!

PATTERNS AND TEMPLATES

THE LITTLE STAR WHO COULD NOT STAY   See Page 89

This little felt star fits in a moon pocket – the felt pocket is a circle with a half-moon shape stitched on the front to create the pocket part.

YOU WILL NEED
- Small oddments of felt
- Toy stuffing (oddments of felt or wool)
- Sewing thread
- Needle

1. Using the templates, cut out two star shapes in yellow felt or wool, and one circle and one semi-circle in blue or purple felt or wool.

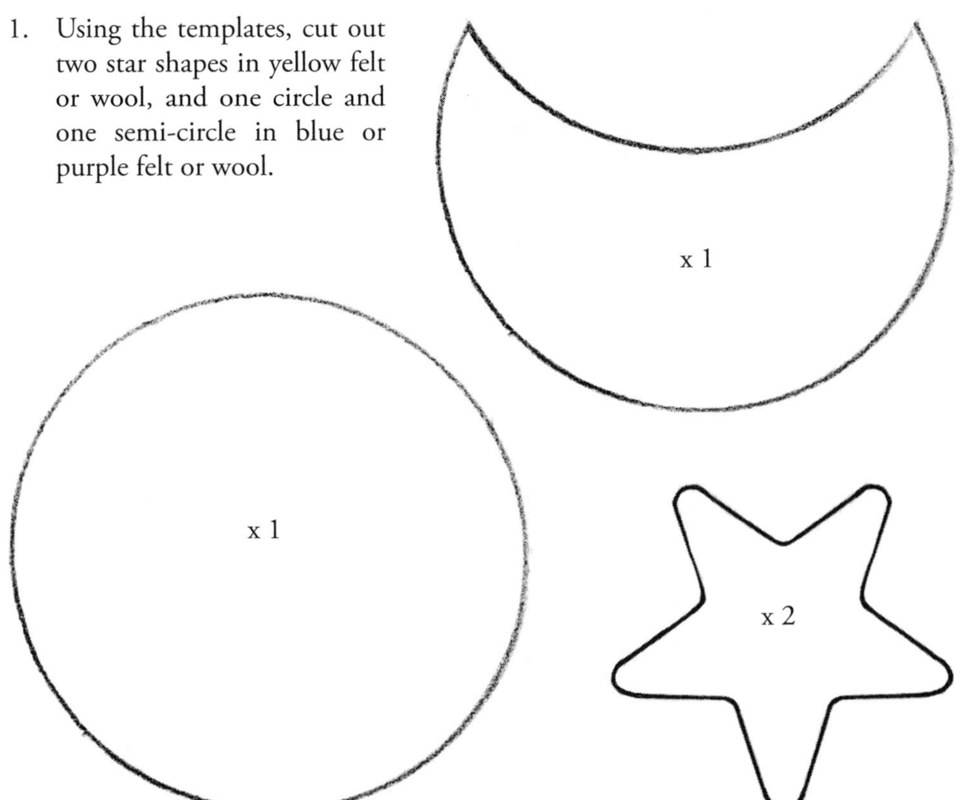

2. Sew the two stars together using over stitch or blanket stitch around the edge. When you are halfway around, stuff gently with your stuffing so it's not too full before sewing all the way.

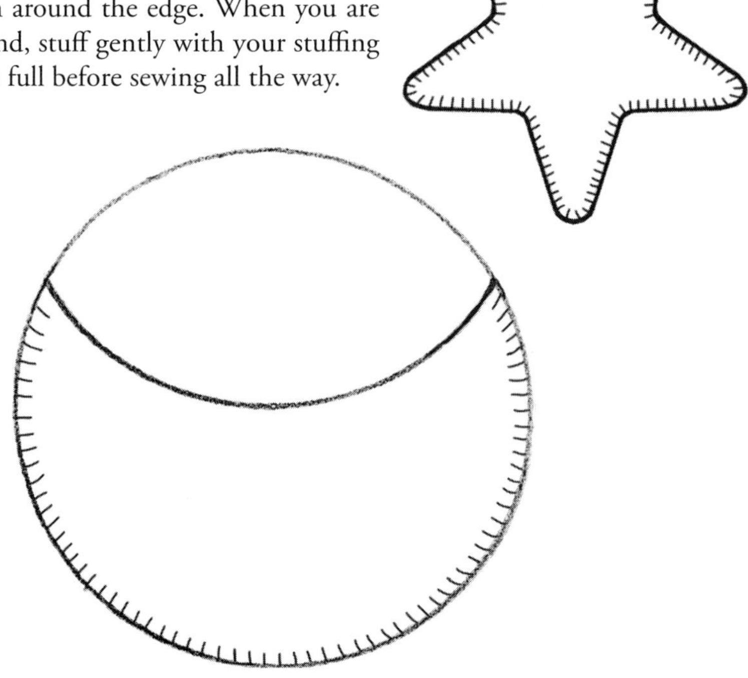

3. Place the semi-circle on top of your circle as shown (see above) and stitch all the way around using over or blanket stitch, making sure that your star fits snugly (see below) in the pocket formed.

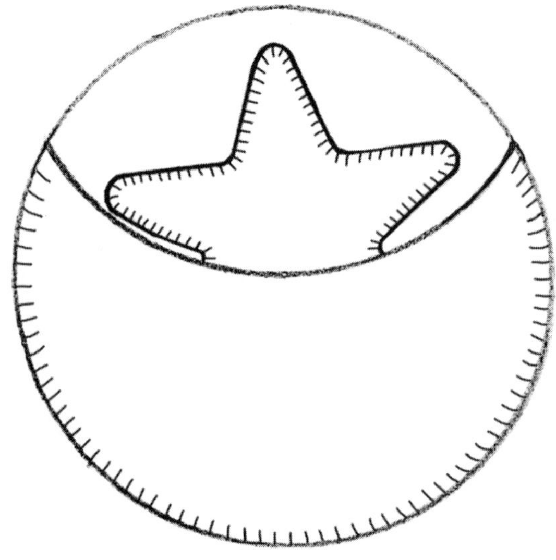

You will need
- Small piece of felt 10 x 8cm (4 x 3¼in)
- Aluminium foil
- Glue
- Sequins or shiny sweet wrappers

1. Using the template cut out a fish shape from the felt.
2. Decorate your fish with sequins and shiny paper.
3. Scrunch up the aluminium foil to make two rock pools – with a connecting passage – for your fish to travel from one pool to the other.

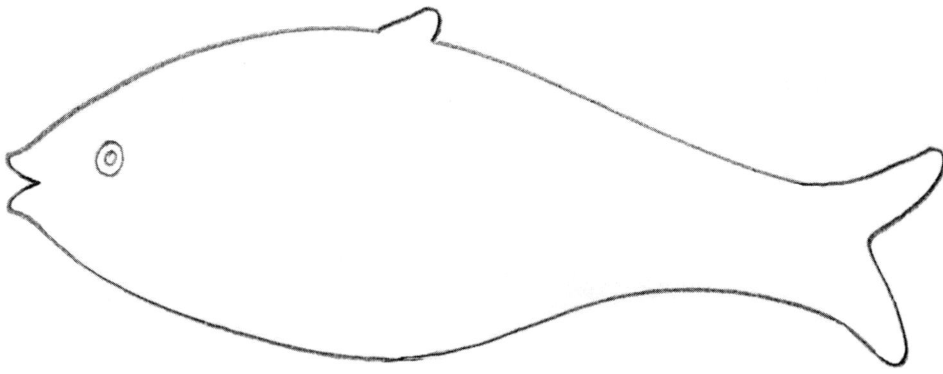

YOU WILL NEED
- Cardboard or strong paper
- Paints and brushes
- Scissors

OR
- Ceramic cups
- Ceramic paints

Design different cups – one for each member of your family; you could do these on thick cardboard (using the template below) and cut them out; or use ceramic paint, and paint the designs on real cups. Choose from the designs below for stars, leaves, waves or flowers, or create your own patterns.

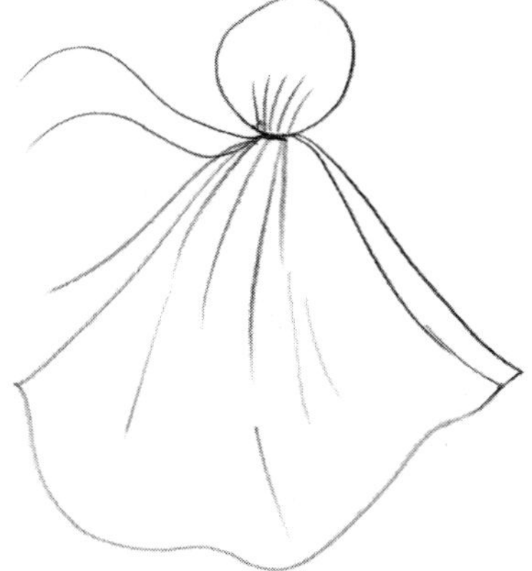

1. Place your stuffing, which could be a small ball of yarn, into the centre and tie for the head.

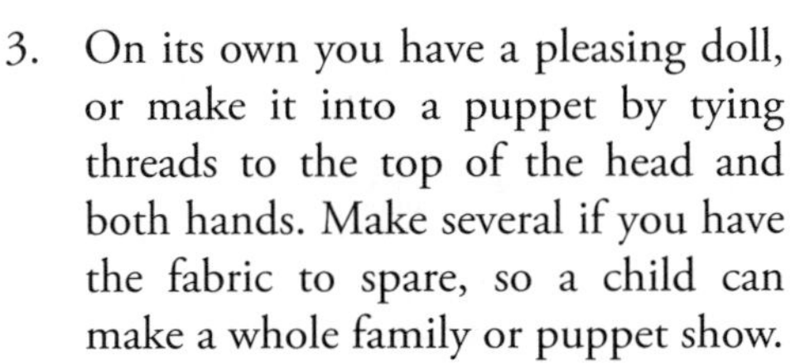

2. Knot the two corners for the hands and the other corners for legs, or leave as a long skirt.

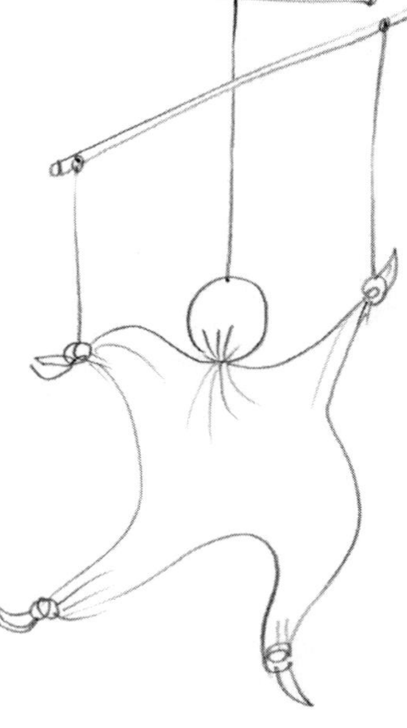

3. On its own you have a pleasing doll, or make it into a puppet by tying threads to the top of the head and both hands. Make several if you have the fabric to spare, so a child can make a whole family or puppet show.

YOU WILL NEED
- Card or strong paper
- Tissue paper 10 x 13cm (4 x 5in)

1. Cut out the bird shape from card. Cut a slot for the wings where indicated.
2. Fold the tissue paper into a concertina as if making a fan.

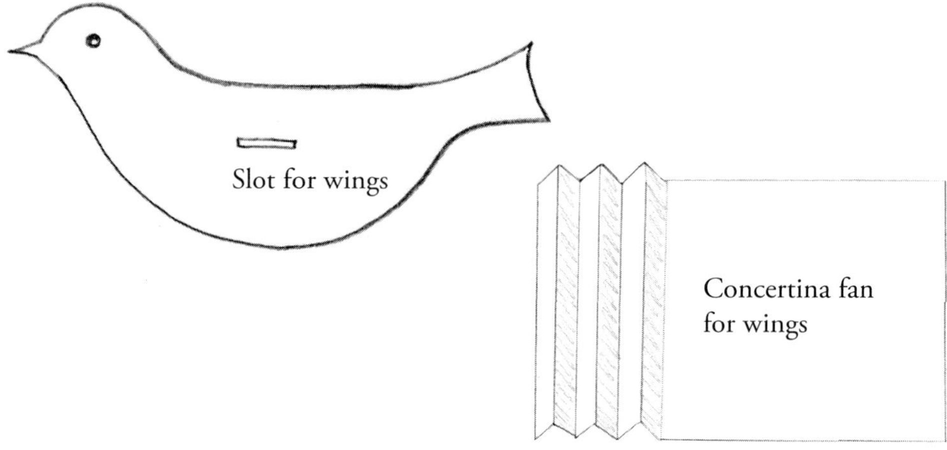

3. Fold pleated paper in half and slip through the slit in the bird's body until half-way point. Pull up the wings so that they meet in the middle.
4. Thread string through a hole in the body where the bird will balance when hanging.

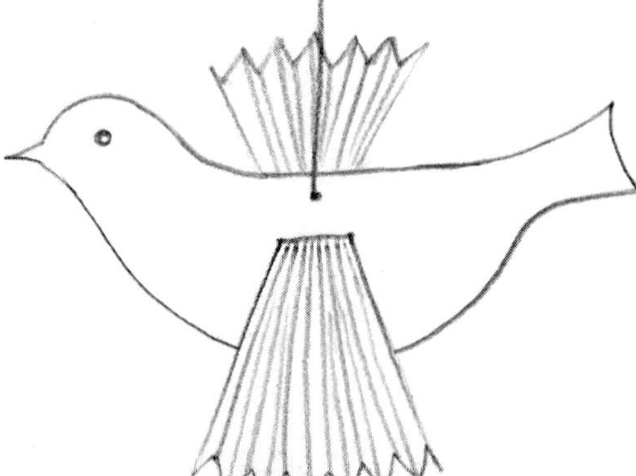

NB: Drawings not to scale

Mini Weaving Pattern

This beautiful story about change and transformation could be accompanied by weaving the colours of the journey. Choose card strong enough not to bend during the weaving process and wool in the colours of water, wind, sand, stones, forests and mountains.

You will need
- Scissors
- Large blunt needle (or small crochet hook)
- Six colours of yarn, double knitting (8 ply)
- Thick cardboard 12 x 19cm/4.8 x 7.5 inches

1. Cut a rectangle from card 12 x 19cm/4.8 x 7.5 inches and make 12 slots roughly 1cm/0.4 inches long, top and bottom.

2. Starting at one edge, wrap the yarn tightly over the card, through each slot to make the warp (foundation) threads. Tie the ends diagonally across the back of your loom.

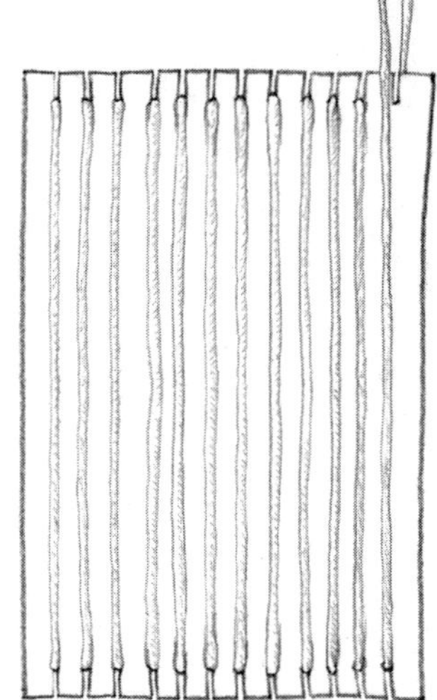

3. Start at the bottom by weaving over and under the threads. When you reach the other side, weave back under or over in the opposite manner. Change colours for the story, leaving the ends to sew in later.

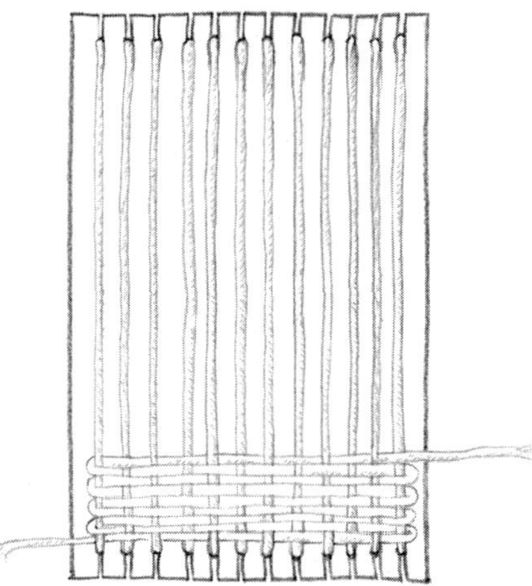

4. When you have finished, remove the warp from the card-loom by cutting the warp threads. Trim to an even length to create a fringe.

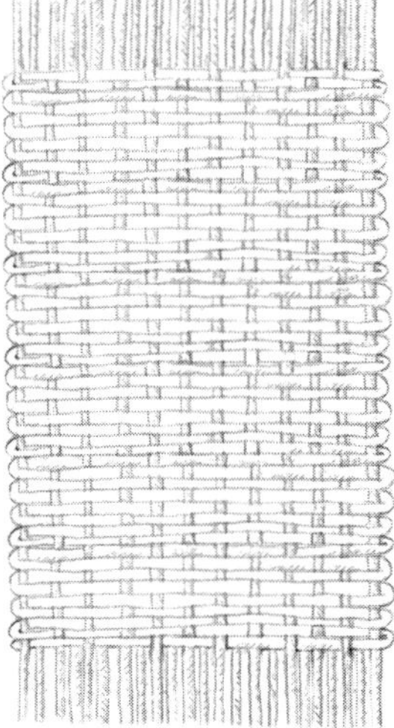

   STORIES TO LIGHT THE NIGHT

There is no right or wrong way to design your snowflake as every one is different.

1. Get a square piece of paper or trim a piece of paper to be square.

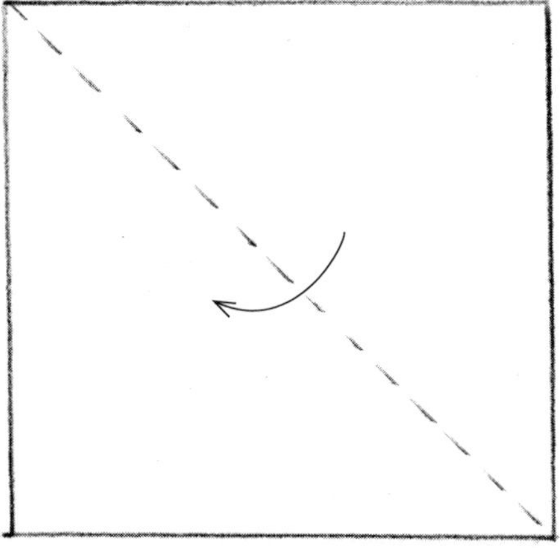

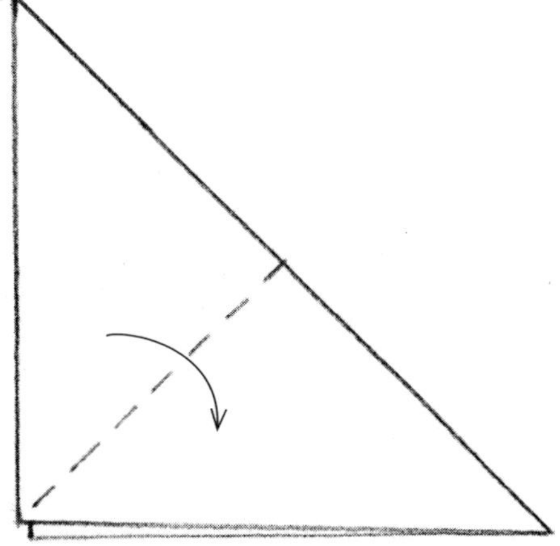

2. Fold your square in half diagonally.   Fold your triangle diagonally in half again.

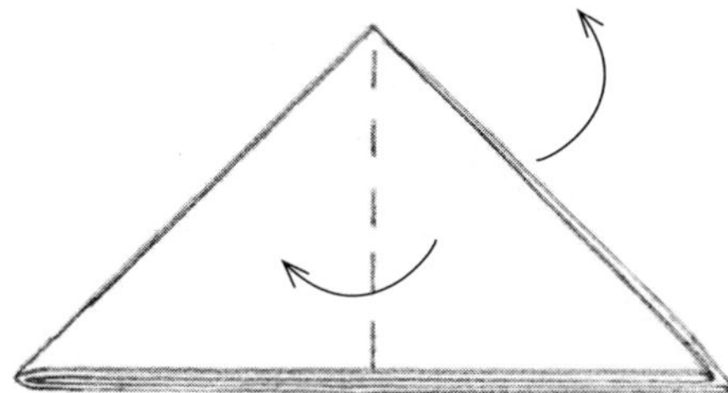

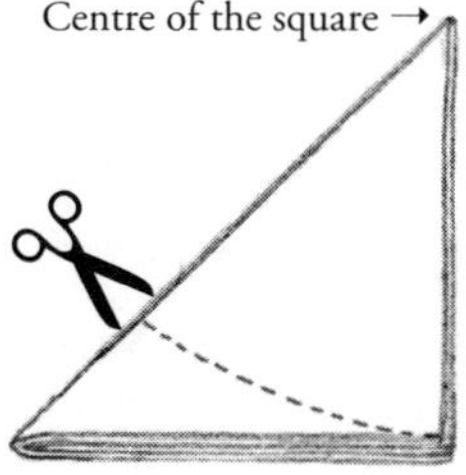

3. Fold the paper in thirds with one side to the front, the other to the back.

4. Trim the extra pieces of paper off the end of your small triangle to create a curve.

5. Cut different shapes all around the outside edges of your triangle – circles, squares, triangles – anything is possible.

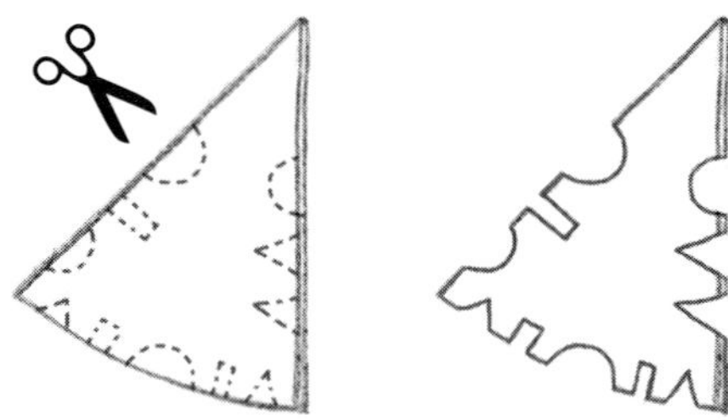

6. Unfold your paper and look at your unique snowflake – hang it in your window or on your wall.

REFERENCES AND RESOURCES

In this section you will find information on bereavement clinics and services for children and their families in different countries around the world – the UK, the USA, Canada, Europe, Australia, New Zealand, South Africa and Hong Kong. There is also a list of books and websites.

If there is something you would like added here, please contact me or Hawthorn Press so it can be inserted in time for the next printing of the book.

Services for Children and Their Families

AUSTRALIA
The National Centre for Childhood Grief: https://childhoodgrief.org.au/
Australian Bereavement Care Centre: http://www.bereavementcare.com.au/
Australian Centre for Grief and Bereavement: https://www.grief.org.au/
Griefline: http://griefline.org.au/
Lifeline: https://www.lifeline.org.au/
Pink Elephants Support Network: a charity created to support women through miscarriage, pregnancy loss and beyond – https://pinkelephantssupport.com/
SANDS (Stillbirth and Neonatal Death Support): www.sands.org.au

CANADA
Bereaved Families of Ontario: https://www.bfotoronto.ca/
Canuck Place Children's Hospice, BC: https://www.canuckplace.org/
The Coping Centre: http://www.copingcentre.com/
Rainbows Canada: http://www.rainbows.ca/

EUROPE
Bereavement Support Network (English language): http://www.bsnvar.org/

HONG KONG
The Jessie and Thomas Tan Centre: www.hospicecare.org.hk/bereavement

INDIA
East-West Centre for Counselling and Training: https://centerforcounselling.org/
Support for Women: https://www.womensweb.in/
Indian Storytellers Healing Network: https://www.facebook.com/Indian-Storytellers-Healing-Network-111967630552639/
A safe space for conversations on mental health in India: http://www.healthcollective.in/
Suicide prevention organization: https://snehaindia.org/

NEW ZEALAND
Lifeline Aotearoa: http://www.lifeline.org.nz
Skylight: A New Zealand organization supporting children and young people with change, loss and grief – http://skylight.org.nz/

SOUTH AFRICA
The Compassionate Friends South Africa: http://www.compassionatefriends.co.za/
Khululeka Grief Support: http://www.khululeka.org/

UNITED KINGDOM
Winston's Wish: https://www.winstonswish.org/
Bereavement Advice Centre: https://www.bereavementadvice.org/
Care for the Family: http://www.careforthefamily.org.uk/
Child Bereavement UK: http://childbereavementuk.org/
The Compassionate Friends: https://www.tcf.org.uk/
Cruse Bereavement UK: http://www.cruse.org.uk/
Hope Again: http://hopeagain.org.uk/
S.P.R.I.N.G. (Supporting Parents & Relatives in Neonatal Grief): https://www.springsupport.org.uk/
SANDS (Stillbirth and Neonatal Death Support): www.sands.org.uk

USA
The Dougy Centre for Grieving Children: https://www.dougy.org/
Association for Death Education and Counselling: https://www.adec.org/
Bereaved Parents of the USA: http://bereavedparentsusa.org/
Grief Share: https://www.griefshare.org/
MISS Foundation: https://missfoundation.org/

Books

Anon (Mrs Wordsmith) (2019). *Storyteller's Illustrated Dictionary: 1000+ Words to Take Your Storytelling to the Next Level.* London: Mrs Wordsmith.

Bassil-Morozow, Helena (2020). *Jungian Theory for Storytellers: A Toolkit.* Abingdon, Oxon: Routledge.

Berthoud, Ella & Elderkin, Susan (2014). *The Novel Cure: An A–Z of Literary Remedies.* Edinburgh: Canongate Books.

Biesenbach, Rob (2018). *Unleash the Power of Storytelling: Win Hearts, Change Minds, Get Results.* Evaston, Ill.: Eastlawn Media.

Boyd, Brian (2010). *On the Origin of Stories: Evolution, Cognition, and Fiction.* Cambridge, Mass.: Harvard University Press.

Bruce, Tina, McNair, Lynn & Whinnett, Jane (eds) (2020). *Putting Storytelling at the Heart of Early Childhood Practice: A Reflective Guide for Early Years Practitioners.* Abingdon, Oxon: Routledge.

Bruner, Jerome (2002). *Making Stories: Law, Literature, Life.* Cambridge, Mass.: Harvard University Press.

Burns, G.W. (2005). *101 Stories for Kids and Teens – Using Metaphors in Therapy.* Hoboken, NJ: John Wiley & Sons.

Crossley, Diana (illust.) and Sheppard, Kate (2001). *Muddles, Puddles and Sunshine: Your Activity Book to Help when Someone Has Died.* Stroud: Hawthorn Press.

Daniel, Alastair K. (2011). *Storytelling across the Primary Curriculum.* Abingdon, Oxon: Routledge.

Denborough, David (2014). *Retelling the Stories of Our Lives: Everyday Narrative Therapy to Draw Inspiration and Transform Experience.* New York: W.W. Norton.

Gersie, Alida (1991). *Earthtales: Storytelling in Times of Change.* Green Print.

Gersie, Alida (1991). *Storymaking in Bereavement: Dragons Fight in the Meadow.* London: Jessica Kingsley Publishers.

Gersie, Alida (1997). *Reflections on Therapeutic Storymaking: The Use of Stories in Groups.* London: Jessica Kingsley Publishers.

Gersie, Alida (2010). *Storytelling, Stories and Place.* Norwich, UK: Society for Storytelling Press.

Gersie, Alida & King, Nancy (1989). *Storymaking in Education and Therapy.* London: Jessica Kingsley Publishers.

Gersie, Alida & Schiefflin, Edward (2014). *Storytelling for a Greener World: Environment, Community and Story-Based Learning.* London: Jessica Kingsley Publishers.

Golding, Kim S. (2014). *Using Stories to Build Bridges with Traumatized Children: Creative Ideas for Therapy, Life Story Work, Direct Work and Parenting.* London: Jessica Kingsley Publishers.

Gottschall, Jonathan (2013). *The Storytelling Animal: How Stories Make Us Human.* Boston, Mass.: Houghton Mifflin Harcourt.

Handke, Peter (2020). *The Jukebox and Other Essays on Storytelling.* New York: Picador USA.

Jones, Pia & Pimenta, Sarah (2020). *Therapeutic Fairy Tales: For Children and Families Going through Troubling Times.* Abingdon, Oxon: Routledge.

Kearney, Richard (2001). *On Stories (Thinking in Action).* Abingdon, Oxon: Routledge.

Lipman, Doug (2005). *Improving Your Storytelling: Beyond the Basics for All Who Tell Stories in Work or Play.* Little Rock, Ark.: August House.

McKissock, Diane & Mal (2018). *Coping with Grief,* 5th edition. Australia: ABC Books.

Marr, Hugh K. (2019). *A Clinician's Guide to Foundational Story Psychotherapy: Co-Changing Narratives, Co-Changing Lives.* Abingdon, Oxon: Routledge.

 STORIES TO LIGHT THE NIGHT

Mellon, Nancy (1998). *The Art of Storytelling*. Shaftsbury, Dorset: Element Books.

Mellon, Nancy (2008). *Body Eloquence: The Power of Myth and Story to Awaken the Body's Energies*. Santa Rosa, Calif.: Energy Psychology Press.

Mellon, Nancy (2013). *Storytelling with Children*, 2nd edn. Stroud: Hawthorn Press.

Mellon, Nancy (2019). *Healing Storytelling: The Art of Imagination and Storymaking for Personal Growth*. Stroud: Hawthorn Press.

Morris, Nicky (2020). *Find Your Way: A Story and Drama Resource to Promote Mental Well-being in Young People*. Shoreham by Sea, West Sussex: Pavilion Publishing and Media.

Perrow, Susan (2008). *Healing Stories for Challenging Behaviour*. Stroud: Hawthorn Press.

Perrow, Susan (2012). *Therapeutic Storytelling – 101 Healing Stories for Children*. Stroud: Hawthorn Press.

Perrow, Susan (2017). *A–Z Collection of Behaviour Tales*. Stroud: Hawthorn Press.

Petrova, Diana (2018). *The Wheat Beetle: Fairy Tale Therapy for Children and Parents*. JustFiction Edition.

Pullman, Philip. (2017). *Daemon Voices: Essays on Storytelling*. Oxford: David Fickling Books.

Ramsden, Ashley & Hollingsworth, Sue (2013). *The Storyteller's Way: A Sourcebook for Confident Storytelling*. Stroud: Hawthorn Press.

Rogers, J. Earl (2007). *The Art of Grief: The Use of Expressive Arts in a Grief Support Group*. New York and London: Routledge (from the series on Death, Dying and Bereavement, Consulting Editor Robert A. Neimeyer).

Rose, Richard & Philpot, Terry (2004). *The Child's Own Story: Life Story Work with Traumatized Children*. London: Jessica Kingsley.

Silko, Leslie Marmon (2012). *Storyteller*. Harmondsworth: Penguin.

Simmons, Annette (2019). *The Story Factor: Inspiration, Influence, and Persuasion through the Art of Storytelling*. New York: Basic Books.

Smith, Chris (2014). *147 Traditional Stories for Primary School Children to Retell*. Stroud: Hawthorn Press.

Smith, Chris (2020). *Stories for this Uncertain Time: Tales and Creative Activities for Teachers and Parents to Help Children Adapt*. Woodmancote, Glos UK: Twinberrow Press.

Sunderland, Margot (2000). *Using Therapeutic Storytelling as a Teaching Tool*. London: Speechmark Publishing.

Walsh, John D. (2014). *The Art of Storytelling: Easy Steps to Presenting an Unforgettable Story*. Chicago, Il: Moody Press.

Yorke, John (2014). *Into The Woods: How Stories Work and Why We Tell Them*. Harmondsworth: Penguin.

Websites

Dr Alys Mendus
Letters from Lesbos: A Recounting of Emergency Pedagogy in Action
https://othereducation.org/index.php/OE/article/view/161.
  Here you will find Alys has written up her experience of working with unaccompanied minors and using storytelling to help refugees on Lesbos in an article for *Other Education Journal.*

George W. Burns
http://www.georgeburns.com.au/
George W. Burns is an Australian clinical psychologist whose innovative work as a practitioner, teacher and writer is recognized nationally and internationally. His website provides information about his workshops and training programmes, books, and the professional development study tours he leads for health professionals. He is especially known for his use of the healing value of metaphor to communicate effective therapeutic strategies.

Healing Story Alliance (HSA)
http://healingstory.org
HSA explores and promotes the use of storytelling in healing. This website offers resources, guidance and practical applications for storytelling, revealing and reflecting the many facets of healing story in the world today and in the past. Many people are drawn to the site searching for answers or resources for dealing with the pain and tragedy of specific life events, such as the shootings of children in Connecticut, the uprooting of families and communities through natural disasters and human-initiated aggression (from bullying to war). This interest is addressed in their compilations of stories:
Healing Treasures: Stories intended to precipitate conversation, and guide teaching and healing with participants.
Stories We Live: Personal stories and methods for gathering and applying life experiences as healing references.
Stories for Children in Crisis: Compiled by Laura Simms, includes stories, articles and links, drawn from years of research and professional work with children.
Stories for Peace: storytelling in pursuit of peace and understanding.
Healing the Earth: featuring stories contributed by storytellers working in environmental settings or on educational projects with an environmental theme.

Nancy Mellon
http://www.healingstory.com/
Nancy Mellon counsels adults who seek new perspectives and greater well-being in their personal, family and professional lives. Applying a broad variety of healing

modalities, she specializes in life coaching, family and generational dynamics, and health concerns. See also Nancy's books listed in the Books section, p. 291.

In her words: 'I am a convener of listening circles, and a tender of plot lines. I help people to find their way through dark woods and briar patches to new freedom and well-being.'

Susan Laing BA (Psych), Adv.Dip. T (Art)
http://www.creativelivingwithchildren.com/
An invaluable website with comprehensive resources developed from parenting four children. Particularly relevant to 'grief and loss' are the following guidelines that can be downloaded from Susan's website:

http://www.creativelivingwithchildren.com/help-for-challenging-times/grief-death-and-bereavement/ (https://tinyurl.com/y2fsx9tl)

http://www.creativelivingwithchildren.com/help-for-challenging-times/grief-death-and-bereavement/helping-young-children-after-a-death/   (https://tinyurl.com/y2d-puj5a)

http://www.creativelivingwithchildren.com/help-for-challenging-times/grief-death-and-bereavement/the-effects-of-grief-and-loss/ (https://tinyurl.com/y45gfcyj)

http://www.creativelivingwithchildren.com/help-for-challenging-times/dealing-with-stressful-times/ (https://tinyurl.com/y649jlnm)

Susan Perrow
www.susanperrow.com
Susan is an Australian author, storyteller, teacher trainer, parent educator – and the author of this book. For the last 30 years she has been documenting stories from other cultures, writing stories and telling stories to groups of children and adults – all this woven in with a career in teaching, lecturing and consulting, both nationally and internationally. See also Susan's other published books listed in the Books section, p. 291.

Dr Margot Sunderland
https://www.margotsunderland.org/
Dr Margot Sunderland is Director of Education and Training at The Centre for Child Mental Health London, CEO of The Higher Education Psychotherapy training college, The Institute for Arts in Therapy and Education (academic partner of University of East London), Honorary Visiting Fellow at London Metropolitan University, Senior Associate Member of the Royal College of Medicine, and Co-Director of Trauma Informed Schools UK. Dr Sunderland is also Child Psychotherapist with over 30 years experience of working with children and families.

Dr Sunderland was a member of the Early Years Commission, Centre for Social Justice, Westminster and co-author of the cross-party advisory report 'The Next Generation' (early years intervention). She is also founder of the 'Helping Where It Hurts' programme which offers free arts therapy to troubled children in Islington primary schools. She directed the Gulbenkian-funded research study, which, in liaison with University of Cambridge School of Education, measured outcomes for this intervention. Dr Sunderland makes TV and radio appearances as a child and parenting expert. Overall, she is concerned to ensure that parents, teachers and mental health professionals alike are offered the most up-to-date psychological and brain-science research on how children and young people can be enabled to thrive. She is passionate about social change for a kinder, warmer world.

Winston's Wish
https://www.winstonswish.org/
A support agency for children and young people after the death of a parent or sibling, Winston's Wish provides specialist bereavement support services, including following a bereavement by accident or illness, suicide, murder or manslaughter and deaths in the military. Their experienced bereavement support team provide bereaved children and families with the tools to come to terms with their grief.

Muddles, Puddles and Sunshine

Your activity book to help when someone has died

Diana Crossley,
illustrated by Kate Sheppard

Muddles, Puddles and Sunshine offers a structure and an outlet for the many difficult feelings which inevitably follow when someone dies. It aims to help children make sense of their experience by reflecting on the different aspects of their grief, whilst finding a balance between remembering and having fun. Beautifully illustrated, it suggests a helpful series of activities and exercises accompanied by the friendly characters of Bee and Bear.

'What a fantastic book. Practical, sensible and fun – it should prove an invaluable tool for those of us whose jobs involve helping and supporting bereaved families.'
Dr. Mark Porter MBE, medical broadcaster and local GP.

Published by Hawthorn Press; 32pp; 297 x 210mm; full colour illustrations.
Paperback ISBN: 978-1-869890-58-2
Hardback ISBN: 978-1-903458-96-9
Ebook ISBN: 978-1-912480-36-4

 STORIES TO LIGHT THE NIGHT

The Good Grief Project

Changing the landscape and language of grief

The Good Grief Project's mission is to give a voice to the bereaved in a culture that often has difficulty talking openly about death, dying and bereavement.

Approximately 6,000 young people under the age of 24 die in the UK every year leaving up to 50,000 newly bereaved parents, siblings and grandparents.

The brainchild of bereaved parents Jane Harris and Jimmy Edmonds, whose son Josh died in a road accident in Vietnam in 2011, *The Good Grief Project* is primarily concerned with supporting families grieving following the untimely death of a loved one, particularly the death of a child. More generally, it has made significant contributions to our understanding of what it means to grieve in contemporary society, in particular the concept of grief as an active and creative process of adjusting to loss.

Jane is a psychotherapist and Jimmy is a BAFTA award-winning filmmaker, photographer and Winston Churchill Fellow. Together they've produced and directed a range of personal yet widely acclaimed films including *Beyond Goodbye* (a reflection on the power of a good funeral), *Gerry's Legacy* (following the final years of Jane's father's life as he struggles with dementia in a psychiatric hospital) and the award-winning feature documentary, *A Love That Never Dies* (a road trip across the USA in honour of their son in which they meet with other bereaved families to discover a wide variety of approaches to grief).

Along with its films and talks *The Good Grief Project* has also developed a series of workshops, courses and retreats designed to help the bereaved to work more actively with their grief, and to find a more comfortable language to express it.

To find out more about screening their films or to join one of their Active Grief Weekends, please go to https://thegoodgriefproject.co.uk/.

Other Books by Hawthorn Press

Healing Stories for Challenging Behaviour

Susan Perrow

ISBN: 978-1-903458-78-5

Therapeutic Storytelling

101 Healing Stories for Children

Susan Perrow

'An inspirational and practical resource'
Sue Hollingsworth, International School of Storytelling

ISBN: 978-1-907359-15-6

An A–Z Collection of
Behaviour Tales
From Angry Ant to Zestless Zebra

Susan Perrow
Illustrated by Allmut ffrench

ISBN: 978-1-907359-86-6

Storytelling for a Greener World

Environment, Community and Story-Based Learning

Edited by
Alida Gersie, Anthony Nanson and Edward Schieffelin
with Charlene Collison and Jon Cree

Foreword by Jonathon Porritt

ISBN: 978-1-907359-35-4

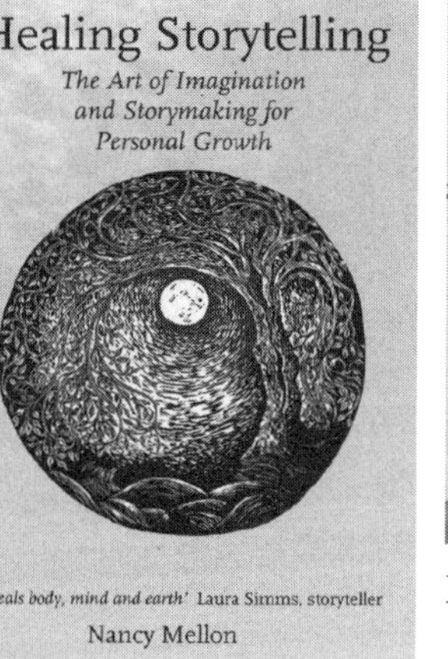

Healing Storytelling

The Art of Imagination and Storymaking for Personal Growth

'Heals body, mind and earth' Laura Simms, storyteller
Nancy Mellon

ISBN: 978-1-912480-13-5

The Natural Storyteller
Wildlife Tales for Telling

Georgiana Keable

ISBN: 978-1-907359-80-4

Ordering Books

If you have difficulties ordering Hawthorn Press books from a bookshop, you can order direct from our website: **www.hawthornpress.com**, or from our UK distributor:

BookSource, 50 Cambuslang Road, Glasgow, G32 8NB

Tel: (0845) 370 0063, E-mail: orders@booksource.net.

Details of our overseas distributors can be found on our website.

Hawthorn Press